Praise for *Learning to Bake Allergen–Free*

"This book will give you the depth of knowledge you need to be a successful allergen-free baker."
—CHEF MING TSAI, chef and owner of Blue Ginger and national spokesperson for the Food Allergy & Anaphylaxis Network

✳

"This amazing collection of lessons and recipes will fast-forward the learning curve for anyone new to cooking with food allergies. Speaking with the voice of experience, Colette Martin offers in-depth but approachable chapters on replacing key ingredients, even seemingly integral baking ingredients like eggs. Her 'Crash Course' subchapters cover everything from using baking soda and baking powder, to proofing yeast breads, to how to tell when the darn thing is done! Learning to Bake Allergen-Free will be a companion you will want to keep close by in your kitchen for frequent reference."
—JULES SHEPARD, author of *Free For All Cooking* and *The First Year: Celiac Disease and Living Gluten Free*

✳

"Colette Martin's book will be a great resource for the home baker hesitant to venture 'out of the box.' Her use of a variety of name-brand gluten-free flours and mixes makes for easy adaptation."
—CHEF RICHARD J. COPPEDGE, JR., CMB, professor of baking and pastry arts, the Culinary Institute of America

✳

"A fabulous education in a cookbook! Learning to Bake Allergen-Free will move you right to the head of the baking class thanks to Colette Martin's thorough and easy-to-understand lessons about allergens, ingredients, and substitutions. Colette's recipes are poised to become staples in your repertoire, so happy baking, and enjoy your new discoveries!"
—LORI SANDLER, founder of Divvies and author of *The Divvies Bakery Cookbook— No Nuts, No Eggs, No Dairy—Just Delicious!*

✳

THE EXPERIMENT

BECAUSE EVERY BOOK IS A TEST OF NEW IDEAS

"*Learning to Bake Allergen-Free* is the guide that I sought for years, and a positively beautiful book. Colette Martin presents all of her secrets, from the most reliable egg substitutes to the best gluten-free baking mixes, and her masterful recipe collection is the icing on the cake!"
—ALISA FLEMING, author of *Go Dairy Free: The Guide and Cookbook* and founder of GoDairyFree.org

*

"Colette Martin shares her favorite, creative recipes and her love of baking with you so you will come to love gluten-free, dairy-free, egg-free, nut-free baking, too."
—LYNDA MITCHELL, President, Kids With Food Allergies Foundation

*

"Colette Martin's *Learning to Bake Allergen-Free* is a welcome addition to the world of allergen-free cooking. Martin's approach to the challenge is masterful and complete. This is more than a cookbook; this is a resource book for families struggling to feed a family member with multiple food allergies. She guides the way, teaching us how to adapt recipes for results that the whole family will enjoy. Kudos to Colette Martin for tackling this challenge head-on and providing families with a much-needed resource."
—WENDY BOOK, President, American Partnership for Eosinophilic Disorders

*

"As a practicing allergy and asthma specialist, I see patients every day who have multiple food allergies, but the diagnosis is just the first step. These families need to modify their diets to avoid wheat, milk, eggs, peanuts, nuts, soy, and other common food allergens. *Learning to Bake Allergen-Free* is exactly the book these families need when they leave my office. It's jam-packed with practical advice, simple baking techniques, and easy recipes that the whole family can enjoy! It will, for sure, bring smiles to many, for years to come."
—DR. ATUL N. SHAH, Medical Director, Center4AsthmaAllergy.com, and author of the AmazingAllergist's Awesome Series for Children, AmazingAllergist.com

learning to bake
Allergen-Free

Colette Martin

learning to bake
Allergen-Free

A CRASH COURSE FOR BUSY PARENTS ON BAKING

WITHOUT WHEAT, GLUTEN, DAIRY, EGGS, SOY OR NUTS

THE EXPERIMENT

NEW YORK

LEARNING TO BAKE ALLERGEN-FREE: *A Crash Course for Busy Parents on Baking without Wheat, Gluten, Dairy, Eggs, Soy or Nuts*

The Experiment, LLC
260 Fifth Avenue
New York, NY 10001–6408
www.theexperimentpublishing.com

The Experiment's books are available at special discounts when purchased in bulk for premiums and sales promotions as well as for fundraising or educational use. For details, contact us at info@theexperimentpublishing.com.

Many of the designations used by manufacturers and sellers to distinguish their products are claimed as trademarks. Where those designations appear in this book and The Experiment was aware of a trademark claim, the designations have been capitalized.

Learning to Bake Allergen-Free is not intended to provide medical advice. While care was taken to provide correct and helpful information, the suggestions in this book are not intended as dietary advice or as a substitute for consulting a dietician, physician, or other medical professional. It is the reader's sole responsibility to determine which foods are appropriate and safe for his or her family to consume. The author and publisher make no claims regarding the presence of food allergens and disclaim all liability in connection with the use of this book.

Library of Congress Cataloging-in-Publication Data

Martin, Colette (Colette F.)
Learning to bake allergen-free : a crash course for busy parents on baking without wheat, gluten, dairy, eggs, soy or nuts / Colette Martin.
p. cm.
Includes index.
ISBN 978-1-61519-053-9 (pbk.)—ISBN 978-1-61519-150-5 (ebook)
1. Food allergy—Diet therapy—Recipes.   I. Title.
RC588.D53M37 2012
641.5'6318 —dc23
2012000611

ISBN 978-1-61519-053-9
Ebook ISBN 978-1-61519-150-5

Cover design by Susi Oberhelman
Cover photograph by Colette Martin
Author photograph by Harry Yudenfriend
Text design by Pauline Neuwirth, Neuwirth & Associates, Inc.

Manufactured in the United States of America
Distributed by Workman Publishing Company, Inc.
Distributed simultaneously in Canada by Thomas Allen and Son Ltd.
First published June 2012
10 9 8 7 6 5 4 3

For Patrick,
my inspiration for this journey

Contents

Foreword

By Dr. Stephen Wangen

FOOD ALLERGIES ARE a huge public health issue. Those of you reading this cookbook likely already have some appreciation for this issue. But millions of people consume foods that are directly or indirectly responsible for their health problems.

It is a relationship that I see played out in my clinic every day. There are literally hundreds of different symptoms that can be caused by food allergies. Potential consequences can range from headaches to heart disease (yes, research really does support this connection), and from canker sores to cancer.

Ironically, the public is far ahead of the medical community when it comes to diagnosing and addressing reactions to foods. Individuals are still far more likely than most doctors to see this connection and to do something about it. Most doctors don't recognize the true power of food and negative reactions to foods except in the case of anaphylaxis. But anaphylaxis, a life threatening reaction to food, is merely the tip of the iceberg.

The single most profound thing that I do for my patients on a daily basis is to help them identify reactions to foods. I never cease to be amazed at how significant an impact a food allergy can have on one's health, or at the extremely wide ranging potential consequences of those allergies.

Let there be no doubt that these reactions to food are indeed allergies. Allergies occur when the immune system is involved in the reaction. This in turn triggers inflammation, and inflammation is at the root of nearly all health issues. Food intolerance, such as lactose intolerance, does not involve the immune system and therefore does not involve inflammation. For this reason it cannot cause inflammatory reactions in the body.

Unfortunately, the growing recognition of gluten intolerance has caused significant confusion with regard to this discussion. Although the word "intolerance" is used, it is indeed an immune reaction. And technically it is therefore an allergy. Expert panels have clarified this, but the knowledge has not yet filtered down through the medical community, much less the general public. So if you are confused, you are in very good company.

Whatever we call them, immune reactions to food are very important. They can affect your digestion, your mood, your energy, your clarity of thought, your neurological system, your skin, your musculoskeletal system…just about anything you can imagine.

In an era where medicine is primarily about treating the symptom, not the cause, discovering that you have a food allergy can have seemingly miraculous results. And the beauty of it is that you control them. Although it may not be easy at first, you can decide whether or not you want to be healthy. All it takes is a little investment in you. And there is no better place to invest.

Adapting to your unique diet has gotten much easier with the expertise shared by Colette Martin. This book is a fantastic resource for understanding reactions to foods and how to bake if you have food allergies.

I am much obliged to Colette Martin for producing a wonderful cookbook that is not only gluten-free but also free of dairy, eggs, soy, and nuts. On behalf of myself and my patients, I thank you. Cookbooks that truly avoid this combination are still relatively rare, but the people who suffer from reactions to these foods are not. In my experience these reactions are just as common as gluten reactions, and cause just as many problems.

I am honored to be a part of this book. I know that you didn't buy it for the foreword, but I appreciate that you took the time to read it. I hope that you learn a great deal from this excellent resource, and live a much happier and healthier life because of it.

STEPHEN WANGEN, ND, known as "The Gluten Free Doctor," is the author of *Healthier Without Wheat*, founder of the Center for Food Allergies, Research Director of the Food Allergy and Intolerance Foundation, and a member of the board of trustees of the Gluten Intolerance Group of North America.

When the Food You Eat Is Making You Sick

LOOKING BACK ON IT now, it's clear that my son suffered from food allergies since birth. He was miserable after he was fed—it didn't matter whether it was breast milk, or the myriad of milk- and soy-based formulas his doctors suggested. The first six months of Patrick's life were an endless cycle of feed, scream, and spit up. I described my son as "the blurpiest baby you have ever seen," and I was afraid to leave him with anyone besides immediate family. He was unable to be comforted and didn't want to be held. But my beautiful baby was nothing short of persistent; he continued to gain weight, and was among the 70th percentile for height and weight. He didn't exhibit any of the most traditional and most visible signs of food allergy: He didn't have rashes, his lips never swelled up, he never turned blue, and he never went into anaphylactic shock. The doctors diagnosed him with extreme colic and prescribed drops.

It was 1990, and eosinophilic gastrointestinal disorders were just beginning to be studied. It would be another ten years before we discovered that Patrick suffered from eosinophilic esophagitis (EE), an autoimmune disorder triggered by food allergies.

Intuitively, I knew that milk was a cause of Patrick's distress, and abandoned all formulas at an early age. I started feeding my son solid foods—oatmeal, fruit purees, and vegetable purees—and juice around six months of age. And he got better. He stopped screaming and was a delightfully happy child. Aside from the occasional birthday party where cake and ice cream were served, the spitting up and vomiting stopped, and he worked his way into the 90th percentile for height and weight. He was a happy, thriving, outgoing kid. Until he went to elementary school.

By the time Patrick was in third grade, it was common for me to receive a call from the school nurse in early afternoon (after lunch) to let me know that my son had thrown up. He never had a fever, and he never wanted to miss class. Of course, milk was served with school lunches, and I was once again suspicious that it could be causing the problem. When Patrick tested positive for lactose intolerance, we eliminated milk from his diet and school officials allowed him to have juice with lunch.

Problem solved? Not quite. A diet without milk helped, but Patrick still complained of chest pain when he ate. He was prescribed the purple pills for acid reflux. Knowing what I know now, I understand that the medication (which reduces the acid in the stomach) was masking the real problem. My son no longer had as much pain in his esophagus because the acid wasn't there to further irritate it, but he still had difficulty swallowing and keeping food down. There were even more tests with no conclusive results.

When Patrick had his first endoscopy, his doctor discovered that his esophagus was severely inflamed. A biopsy confirmed the very high presence of eosinophils (a form of white blood cells that are normal in small amounts but can cause inflammation when abundant), which led to the diagnosis of EE. Through a combination of blood testing and observed reactions to food, we discovered that in addition to milk, Patrick was allergic to the proteins in wheat, soy, peanuts, and eggs. I was relieved that we finally had an answer—after ten years of symptoms, we finally knew what the problem was. But let's be clear about one thing: Nobody wants to have food allergies. Nobody wants to order a salad instead of having pizza with the team. No child wants to sit at the food allergy table or miss out on cupcakes at a party. No parent wishes that for his or her child. Food allergies are a real and growing problem, and we need solutions.

Patrick's food allergy diagnosis was a sobering moment. While I had been baking my entire life with wheat, milk, eggs, and butter (as most bakers do), I realized that I would need to find new ingredients and techniques, and began my own journey in learning to bake allergen-free. Since then I have been on a quest to find the best allergen-free ingredients, flour blends, and baking mixes, and to create great recipes so I can keep my family safe. Along the journey, I stumbled upon my own allergies to gluten and soy. When I eliminated my son's food allergens (and later gluten), I was happy to discover that my own lifelong symptoms disappeared.

As food-allergy parents, our challenges will vary. While the most severe food allergies are the easiest to diagnose—anaphylaxis is nearly always immediately evident—parents of children with life-threatening symptoms will need to be the most vigilant. Those of us with children with less visible symptoms (e.g., my son's EE, celiac disease, or delayed symptoms) may have a harder time getting a diagnosis. Others may have difficulty determining which foods are causing the problem. Support organizations such as Kids with Food Allergies can be extremely helpful throughout the process of diagnosis (see page 267 for more resources).

If you are reading this book, you have your own story to share. Either you suspect that food is making you or a family member sick, or you already have a diagnosis of food allergies or intolerance. Congratulations. That's the hard part. And you're in good company. One in two thousand people suffers from EE. One in 133 suffers from celiac disease, an autoimmune response to the gluten found in wheat, rye, and barley. Even more—up to one in 25—suffer from traditional food allergies,[1] an autoimmune response to the protein in certain foods. There are countless others who have food intolerances.

Whether it's an autoimmune response or not, we all have one thing in common: We must avoid the foods that make us sick. I am not a doctor and will not offer medical advice. What I will do—with pleasure—is share the secrets I have learned as an allergen-free baker to help make your journey easier.

learning to bake
Allergen-Free

PART

1

baking
Lessons

Raspberry Brownie Bites (page 250)

1

A New Adventure

YOU JUST RECEIVED A phone call from the doctor and your son's blood test indicates he is allergic to wheat, eggs, soy, and milk, *or* you just came home from the allergist's office where your daughter's scratch test showed allergies to milk, wheat, and peanuts, *or* the oral food challenge you just completed in the doctor's office confirms that your child now needs to avoid eggs and tree nuts—in addition to the three other foods previously diagnosed.

Your child has food allergies. You are asking yourself, *Now what?*

※ *What am I going to make for breakfast without wheat, milk, or eggs?*
※ *How can I make school lunch tomorrow without traditional bread?*
※ *Is there a safe snack I can bring to the classroom party next week?*
※ *How are we going to get through this?*

One of the questions I am asked most frequently when people learn of my son's food allergies is, "What *do* you eat?" The truth is, the journey becomes much easier when you focus on what your family *can* eat.

Whether you've just received a food allergy diagnosis, you're following an elimination diet to determine which foods your son is allergic to, or you're adding new food allergies to the list you knew your daughter already had, you've come to the right place. Whether you have been baking all of your life with foods you must now avoid, or you've never even pre-heated an oven, you've come to the right place.

Yes, you may have to start baking at home. I know that it's hard to add another chore to the list—but the baking itself doesn't have to be tedious. And you don't have to figure it out for yourself—I've done the experimenting for you.

This book will help you understand how to replace the most common food allergens used in traditional baking (including wheat, milk, butter, and eggs), and teach you what works and why. You will learn the best techniques to use to get great results, and the specific products to look for at the grocery store or health food store. The recipes are quick and easy, with basics that you will be able to rely on as you take your family from breakfast through dinner.

You might be questioning the purpose of ingredients that you had previously taken for granted, such as baking soda and baking powder—*What do they do, how much do I need, and which should I use?* Or you might be looking at ingredients you see in allergen-free recipes, such as xanthan gum, or egg replacer, and wondering what they are—or how to use them. Again, you are in the right place. You will find the answers to these questions and more, right here.

This crash course in baking allergen-free teaches you what you need to know—now. The "Baking Lessons" include an explanation of ingredients and substitutions for families who need to avoid wheat, milk, eggs, soy, nuts, and gluten—families just like yours and mine. After some basics (e.g., how to read product labels, page 6, and how to avoid contamination, page 68), you will learn about gluten-free and wheat-free grains and how to use them effectively, the choices you have to replace cow's milk and butter, how to bake without eggs—and much more.

In "The Allergen-Free Baking Lab," you will be getting your hands dirty and, yes, baking in your own kitchen! The baking lab is organized by the methods used, and in each chapter, crash courses provide just-in-time lessons, describing the techniques to use and explaining what works and why. If you make one or two recipes from each chapter you will be able to build on your skills as you go.

I start with the easiest recipes using simple batters; you will be making fresh Blueberry Muffins (page 93) and Vanilla Pound Cake (page 108) before you know it. Next you will learn how to form scones and doughnuts (and more) from thick batters that hold their shape when molded.

Once you're comfortable with batters, you will learn how to make dough for a pie crust and how to prepare your own allergen-free cookie dough to keep in the fridge (page 131). When you're ready to tackle breads and rolls, you will learn how to use yeast to make everything from Basic Dinner Rolls (page 157) to Basic Sandwich Bread (page 161) to Cinnamon Rolls (page 181).

Chocolate (a special topic) takes center stage next, but you don't have to wait to learn about chocolate—Double Chocolate Muffins (page 197) can be made from a simple batter, so feel free to skip ahead if your child is begging for chocolate. In "Extra Credit," you will also find a few more great comfort foods and snack bars that take minimal time and effort to prepare. This book is chock-full of basic, customizable recipes and variations that use the same ingredients and techniques.

The final chapter in "The Allergen-Free Baking Lab" focuses on off-the-shelf baking mixes. If you've never baked before (or just need a quick solution), you may want to turn to page 221 to learn how to adapt off-the-shelf gluten-free baking mixes with allergen-free substitutions—or to kick them up a notch for a special treat such as Chocolate Mousse Tarts (page 248).

As you explore the book, you will discover that it's still possible to make pudding without eggs and that coconut oil makes a great replacement for butter. You will learn that it's easier to make gluten-free pie crust than traditional pie crust made with wheat—and why. You will discover the nuances of chocolate, shortening, and so much more. While this is a cookbook, it is also a reference. If you come back to this book to learn about yeast while using another recipe or cookbook, I will be delighted and honored.

Some of the baking books that you have in your kitchen may caution you to follow the recipe exactly. But that's simply not practical for families like yours and mine. We know that while multiple food allergies are common, the specific allergies vary. I have chosen to avoid the eight most common food allergens and gluten in my recipes, and I try to point out where other less common allergens may lurk. If you need to substitute more ingredients, then (please!) do so. If you want to substitute back in an ingredient I have left out (only if you're not allergic to it), I encourage you to do so, and have some tips you may find helpful (see page 257). You have my permission to substitute. The only requirement I have as you learn to bake allergen-free is to have fun. Don't beat yourself up if you forget an ingredient or miss a step. I've done it many times myself. Just enjoy the adventure and keep baking!

Reading labels

Learning to bake allergen-free starts with the ingredients. There's more to the labels that the US Food and Drug Administration (FDA) requires on packaged food products sold in the United States than just calories and nutrition facts; a detailed list of ingredients is also required. Whether you are buying products to make muffins from scratch, looking for a baking mix to make a quick dessert, or planning a dinner for your family, your first concern when shopping for groceries is to understand what's in the food you're buying. To do that, you must always read the detailed ingredients labels.

When my son was first diagnosed with food allergies, I had limited experience in reading food labels. I sometimes checked for the calories per serving, and scanned the labels to avoid products with high-fructose corn syrup in the first few ingredients, but I rarely paid attention to—or understood—what most of the ingredients in my food were. I quickly had to learn that casein and whey were both milk proteins that could cause allergic reactions, and I learned to avoid products with ingredients such as hydrolyzed vegetable protein, because they may be hidden sources of wheat or soy.

Today, reading food labels is much easier, thanks to the Food Allergen Labeling and Consumer Protection Act of 2004 (FALCPA).[2] The act spells out how packaged food products sold in the United States must list ingredients on their labels when they contain any of the top eight food allergens—wheat, milk, soy, tree nuts (which includes almonds, cashews, walnuts, pecans, and other nuts), peanuts, eggs, fish, and shellfish. This legislation was a breakthrough for families with food allergies, making it much simpler for us to identify the products we can eat safely, and those to avoid.

Understanding what the law requires (and what it doesn't) is key to reading labels. First you should know that the labeling requirements only apply to food (not cosmetics or cleaning products), and they only apply to packaged food (not produce, meat, or fish bought at the fish counter). If it's meant for humans to eat and it has a label, the law applies.

The primary focus of the law is clarity—food vendors need to spell out what is in the food you are buying, and can no longer hide ingredients. Specifically, if a product contains one of the top eight allergens, that food must be clearly listed on the ingredients label using the common name for the food. For example, a label that previously listed "casein" as an ingredient must now use the word "milk." Milk is the common name.

Food vendors can comply with the law by listing ingredients in one of two ways: They can either list the common name for the food allergen in the complete list of ingredients, or they can call out the food allergen just below the ingredients list using a "contains" statement. Here are two examples of the way that the milk ingredient "whey" may be listed:

INGREDIENTS: vegetable oil, water, whey (milk), salt

INGREDIENTS: vegetable oil, water, whey, salt
CONTAINS: milk

Notice that I said the food allergen *may* be listed either of these two ways. It is becoming more common for food vendors to list the ingredients using both methods, but the law doesn't require it. While some food vendors precede the "contains" statement with the words "allergen information," that is also not required by the law. If you don't see a "contains" statement or an "allergen information" statement, that does not necessarily mean the food is safe. What this boils down to is that you must read the entire ingredients list, even if the "contains" statement does not list anything you are allergic to, and even if there is no "contains" or "allergen" statement following the ingredients.

And you might want to get used to carrying reading glasses with you to the grocery store, as the size of the font used to list the ingredients is sometimes very small. Some food vendors list the allergen information in bold print, making it easier for you to spot, but that isn't required.

Any food that your family is allergic to that is *not* one of the top eight food allergens must be listed as an ingredient but does not need to follow the FALCPA rule to use the common name. That means that an ingredient such as corn might be present if the ingredients label includes such items as maltodextrin or hydrolyzed vegetable protein (or any number of other foods derived from corn). Parents of children with less common food allergens need to become detectives when it comes to reading labels and will need to call product manufacturers more often. Support organizations such as Kids with Food Allergies and the Food Allergy and Anaphylaxis Network (FAAN) can be very helpful (see page 267 for more resources for families with food allergies).

Keep in mind that food vendors change their formulas, and ingredients do change. I can't stress enough that you must read the ingredients label *every time* you buy the product, even if you have bought it before and haven't had any allergic reactions. Food vendors also change their manufacturing processes, which can affect how safe a product is for you. This brings us to the topic of cautionary or advisory statements on food labels.

What we've discussed so far refers to the law concerning the ingredients that are intended to be in your food. With food allergies, you also have to be concerned about the ingredients that may make their way into your food *unintentionally*—this is referred to as cross-contamination and happens when foods are processed on the same equipment or in the same facility as a food allergen.

Some of the most common cross-contamination issues occur with these foods:

* **PEANUTS AND TREE NUTS:** The equipment used to process nuts of all kinds is the same, and they are often processed together.
* **WHEAT AND OATS:** Vendors that process both of these grains tend to process them in the same facilities and often on the same equipment.
* **CHOCOLATE AND MILK OR NUTS:** While it's not too hard to find chocolate that is pure cocoa liquor and cocoa butter, most chocolate vendors also produce milk chocolate, with (you guessed it) milk ingredients. Chocolate factories also tend to use nuts.

The current food allergen labeling requirements do not address cross-contamination. In 2008, the FDA held hearings on the use of advisory labeling for food allergens, and the food-allergy community continues to lobby for even more clarity and change, but as of this writing there is no consistency in these advisory labels. It is entirely up to the discretion of the food manufacturers to provide additional allergen information.

Nevertheless, more and more food vendors, especially those who are catering to the food-allergic, are stepping up to the plate and voluntarily providing more information on their labels. These statements come in many forms and can easily be misinterpreted, so let's take a look at some of the most common:

MAY CONTAIN (FOOD ALLERGEN) OR MAY CONTAIN TRACES OF (FOOD ALLERGEN): A "may contain" statement does not mean that this ingredient is in the product. In fact, the vendor does not intend for that ingredient to be in the product. Usually these warnings are due to either shared equipment (e.g., a tree-nut product from a vendor that also produces peanut products) or same-facility processing (e.g., the milk and chocolate example), and usually require your digging further to determine whether the food is safe for you or your child.

PROCESSED IN A FACILITY THAT ALSO PROCESSES (FOOD ALLERGEN): While this advisory statement gives you more information, it still may not be enough information to determine if the product is safe for your family. It's possible that the food is being processed in a 10,000-square-foot facility and the product with the food allergen is being processed nowhere near the product you plan to buy. It's also possible that these products are being produced side by side. Again, further research is required before you decide this is safe.

PROCESSED ON SHARED EQUIPMENT WITH (FOOD ALLERGEN): In my opinion, this advisory statement is one of the most clear. The risk of cross-contamination grows dramatically when processed on shared equipment. This is a product I would avoid if the warning applied to one of my family's food allergens.

PROCESSED IN A DEDICATED FACILITY FREE OF (FOOD ALLERGENS): This allergen statement is the one that food-allergy moms and dads can rejoice over! When a food is processed in a dedicated facility, the risk of cross-contamination goes way down. Think about it this way—if your son is allergic to peanuts, and you don't allow any peanuts in your house, you will be quite confident that he will not be accidentally exposed in your home. These are products you should feel confident buying.

NO ADVISORY STATEMENT: You might think that just because a food vendor chooses not to use an advisory label, that this product isn't any safer than one that does contain a voluntary warning. In August 2010, the Food Allergy Initiative shared the results of a study on the use of advisory labeling and product contamination,[3] with some surprising results. The allergens they tested for (egg, milk, or peanut) were found in 5.3 percent of products with advisory statements and in 1.9 percent of similar products without advisory statements. These results suggest that products without food allergens listed in the ingredients and without warning labels are indeed a little bit safer.

Some food vendors choose to share information prominently on the front of their packages. Front-of-package statements such as "wheat-free," "dairy-free," or "processed in a dedicated facility containing no [wheat, dairy, nuts, etc.]" are not regulated by the FDA.

While these front-of-package labels do provide a good source of additional information, ultimately it is up to you to determine whether a product is safe for you and your family. It's a very personal choice that you need to make, with advice from your doctor. My own decision on whether to purchase products that contain advisory labels is tempered by a number of factors, including the severity of our allergic reactions. If you know that your daughter will go into anaphylactic shock if she even gets a whiff of peanut dust, then you will be sure to avoid any products with warning labels for peanuts, and opt instead for a product that is made in a dedicated facility that does not process nuts.

If the labels are confusing, or conflicting, or you're just not sure, you must seek additional information. Many food vendors provide detailed allergen information on their websites, and some now provide a phone number right on the product package to contact their consumer information center. Most are more than happy to help you determine if a product is safe for your family. If you are unable to get clear answers to your questions, don't purchase the product. Always err on the side of caution when it comes to food allergies.

Now that you understand the basics of reading food labels, there are two exceptions worth noting:

COCONUT: The FDA's list of nuts that are considered "tree nuts" includes coconut. Most botanical experts classify coconut as a drupe, a fruit with a hard, stony covering enclosing the seed. Examples of drupes include peaches and avocados. Others refer to coconut as a seed. While it is possible to be allergic to coconut, being allergic to tree nuts (e.g., almonds, cashews, hazelnuts) does not necessarily mean that you are allergic to coconut. According to the Food Allergy and Anaphylaxis Network (FAAN), "Coconut, the seed of a drupaceous fruit, has typically not been restricted in the diets of people with tree nut allergy. However, in October of 2006, the FDA began identifying coconut as a tree nut. The available medical literature contains documentation of a small number of allergic reactions to coconut; most occurred in people who were not allergic to other tree nuts."[4] FAAN recommends checking with your doctor to determine whether you need to avoid coconut.

For those allergic to tree nuts but *not* to coconut, the confusion in labeling comes when coconut is present, yet no other tree nuts are listed in a product's ingredients. You may see a "contains tree nuts" statement on a label when coconut is included in the ingredients, or a "may contain tree nuts" advisory statement even if there are no true tree nuts processed in that facility. This is a case where you may need to check the vendor website or call the customer support center to determine whether the warning is strictly for coconut or whether other tree nuts are indeed used in the facility.

For most people, coconut is a great alternative to milk and butter when baking (see pages 40–49), so I have chosen to use coconut products in some recipes. If you are allergic to coconut, see page 258 for alternatives.

OILS: The FALCPA exempts highly refined oils derived from one of the eight major food allergens from being called out on ingredients labels. This makes sense because almost all food allergies are due to the protein in the food. Most oils, when refined, contain such a small amount of protein that even those with food allergies may be able to safely consume them.

Soy lecithin is an emulsifier that is derived during the processing of soybean oil. In 2006, the FDA issued additional labeling guidance for soy lecithin,[5] saying that it must now be called out on the product labels. Even if the soy lecithin was derived from highly refined soybean oil, soy or soybeans will be listed as an allergen on products containing it. While soybean oil does not have to be listed as an allergen, lecithin derived from soy *does* have to be called out. You should consult with your doctor to determine whether you need to avoid oils or lecithin derived from a food you are allergic to. Note that some of the shortenings I use in my recipes do contain soybean oil, and some of the chocolate products I use do contain soy lecithin. If you need to avoid these products, alternatives are available (see pages 48 and 192).

Always keep in mind that the FDA food allergen labeling requirements only apply to the top eight food allergens, and you must always work with your doctor to determine which ingredients are safe for you to consume. Now let's talk about a few other designations on product labels that may be helpful to you as you look for products without food allergens.

First, let's look at the term *gluten-free*. Gluten is a protein found in wheat, rye, and barley. Those who need to eat gluten-free typically suffer from celiac disease or gluten intolerance rather than traditional food allergies. (See page 18 for more on the differences between wheat and gluten.) Because of the complexity in establishing a standard acceptable threshold for the presence of gluten in products labeled gluten-free, the FALCPA did not include gluten as an allergen, but required the FDA to create a standard definition for *gluten-free*. As of August 2008, the deadline established to implement rules for voluntary gluten-free labeling guidelines, the FDA had provided no guidance.

Some independent certification organizations, including the Gluten-Free Certification Organization (GFCO), provide their own guidelines and test vendor products to ensure that they do not exceed a gluten threshold measured in parts per million (ppm). The GFCO standard threshold is 10 ppm.

Inspired (in part) by a gluten-free labeling summit in Washington in May 2011 (and the building of the world's tallest gluten-free cake), the FDA reopened previously proposed gluten-free labeling legislation[6] for comment in August 2011, with the intent of establishing a standard within the next year. If enacted, manufacturers will be able to label a product "gluten-free" only if it is at or below the defined threshold of 20 ppm, a number that (according to the FDA) is generally accepted by experts as safe for those with celiac disease. It's important to note that this labeling will be voluntary—if a product is labeled "gluten-free," it will have to meet the minimum threshold for gluten, but (unlike the labeling for food allergens) products that do contain gluten will not require special labeling.

While there is no legislation for the use of the label "vegan" on food products, a product that is labeled "vegan" may be helpful to those looking to avoid milk or eggs. *Gluten-free* and *vegan* designations do not exempt you from the need to read ingredient labels, but they do signal products that you may want to investigate further.

Redefining healthy eating

When you start reading labels at the grocery store, you will notice that a very large portion of the processed foods available contain wheat, milk, and/or soy. Just as I did when we first learned of my son's food allergies, you may be thinking that there is nothing your family can eat. Foods that we have been told are healthy and good for us, including whole wheat bread, yogurt, and soy milk (to mention just a few), may suddenly be off-limits. Even the new dietary guidelines for Americans released by the USDA in January, 2010,[7] recommend that healthy adults consume three cups of milk per day. Milk is defined as milk, cheese, yogurt, or their lactose-free cousins—all options that the milk-allergic need to avoid. Clearly, those of us with food allergies need another definition of healthy eating.

In my family, healthy eating means eliminating the foods that make us sick and replacing them with nutritious foods that we can safely eat. The good news is, despite what we commonly find on the grocery store shelves, there are many foods to choose from. As I look for allergen-free ingredients to bake with, I follow these guidelines:

* **WHENEVER POSSIBLE, CHOOSE WHOLE FOODS.** Whole foods are foods that have not been processed. Fruits, vegetables, and meats are whole foods, as are unprocessed grains, seeds, and beans. The baking ingredients I use most often are non-wheat/non-gluten whole grains and milks that are made from seeds or grains.

* **WHEN BUYING PROCESSED FOODS, LOOK FOR PRODUCTS WITH THE FEWEST INGREDIENTS.** In Michael Pollan's book *Food Rules*, his sixth rule for eating is, "Avoid food products that contain more than five ingredients,"[8] contending that they are healthier for you. I agree. When you are eating allergen-free, this rule is even more critical. The fewer ingredients there are in a product, the less you need to worry about possible contamination. (See page 68 for more on contamination.) Why buy a package of chocolate chips that contains sugar, chocolate, cocoa butter, butterfat, soy lecithin, artificial flavoring, and natural flavoring, when you can buy one that contains just cane juice, chocolate liquor, and cocoa butter? Even if I didn't need to avoid the milk, I'd rather avoid the added flavorings.

* **OPT FOR PACKAGED FOODS.** It's important to make a distinction between processed and packaged. Processing refers to chemically changing the composition of the food. Packaging refers to how it is wrapped for sale to the consumer. While we all want to be environmentally conscious, if you have food allergies you need to avoid the open bins, as well as grains and flours that have been packaged at the point of sale. Packaging from the manufacturer provides another layer of protection—helping to keep foods that are intended to be allergen-free safe from contamination.

As you select foods, keep in mind that your primary focus is on keeping yourself and your family healthy. The new healthy diet you will follow is a lifestyle diet—one where you are consciously choosing foods that are safe for your family and that provide the best fuel for your body.

Eating together

So much of our lives revolve around food. We plan our days around breakfast, lunch, and dinner. Our kids look forward to a freshly baked cookie when they get home from school. We linger in the kitchen after a satisfying meal, maybe finishing that last bit of bread. Most holidays revolve around food. We associate Valentine's Day with chocolate and roses, and birthdays with cake and presents. When we want to reward ourselves after a hard day at work or a major accomplishment, it is so often with food—and usually food that is full of wheat, milk, and eggs. When one family member has food allergies or restrictions, all of the joy of those happy occasions and gatherings can quickly turn to stress.

It wasn't until my son was in his teens and able to verbalize his feelings about food allergies that I truly understood how difficult mealtime could be for a food-allergic child. Yes, both you and your child are worried about what they are eating, and worried about a possible reaction, but there's a serious social impact here as well. A 2011 survey by the Food Allergy and Anaphylaxis Network (FAAN) and Galaxy Nutritional Foods found that seven out of ten parents of children with food allergies felt that their child's quality of life had been impacted at least "somewhat" by food allergies.[9] Food-allergic children may already feel isolated from friends at school because they have to sit at the "allergy table" or can't eat the cupcakes when there's a birthday party. Most of all, they don't want to be a burden. It can be very stressful for food-allergic children when every meal, every restaurant choice, and even every trip to the mall has to be planned around their food restrictions. It's a fact of life that those of us with food allergies have to adapt when we are out, which is why I feel so strongly that we should strive to be stress-free when eating at home.

When one family member has food allergies, it's tempting to make two different meals—and in some cases (e.g., multiple family members with food allergies, or conflicting allergies) that may be necessary—but whenever possible, I like to make the same meal for the whole family. Depending on your family's needs (and whether all family members are willing to follow an allergen-free diet), you may need to adapt selected items; for example, if you're making hamburgers, substitute an allergen-free dinner roll for the wheat bun on your daughter's plate. Be sure to fill the plate for the food-allergic child first, before handling any potential food allergens.

If possible (and if your plan to keep your family safe allows), let your food-allergic child sit at the dinner table with the family and enjoy the dynamic that is your unique family experience. If you're worried about little hands getting into food that they shouldn't, I suggest keeping the serving dishes off the table and seating that child strategically to avoid problems.

Holidays and family gatherings are even more critical. I like to host Thanksgiving dinner at my house, and nothing goes on the menu unless it's allergen-free and safe for everyone at the table. After all, there should be at least a few days a year when every warmed dinner roll, every savory side dish, and every delicious dessert can be passed around the table and everyone can eat as much as they want!

Breaking the rules

There are few cases where the ingredients in a recipe need to be followed to the letter. Unless you're whipping eggs to make a meringue, or making a dish that centers around the egg or cheese itself (e.g., omelets or cheese-cake), chances are there is a way to substitute for most ingredients, and I encourage you to do just that. If a recipe calls for hemp milk, feel free to try rice milk instead. There's no penalty. Really. Experimenting is not only encouraged, it's a necessity when you need to substitute for food allergens.

It's lucky that I have a rebellious streak, because I've always looked for ways to modify recipes or switch them up a bit. Once I started baking allergen-free, even more substitutions were necessary. I began to look at recipes as a blueprint or a guide, rather than a rule. I first started adapting recipes by tentatively substituting to avoid allergens, but still sticking to basics. Often, I was disappointed with the results. I wanted them to look and taste like they had in the past. It wasn't until I started to embrace new foods that I really started to enjoy baking again. Instead of baking *without* wheat, milk, soy, eggs, and nuts, I was baking *with* amaranth, oats, millet, hemp, coconut, flaxseeds, and a variety of new foods—and soon, you will be too!

While the ingredients provide a blueprint, the techniques and methods used to bake do matter. Throughout the book I share twelve years' worth of hints, tricks, and tips to help your allergen-free baked goods be the best they can. Some of these techniques take a little bit of practice, but once you've tried them a few times you will be able to fool everyone into thinking that you've been baking forever, even if you're baking for the first time. You may even develop some techniques of your own, and I'd love to hear about them.

I have used a variety of ingredients in my recipes to give you a flavor of what is possible. If I suggest sunflower oil and you prefer canola oil, go for it. If you need to avoid coconut or flaxseeds due to an allergy, go ahead and substitute for them. If you want to try to make a recipe sweeter, add ¼ cup of sugar or honey and reduce the liquids a bit to compensate (see page 140 to learn why). The more you understand the ingredients you are using, the easier it will be to substitute them for the foods you are allergic to. There are endless possibilities and ways to combine wheat-free grains with non-dairy milks, sugars, and egg replacements to create just about any baked good you may be craving.

Go ahead, break the rules!

Key Lessons

✓ Wheat, milk, soy, eggs, tree nuts, peanuts, fish, and shellfish (the top eight food allergens) must be clearly identified in the ingredients lists on food labels in the United States.

✓ Always read the detailed ingredients list on every product label every time you buy the product to ensure that it is safe for your family.

✓ Vendors may include warnings about cross-contamination (e.g., "May contain nuts"), but they are not required to.

✓ Err on the side of caution when selecting products; if you're not sure, leave it on the shelf.

✓ If you are allergic to tree nuts, consult your physician to determine whether coconut is safe for you. If you are allergic to soy, consult your physician to determine whether soybean oil and soy lecithin are safe for you.

✓ "Gluten-free" and "vegan" designations on product labels are helpful to indicate products that may be wheat-free and dairy-free (respectively), but you must still scrutinize the detailed ingredients list to be sure.

✓ Whenever possible, choose packaged whole foods with the fewest ingredients; avoid the open bins and products that have been packaged at the store.

✓ Healthy eating means choosing foods that will keep your family safe.

✓ Experiment with ingredients and enjoy exploring new foods!

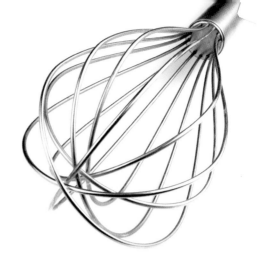

Replacing Wheat

WHEAT IS EVERYWHERE. Of the foods we eat in the United States, more are made with wheat than with any other grain.[10] Wheat is grown in forty-two of our fifty states. One acre of farmland yields forty-two bushels of wheat, and each bushel of wheat yields between forty-two and ninety loaves of bread. The result is a whole lot of bread, and a massive number of products in our grocery stores based on wheat. Our food supply is heavily wheat-based because it is available and affordable to produce.

As Americans, we didn't always eat as much wheat as we do today. In fact, wheat is not indigenous to the United States; it was first grown in this country in the late 1700s. Wheat is believed to have made its way to Europe from the Middle East (Syria and Turkey), and later brought to the United States.

Yet, wheat makes so many of us sick. In his book *Healthier Without Wheat*, Dr. Stephen Wangen writes that "many millions of (Americans) have not been fortunate enough to inherit the genetic makeup that allows us to enjoy the nutritional benefits of wheat without suffering from one or more of the many potential illnesses that a reaction to wheat can cause."[11] Those illnesses include autoimmune reactions such as food allergies and celiac disease, as well as intolerances (where a person lacks the enzyme needed to properly digest the food).

When you walk the center aisles of the grocery store, a large proportion of the processed foods you inspect will contain wheat. So much of what we eat every day, including bread, pasta, and desserts, is made from wheat. Even a loaf of bread that is sold as oat bread most likely has wheat as an ingredient, possibly even the first ingredient. That's the bad news.

The good news? There are many great grains (some you may be hearing about for the first time) that can replace wheat, and these foods are becoming more readily available. Before we take a look at the grains that you can eat, let's explore what to avoid.

Gluten-free versus wheat-free

Common wheat belongs to a genus of grasses known as *Triticum*. The genus itself is also sometimes referred to as wheat. Those who are allergic to wheat need to avoid all of the *Triticum* grains, including triticale, durum wheat, kamut, spelt, and einkorn. While these grains are sometimes suggested as alternatives to wheat in recipes, if you are allergic to wheat you must avoid them all. Any grain in the wheat or *Triticum* family must be labeled "wheat" on processed food packages, as discussed earlier (see page 6).

Gluten is a protein found in certain grains, which gives the grain special properties. First, gluten brings elasticity to the flours made from these grains, which gives them the fluffiness and stretchiness we typically associate with bread. Gluten also traps the gases released by yeast, both before and during the baking process. When you bake with gluten-free grains, you will use some different techniques than traditional bakers use.

Wheat contains gluten. Rye and barley also contain gluten. If you are allergic to wheat, you may be able to eat rye and barley, but there is a strong association of cross-reactivity with wheat, rye, and barley allergies. If you are gluten-intolerant or have celiac disease, you must avoid all of the gluten grains (wheat and its brothers, rye and barley). If you are allergic to wheat, you should work with your allergist to determine whether you also need to avoid rye and barley. While some people believe that oats also contain gluten, this is incorrect; oats are naturally gluten-free, but are often subject to contamination (see page 8).

If a grain is gluten-free, we know it's not wheat. But here's the catch—while most products on the grocery store shelves that are labeled "gluten-free" are indeed wheat-free, the proposed gluten-free labeling laws in the United States and established laws implemented in other parts of the world *do* allow for a small amount of gluten to remain in products labeled "gluten-free." That opens the door for manufacturers to process wheat and create wheat-based products with most of the gluten removed. One example is a product available in the United Kingdom known as Codex wheat starch, a wheat starch that has been processed to remove the gluten to a level that is within the United Kingdom's Codex gluten-free standard. Even though this product is considered gluten-free, it is not safe for someone with a wheat allergy.

If a product is wheat-free, that does not necessarily mean that it is gluten-free, as it may still contain other gluten grains. Remember that while all food products containing wheat must be clearly labeled, there is not yet an FDA labeling standard for gluten; you must still read the detailed ingredients list when a product is labeled "gluten-free." Also, as noted earlier, keep in mind that the proposed gluten-free labeling standard will be voluntary and will still allow a small threshold of gluten (and therefore possibly wheat) to be included in the product (see page 11). Both the wheat-allergic and those who need to eat gluten-free should avoid all products that have wheat listed as an ingredient.

All of the recipes I share with you in this book are intended to address the needs of both the food-allergic and the gluten-intolerant. For that reason, and because rye and barley are usually processed side by side with wheat (leading to a high possibility of contamination), I have focused on grains that are both wheat-free and gluten-free in my recipes.

Great grains

The only bread we had in my childhood home was white bread. I actually believed that bread in its natural state was white. Imagine my surprise when I started exploring alternative grains and discovered that they came in all shapes, sizes, colors, and flavors. Let's take a look at some of the many grains you can eat, and the flours you will be using as you bake allergen-free.

RICE: Rice flours are among the most commonly used flours in gluten-free and allergen-free baking. They can be made from any of the rice grains by grinding down the grains. Common rice flours include white rice flour, brown rice flour, and sweet rice flour. Brown rice flour is a whole grain, whereas white rice flour is the processed version of that grain (with the bran and germ removed). A simple way to think about it is using this analogy: White rice flour is to brown rice flour as traditional white flour is to whole wheat flour. Sweet rice flour comes from a sticky type of rice, and will perform differently from its cousins. You should be aware that rice flours of all varieties are high in carbohydrates and calories, and low in fiber.

Rice flours are commonly used in gluten-free flour blends. One of the reasons for this is the flour's mild taste, which helps it to mimic a traditional taste in breads and baked goods. On the flip side, rice flours can be grainy. All rice flours perform best when they are very finely milled. The finely milled rice flours will be more expensive, but they are worth it.

OATS: Oats have gotten a bad rap. I mentioned earlier that some people believe oats contain gluten. The reason for the confusion is that most oat crops are processed in the same facilities and on the same equipment as wheat, making them off-limits to those with wheat allergies and celiac disease. Until recently, gluten-free oats have been difficult to find, but some manufacturers are stepping up to the plate and offering oatmeal and oat flours that are certified gluten-free; I have used these products with great results. Oat flour is simply ground oats (you can easily make your own with a food processor or high-speed blender). It offers a nice consistency for baking, as well as additional protein.

Oat flour has a somewhat sweet taste, and works extremely well in baking when combined with other flours. If you want an oat taste in your baked goods, I recommend replacing up to half of the flour blend you are using with oat flour; one example of this combination is in the Banana Bread recipe (page 94).

CORN AND MILLET: Corn (also known as maize) is one of the most widely grown crops in the Americas. Corn flour is finely milled from corn grain. Cornmeal is a coarsely grained version of the same crop. Like most non-gluten grains, corn flour and cornmeal perform best when combined with other flours. For example, the corn bread and muffin mix I use to make Spicy Corn Bread (page 235) combines cornmeal with rice flours and starches.

sorghum

brown rice

buckwheat

millet

garbanzo bean

oat

When a recipe calls for cornmeal, look for a product with a medium grind unless the recipe specifies otherwise.

Most people associate millet with birdfeed, but is it just for the birds? I don't think so. Millet is a highly nutritious grain with approximately 3 grams of protein per ¼ cup serving (similar to wheat) and is rich in iron, thiamine, and riboflavin. It can easily be grown without pesticides, and it's considered one of the easiest grains to digest. In fact, given these great characteristics, it's surprising we don't eat a lot more of it.

One of the first over-the-counter breads I found that my son could eat (one that didn't contain wheat, milk, soy, or eggs) was millet bread by Food for Life. Since that time, millet has become a favorite in my home. It has a distinctive whole-grain taste, similar to corn. For that reason I like to use it as a featured grain, combining millet with a favorite gluten-free flour blend, as you will see in Millet Baguettes (page 169). Because corn and millet are related grains, those with corn allergies will usually need to avoid both.

SORGHUM, BUCKWHEAT, QUINOA, AMARANTH, AND TEFF: These whole grains are used to make flours that pack a powerful punch. While each of them has its own unique taste, they are all nutrient-rich, with generous amounts of protein, fiber, and minerals. Sorghum has a rather bland flavor, but mixes well with rice and bean flours. Buckwheat has a strong, nutty taste, and is one of my favorites. Despite its name, buckwheat is not wheat—in fact, it's not even a close relative, being far removed from wheat in the family of grasses.

Quinoa and amaranth are becoming more popular and more widely available. They can be found in cereals and pastas, as well as flours. In my experience, people either love these grains and can't get enough of them, or they have a strong preference for other flours.

Teff is very fine—the smallest grain in the world. It has a brownish-gray hue, and a slightly sweet (yet still mild) nutty taste.

As with all gluten-free varieties, flours made from these grains perform best when mixed with others. Some of my favorite gluten-free multigrain flour blends contain many of them. Although the recipes in this book use flours made from buckwheat, amaranth, quinoa, and teff, they can all be cooked in their whole, pre-ground form and served as side dishes or the basis for a meal, similar to rice.

BEANS: In addition to grains or grasses, flours can also be made from beans, including fava and garbanzo beans (also known as chickpeas). Bean flours are far more popular in parts of Asia and India than in the United States and are commonly used in Indian cuisine. They are high in carbohydrates, but also high in protein, making them a more balanced replacement for wheat than the popular rice flours. Garbanzo and fava bean flours are sometimes combined into a single flour blend, called garfava. You might expect bean flours to come on strong, but they have a surprisingly mild taste. This makes them a great replacement for rice flours in your flour blends, especially if you are looking for more protein.

As you consider using bean flours, keep in mind that beans are legumes, as are peanuts. Please check with your doctor, as there is potential for cross-reactivity to beans if you are allergic to peanuts.

STARCHES: Starches are, by definition, not whole foods; flours referred to as starches are produced by extracting a portion of the whole food from the heart of the plant. Popular starches used in baking are tapioca, potato, and corn starch.

Tapioca starch is derived from the root of a cassava plant. There is no difference between tapioca flour and tapioca starch; you will find this product referred to by both names on the market. Potato starch, on the other hand, is different from potato flour. Potato flour is made from whole potatoes (including the skins), and should be used when you want flour with a potato taste. (One example would be for potato pancakes.) Potato starch is the starch extracted from the potato. Likewise, corn starch is the starch extracted from corn. These starches are essentially tasteless and won't affect the flavor of your baked goods.

Starches provide little in the way of flavor and even less in terms of nutrition. They are nearly pure carbohydrates, with virtually no protein and minute amounts of fiber. However, starches play a very special role in gluten-free baking as thickening agents. They are used to thicken fruit fillings and sauces, and—even more important—to help hold gluten-free flours together. Note that when mixing your own flour blends you should always include at least one starch. Take care to not use corn starch if you are allergic to corn, or potato starch if you are allergic to nightshades.

It's important to note that the buckwheat pancakes at the pancake house or the corn tortillas at the Mexican restaurant may contain as much wheat as they do buckwheat or corn. Never assume ingredients based on the name of a dish; always check to be sure they are safe for you.

Even when made from the same grain, not all flours are equal, and that is especially evident when it comes to rice flours. I learned this the hard way as I attempted to make Poured Pizza Crust (page 124) with an off-the-shelf (rice-based) gluten-free flour blend. After partially baking (when it was time to add the pizza toppings) I flipped the crust and watched it crumble in my hands. Instead of wasting my toppings on a subpar crust, I decided to start over with King Arthur Flour Gluten Free Multi-purpose flour, another rice-based flour blend. This time my crust held together and browned nicely, creating a perfect pizza. As you work with flour blends, you will discover your own favorites. A superfine rice flour will give you a better result. King Arthur Flour, Bob's Red Mill, and Authentic Foods all market finely milled rice flours.

Many flours, including gluten-free flours, pick up moisture easily, and should be stored in an airtight container in a cool dry place. Most packaged flours are safe in the pantry until opened. Once opened, I suggest storing flours that you use frequently in the refrigerator. Those you use infrequently can be stored in the freezer. Whether refrigerated or frozen, flours perform best in most recipes when brought to room temperature before baking. Note that flours can go rancid; if you notice a foul odor when you scoop out your flour, you know it is time to replace it.

A friend asked me recently whether a flour blend I had recommended would have "that gluten-free taste," reminding me to let you know that many of the gluten-free flours mentioned here, especially the whole grain and bean flours, do not taste like wheat. Of course, there is no such thing as a gluten-free taste; it's the flavor of the various grains and the unfamiliar texture that she was experiencing. There is a world of grains to explore, and you and your family will have your preferences. I love buckwheat and oat, while my son craves millet. I know some families that swear by quinoa, while others like to stick to the more mild-tasting rice grains. Keep experimenting until you discover what you love—there's a grain out there for everyone.

There's one final point to consider as you select flour: Avoid buying flour that has been packaged at the store. One of the first things I see when I enter my local health food store is a refrigerated section that contains all variety of flours in plastic bags with twist ties. Opt for flours that are packaged and sealed at the manufacturing site, instead of these. There's just no way to ensure that the scoop used for the rice flour or the buckwheat flour wasn't the same scoop used for the spelt or wheat flours. The same caution goes for cereal, granola, and other products packaged locally. Even if the ingredients appear safe, and even if their label says "gluten-free," unintentional contamination is what you need to be concerned about here.

The role of gums

Nearly all recipes for wheat-free baked goods and gluten-free baking mixes will include an ingredient called a gum; most often this is xanthan gum. Xanthan gum is a polysaccharide (a chain of three different forms of sugar) created by combining bacteria with corn sugar. That sounds kind of yucky, so let's look closer. Xanthan gum is a carbohydrate. It's made from all natural ingredients, and is similar to more familiar polysaccharides, including corn syrup. Are you concerned that xanthan gum is made from bacteria? Consider that yogurt is made from combining bacteria with milk. Similarly, adding lactic acid bacteria to milk makes buttermilk. They are all made using fermentation processes.

Because it's a created food, some may think that xanthan gum should be avoided, but it's very helpful (possibly even indispensable) when baking without gluten. Like starches, gums will help thicken a batter or sauce, but they go a step further: they have binding properties that help bring back some of the elasticity we lose in our flours when we eliminate gluten. The same recipe made with and without xanthan gum will have very different results: the quick bread made without xanthan gum will fall to pieces as you bite into it, whereas the bread with xanthan gum will have a bit of springiness to it—not quite like a wheat bread, but enough to allow you to slice it.

If you can't use xanthan gum (those with corn allergies may need to avoid it), an alternative is guar gum. Guar gum is less commonly used in packaged flour blends and baking mixes, but can be found in specialty food stores and online. Like xanthan gum, this product (which is extracted from the guar bean) has thickening and binding qualities. If you need to forgo the gums completely in your gluten-free baking, I suggest that you choose flour blends that are high in protein and increase the amount of starch (tapioca, potato, or corn starch) you add to your flour blend.

When you go shopping, you will quickly notice that gums are very expensive. Xanthan gum costs as much as three dollars per ounce, but keep in mind that you will use very little (¼ to ½ teaspoon) in each baking project. Depending on the amount of baking you do, one 2-ounce cylinder of xanthan gum could last you many months. Resist the urge to buy larger quantities to decrease the cost, as xanthan gum does go bad after about a year. Store opened containers of xanthan gum in the refrigerator.

How to use gums

Not surprisingly, there's a right way and a wrong way to use gums. The first key to using gums is to use the right amount. Only a tiny amount is needed to achieve the desired result. I recommend no more than ¼ teaspoon per cup of flour used. While some gluten-free recipes suggest much more, I find this ratio to be just enough to achieve the desired result—great baked goods that hold together.

The next thing to keep in mind when baking with gums is that they glob up very quickly when the powder mixes with liquid. No, *glob* is not a technical baking term, but it's appropriate to describe what happens. Try this experiment:

THE EFFECT OF XANTHAN GUM

Mix ¼ teaspoon of xanthan gum with 1 teaspoon of warm water in a small glass or stainless-steel bowl. Use a toothpick to mix the powder with the water. Notice that within seconds, the mixture thickens and a gel forms. Within five minutes you will have a gluey ball, and within fifteen minutes you will be able to easily lift that ball out of your container with just a toothpick. (If you wait longer, it will be harder to lift because the ball will stick to the bowl.)

If a lump of xanthan gum is left in your cake before you put it in the oven, it will harden when baking, creating a mass that certainly won't taste good but could also be a choking hazard. I'm not trying to scare you, but I do want to stress that gums must be used properly. The right way is to use a tiny amount and mix it in extremely well with your dry ingredients. When this very fine powder is well blended with your flour, in the right amounts, it will do wonders for your breads, muffins, and cakes.

Off-the-shelf gluten-free flour blends

When I was baking with wheat I rarely thought about the flour I used; simple all-purpose baking flour (made from one grain—wheat) would usually do. When I started baking wheat-free, selecting flours became more complicated. I found myself buying lots of individual packages of flour—rice, potato, tapioca, sorghum, quinoa, teff—and in different varieties—sweet rice, brown rice, white rice, and so on. Who knew there were so many grains, varieties, and brands to choose from? We're certainly lucky that we have that choice, but trying to find the right flour for the job can be a challenge.

One thing that all gluten-free bakers agree on is that flours must be blended together to get great results. If you try to make muffins with just rice flour, they will be bland, dry, and crumbly. If you attempt to make yeast bread with just millet flour, you will have a rock-hard loaf. Even a quick bread with just oat flour will result in too strong a taste and a bread that sinks to the bottom of your stomach. Flours must be mixed to get the best results.

Gluten-free flour blends take a lot of the guesswork out of that task. These blends, now available from food vendors that focus on the gluten-free and allergen-free markets, as well as from many larger food vendors that are expanding their product lines, make life much simpler for allergen-free bakers—and they take up a lot less room in the pantry and the refrigerator.

Many gluten-free bakers also suggest that more than one flour blend is needed to address the varying needs of cakes, cookies, pies, and breads. Richard Coppedge, a certified master baker at the Culinary Institute of America, suggests five different flour blends in his book *Gluten-Free Baking with The Culinary Institute of America*, ranging from weak (high carbohydrate) to strong (high protein).[12] Although some of Chef Coppedge's blends won't be options for the food-allergic (as they contain soy and milk proteins), the concept he teaches makes sense. Depending on what you are baking, different flour blends will work better than others.

To simplify this for you, I have chosen to classify flour blends in two categories: Those that I am calling "white" flours are primarily rice flours and starches, and those that I am calling "multigrain" contain flours made from higher-protein grains and beans.

One of the ingredients you need to pay special attention to in a flour blend is xanthan gum (or other gums). Some flour blends include them, others do not. If the flour blend you choose contains xanthan gum, then you should leave out the xanthan gum in your recipe. There's no need to double up on this ingredient.

Even if they have similar ingredients, not all flour blends perform equally. I have tried dozens of gluten-free flour blends, and have selected the ones that follow to share with you here. I recommend these because they perform consistently, taste great, and are readily available, but new gluten-free flour blends are popping up on the grocery store shelves as food vendors address this growing need. Always make sure that any flour blend you choose—these or others—will be safe for *your* family's food allergies, but once you're comfortable with baking, feel free to experiment with new flour blends as you find them. I'll be trying them, too! I always keep my pantry stocked with at least one white flour blend and one multigrain flour blend.

RECOMMENDED WHEAT-FREE AND GLUTEN-FREE FLOUR BLENDS

	WITH XANTHAN GUM	WITHOUT XANTHAN GUM
White flour blends	Authentic Foods Multi Blend Gluten Free Flour Jules Gluten Free All Purpose Flour	King Arthur Flour Gluten Free Multi-purpose Flour Authentic Foods GF Classical Blend
Multigrain flour blends	Namaste Foods Perfect Flour Blend	Bob's Red Mill Gluten Free All Purpose Baking Flour King Arthur Flour Gluten Free Whole Grain Flour Blend

Let's take a closer look at each of them:

Authentic Foods Multi Blend Gluten Free Flour	Contains: Brown rice flour, sweet rice flour, tapioca starch, corn starch, potato starch, and xanthan gum This is a finely milled flour blend.
Jules Gluten Free All Purpose Flour	Contains: Expandex modified tapioca starch, potato starch, corn starch, corn flour, white rice flour, and xanthan gum This flour is unique in its use of a special starch that emulates the properties of wheat.
King Arthur Flour Gluten Free Multi-purpose Flour	Contains: Rice flour, tapioca starch, potato starch, and brown rice flour This is what I would describe as a white flour using only the finest ingredients.
Authentic Foods GF Classical Blend	Contains: Brown rice flour, potato starch, and tapioca flour Very similar to the Multi Blend Gluten Free Flour by the same brand, this flour contains no corn ingredients or xanthan gum.
Namaste Foods Perfect Flour Blend	Contains: Sweet brown rice flour, tapioca flour, arrowroot flour, sorghum flour, and xanthan gum This flour combines rice with other grains.
Bob's Red Mill Gluten Free All Purpose Baking Flour	Contains: Garbanzo bean flour, potato starch, tapioca flour, white sorghum flour, and fava bean flour This higher-protein flour blend swaps out the rice in favor of bean and sorghum flours.
King Arthur Flour Gluten Free Whole Grain Flour Blend	Contains: Sorghum flour, brown rice flour, amaranth flour, quinoa, millet, teff, and tapioca flour You may not be able to find a better combination of whole grains than with this flour blend.

While almost all of these flour blends describe their usage as "all purpose" they vary considerably in their ingredients, taste, and performance in different recipes. Jules Gluten Free All Purpose Flour is, hands down, the best I have found for baking yeast breads. The Expandex modified tapioca starch in this blend gives bread an elasticity that I haven't found with any other flour blend on the market today. When I want white flour for cakes or muffins, I reach for King Arthur Flour Gluten Free Multipurpose blend. However, I often find myself choosing the Namaste Foods Perfect Flour Blend or the King Arthur Flour Gluten Free Whole Grain blend; these two flours are my favorite everyday gluten-free all-purpose flours. Note that they both contain multiple whole-grain flours, one with and one without xanthan gum.

To keep things simple, I suggest using gluten-free flour blends in my recipes. Any of the blends recommended here will work. I have made each of my recipes dozens of times, and each of them with at least two (often three) of these flour blends. I suggest you try a few and see which you and your family like best. Availability of each of these flours varies depending on where you live; in the United States today, Authentic Foods products are easier to find on the West Coast, while King Arthur Flour is easier to find on the East Coast. Which you select is up to you. Always check the ingredients and scrutinize the warning labels. Choose flour blends that are safe for your family and stock your pantry with at least two or three of them. If you live outside the United States, look for gluten-free flour blends with similar ingredients, paying special attention to whether the gums are already added.

One technique I like to use is to combine a flour blend with a featured flour. You can see examples of this in the Millet Baguette recipe (page 169), where I combine millet flour with a gluten-free flour blend, and the Banana Bread recipe (page 94), where I use half oat flour and half gluten-free flour blend. This technique really gives your baked goods some variety with a pop of flavor.

Mixing your own flour blends

While many great gluten-free flour blends are available on the market today (and more are being introduced every month), there are a few reasons why you may want to mix your own. It's possible that you aren't able to find a blend that addresses your family's particular food allergies, they may not be available in your local markets and you don't want to purchase them online, or you may just prefer a different combination of flours than you can find in a packaged blend. You may be a do-it-yourselfer who wants to control the exact ingredients of your blend. Whatever the reason, you should keep in mind the following when mixing your own flour blend:

* PROPORTION MATTERS. If you want consistent results, you will need to consistently use the same amounts of each type of flour in your blend. Gluten-free bakers will typically combine rice flour (either brown rice or white rice) with potato starch (not flour) and tapioca starch to create a white flour. In recommendations for a 2-cup blend of flour I have seen proportions ranging from high to low starch, as in the chart below.

FORMULAS FOR A 2-CUP WHITE GLUTEN-FREE FLOUR BLEND

HIGHER-STARCH FORMULA	LOWER-STARCH FORMULA
1 cup rice flour ½ cup potato starch ½ cup tapioca starch	1⅓ cups rice flour ⅓ cup potato starch ⅓ cup tapioca starch

If you are mixing a rice-based flour blend, I recommend you stay within the above proportions. If you prefer more protein in your flour blend, you can reduce the total starch within your blend to as little as ½ cup per 2 cups of flour. The protein in conjunction with the starch will help to hold your baked goods together. Here are a couple of suggested multigrain flour blends for you to try:

FORMULAS FOR A 2-CUP MULTIGRAIN GLUTEN-FREE FLOUR BLEND

SORGHUM BLEND	AMARANTH/QUINOA BLEND
¾ cup brown rice flour ¾ cup sorghum flour ½ cup tapioca starch	½ cup brown rice flour ⅓ cup quinoa flour ⅔ cup amaranth flour ½ cup tapioca starch

As you experiment with your own flour blends, always try to keep at least 25 percent of the blend as a starch.

* MIX IN ADVANCE. Once you find a blend you like, mix up large batches so you don't have to mix every time you bake. Always be

sure to blend the flours together extremely well and store them in airtight containers in the refrigerator.

✳ HOLD THE XANTHAN GUM. Don't add the xanthan gum directly to your blend; save this step for when you are ready to bake. I find it difficult to ensure that small amounts of xanthan gum are well blended when dealing with large volumes of flour.

Gluten-free biscuit and baking mixes

Some gluten-free product vendors have introduced what they call a biscuit and baking mix—an all-purpose mix with which you can make a variety of baked goods. These are sometimes called pancake and baking mixes. They differ from the all-purpose flour blends (which are typically just flours or flours and xanthan gum) in that they include baking powder, baking soda, and salt right in the mix. They are the gluten-free world's response to the classic Bisquick baking mix.

Biscuit and baking mixes are convenient to have on hand, but note that they do vary—each with a different blend of flours. I have featured one of these mixes in chapter 12, with the Blueberry Pancakes (page 230), to show you how easily these can be used in allergen-free baking. They can also be used to make simple biscuits, or crusts. Try this simple recipe for a mock potpie crust:

Mock Potpie Crust

MAKES ONE CRUST

⅔ cup gluten-free biscuit and baking mix

1 cup hemp or rice milk

3 teaspoons Ener-G Egg Replacer mixed with 4 tablespoons
   warm water (equal to 2 eggs; see page 62 for instructions)

Whisk all of the ingredients together well. Pour the mixture over your potpie and bake in a preheated 350°F oven for 25 to 30 minutes, until the crust is lightly browned.

Most of the recipes I share with you in this book call for a gluten-free flour blend, but you can substitute one of these biscuit and baking mixes by eliminating the added salt, baking powder and/or baking soda, and xanthan gum.

Measuring flour

Every baking class I have taken has included a discussion on baking by weight rather than volume. The rationale of the master bakers who teach these classes is that weights don't lie. Your cup of flour may not weigh the same as my cup of flour. One of us may be packing it down, while the other is sifting or keeping it loosely packed; we all measure differently.

When working with gluten-free flour blends and different grains, the problem is further complicated. Consider that King Arthur Flour All-Purpose [wheat] Flour and King Arthur Flour Whole Wheat Flour both weigh 120 grams per cup. One cup of oat flour weighs just 110 grams, whereas rice flour is very heavy, some varieties weighing upward of 160 grams per cup. That is a huge variation, and it does make a difference when you are baking. A rice-based flour blend that weighs considerably more per cup than another flour will suck up the liquids in your muffins, leaving them too dry. Conversely, a flour blend that is too light will leave your cake a bit soggy.

Master bakers usually advocate weighing all of your ingredients, from the baking powder, to the eggs, to the flour. I am going to make it simple for you and suggest that you only need to worry about the weight of the flour. Why? You're not using eggs, so you don't have to worry about the difference between a large and a medium egg, and the weights of most of the other ingredients you will be using are fairly standard. Furthermore, flour is the top ingredient in most baked goods, causing it to have the greatest impact on the end result. It's primarily the flour-to-liquid ratio that you need to be concerned about, and the way to take care of that is by adjusting the amount of flour used.

Note the variance in the weights of the flour blends in the following table; there's a full 40-gram difference between the heaviest of these flour blends and the lightest.

I know what you're thinking—*Does it really matter?* Yes, it does. To give you an example, I made Double Chocolate Muffins (page 197) dozens of times with the Namaste Foods Perfect Flour Blend, and they were indeed perfect. I tried them with the King Arthur Flour Gluten Free Multi-purpose Flour (without adjusting for weight) and they were so dry that even the deer scavenging in our backyard didn't want them. When I adjusted for the weight of the flour, they fluffed up and tasted great. It may seem counterintuitive, but my muffins were larger when I reduced the amount of flour because the ingredients had the proper space to interact and do their job.

There's no need for you to make the same mistake. The recipes in this book have been developed to work best with a flour blend that weighs between 128 and 130 grams per cup. Does that mean you should only use the blends in that range? Absolutely not! The key is to adjust. You can do this either by using a kitchen scale (see page 73) and weighing as you go, or by making adjustments per the table below. It doesn't have to be perfect, just close.

WEIGHT ADJUSTMENTS FOR GLUTEN-FREE FLOUR BLENDS

	GRAMS PER CUP OF FLOUR	HOW TO ADJUST
Authentic Foods Multi Blend Gluten Free Flour	160	Reduce each cup of flour by 3 tablespoons
Jules Gluten Free All Purpose Flour	148	Reduce each cup of flour by 2 tablespoons
King Arthur Flour Gluten Free Multi-purpose Flour	160	Reduce each cup of flour by 3 tablespoons
Authentic Foods GF Classical Blend	128	Use 1 to 1
Namaste Foods Perfect Flour Blend	129	Use 1 to 1
Bob's Red Mill Gluten Free All Purpose Baking Flour	136	Reduce each cup by 2 teaspoons
King Arthur Flour Gluten Free Whole Grain Flour Blend	120	Add 1 tablespoon per cup

To measure flour for your recipe, simply add or reduce by the amount listed in the table. For example, if you choose to use King Arthur Gluten Free Multi-purpose Flour, and the recipe requires 2 cups of flour, reduce the amount you use by 6 tablespoons. Keep in mind that it's easier to compensate for too much liquid than too much flour once you've started baking. Err on the side of a bit less flour if you're not sure how much to use; you can always keep your baked goods in the oven a little longer. If you are mixing your own flour blend, aim for one that is in the range of 128 to 130 grams per cup.

When a recipe calls for a featured flour (e.g., the Sugar Cookies on page 131, which use ½ cup of buckwheat flour and ¾ cup of a gluten-free flour blend) adjust the weight for only the flour blend. Single-grain flours can vary dramatically in weight due to the differences in the grains. For example, oat flour is a lightweight at just 110 grams per cup, whereas buckwheat flour, at the other end of the spectrum, weighs in at 180 grams per cup. The recipes I have developed for you have taken the weight of these flours into consideration; there is no need to adjust for weight, unless you choose to use them to replace the gluten-free flour blend. See Appendix D on page 263 for the appropriate weights of these featured flours and other key ingredients.

Key Lessons

✓ If you have a wheat allergy, you must avoid all forms of wheat (including durum, kamut, spelt, and einkorn). Those who have celiac disease or a gluten intolerance must also avoid rye and barley. Work with your doctor to determine which grains are safe for you.

✓ There are many wheat-free and gluten-free flours to choose from, including rice, oat, corn, millet, sorghum, buckwheat, quinoa, amaranth, teff, and bean flours. Keep experimenting until you find the ones your family likes best.

✓ Opt for gluten-free oat flours and oatmeal to avoid possible cross-contamination.

✓ Gluten-free flours must be blended (rather than used on their own) to get the best results. Include at least ¼ cup of starch per cup of flour blend.

✓ Off-the-shelf gluten-free flour blends can simplify the job and save you time. Be sure to check all ingredients and warning labels and choose flour blends that are safe for you and your family.

✓ Xanthan gum is used in gluten-free baking to help bind ingredients and provide elasticity. Use ¼ teaspoon of xanthan gum per cup of flour; be sure to mix it in well with the flour before adding the wet ingredients.

✓ Gluten-free flour blends vary considerably in terms of weight. You will need to adjust the amount of flour you use accordingly (see page 33).

3

Replacing Milk and Avoiding Soy

COW'S MILK IS ANOTHER staple of the American diet. Cereal and milk are served at most breakfast tables. That standard school cafeteria lunch—the one that caused my son's distress in elementary school—comes with milk. Almost all baked goods contain—you guessed it—milk. If you suffer from multiple food allergies, the problem is compounded. The most common replacement for cow's milk is soy milk, but that's not an option for those with a soy allergy. Soy milk is also used in some dairy-free baked goods, but less so in recent years as more alternatives to milk have become available and more food vendors aim to eliminate the top allergens from their products. You can also find non-dairy milk made from nuts (including almonds and hazelnuts), but these aren't options for those allergic to tree nuts. Even with cow's milk, soy milk, and nut milks off the table, there are still plenty of non-dairy milk alternatives readily available at your local store.

Most grocery stores have a few shelves dedicated to milk alternatives. Many of the non-dairy milks can be found on a non-refrigerated shelf where you would also find the soy milk. They may be near the breakfast cereals, the baking aisle, or—if your grocery store has a health food or specialty food section—you might find them there. And you might be surprised to see all of the choices you have!

Technically, milk is produced by mammals (including humans, horses, cows, and goats), and while that would make the products I am about to discuss "alternatives to milk" or "milk substitutes," for simplicity I will refer to them simply as milk(s). These milks are actually made from seeds or grains, which are soaked in water, then pressed and strained to extract the milk. It's a bit like the process used to create wine from grapes (but without the fermentation and aging). In fact, it's quite possible (but time-consuming) to make your own milk from seeds and grains.

One big advantage to non-dairy milks is the packaging. They are typically sold in unrefrigerated boxed containers, just as you would find many brands of soy milk or the stock you buy for making soup. A quart-size (32-ounce) non-dairy beverage usually comes in a 7¾ by 3½ by 2¼-inch container. The aseptic packaging techniques allow the milk to remain shelf-stable without refrigeration—and without artificial preservatives. The cartons are easy to store and their shelf life is up to a year. They should be refrigerated once opened, and most will keep for up to ten days in the refrigerator (or even longer). If you use your favorite non-dairy milk on a daily basis, it's unlikely that you will need to toss it because it has spoiled. Be sure to check the expiration date before you buy.

While you may be longing for something that tastes just like cow's milk, you won't find exactly that. Each non-dairy milk has a unique flavor. Most don't look like cow's milk, either, but you'll soon forget that when you start to think of them as a great addition to an allergen-free diet, providing high-quality nutrients and calories. We'll explore some of the choices you have in more detail below, but first, let's take a closer look at cow's milk.

Cow's milk consists of fat (butterfat), sugar (lactose), and proteins. The two proteins in cow's milk—casein and whey—are most often responsible for milk allergies. In fact, it is nearly always the proteins in food that trigger allergic reactions. While we commonly consume cow's milk in its whole form, it is often broken down into components when added to processed food. If you have a milk allergy, you need to steer clear of casein and whey. These ingredients are commonly used in baking mixes, protein shakes, energy bars, and more. As discussed in chapter 1, thanks to the Food Allergen Labeling and Consumer Protection Act of 2004, food labels must now also contain the word *milk* when the product contains any milk ingredient (see page 6).

So what about Lactaid, a milk that was developed for the lactose-intolerant? Those of us who are lactose intolerant have an inability to digest the lactose (the sugar) in milk; our bodies lack the enzyme lactase that is required to break down the sugar. Lactaid brand milk (usually found in the refrigerated section of the grocery store, next to the cow's milk) has the lactase enzyme added. That's great if you only suffer from lactose intolerance, but this milk contains all of the same proteins that cause food allergies and is not an option for those allergic to milk.

Keep in mind that all forms of cow's milk—reduced-fat milk, low-fat milk, powdered milk, condensed milk, organic milk, raw milk—are still milk, and are not options for the milk-allergic.

You may be tempted to turn to goat's milk as an alternative to cow's milk. Here's what you need to know: The proteins in milk from goats are very similar to the proteins in cow's milk that cause allergic reactions; clinical studies have shown that up to 92 percent of those allergic to cow's milk are also allergic to goat's milk.[13] Consult your doctor if you want to try goat's milk.

Non-dairy milk options

Substituting for cow's milk when baking is simple. With all of the milks discussed here, you will replace cup for cup; if a traditional recipe calls for 1 cup of milk, you may substitute 1 cup of any non-dairy, non-soy, nut-free milk. It's important to consider the role that milk ingredients play in baking. First and foremost, milk provides liquid to mix with dry ingredients and helps hold your baked goods together. Milk also provides nutrients and taste, which will vary depending on the non-dairy milk you choose. Here are some of the options you have:

RICE MILK: Rice milk is the most widely available of the non-dairy and non-soy milk alternatives. It is made from rice grains (usually brown rice) and comes in a variety of flavors. The most popular and widely available rice milk brands include Rice Dream from Imagine Foods (part of the Hain Celestial Group) and Rice non-dairy beverage from Pacific Natural Foods.

Rice Dream milks are available in original (think of this as plain versus flavored), vanilla, and chocolate, as well as a couple of exotic flavors including horchata and carob. In the refrigerated section of the grocery store you will also find Rice Dream milks that are essentially the same as their non-refrigerated cousins—the difference is the packaging. The refrigerated versions come in a traditional milk carton, and stay fresh unopened for forty-five days.

Pacific Natural Foods Rice milks come in low-fat plain and low-fat vanilla varieties. While Pacific Natural Foods calls their product low-fat, most rice milks have a relatively low fat content (between 2 and 3 grams per serving). Both Pacific Natural Foods and Rice Dream's rice milk products are gluten-free, but you should be aware that most companies that make rice milk also make soy milk, including these two. Always read the label and check with the food vendor for their most recent allergen statement to determine if the product is right for you.

So what does rice milk taste like? Plain rice milk has a light, sweet taste, with a smooth consistency that closely resembles that of cow's milk. Due to its mild taste, rice milk is very versatile and can easily be substituted for cow's milk in recipes. The flavored varieties take on the flavor of their name—for example, chocolate rice milk has a chocolate taste. The flavored milks also pack more calories and sugar.

While the calorie content of rice milk and most of the other milks discussed here is similar to that of cow's milk, the milks vary considerably in nutritional makeup. Rice milk is high in carbohydrates—not surprisingly, as rice is indeed a grain. While the nutritional content of rice milks vary little from vendor to vendor, the newest formulas of these rice milks are enriched with vitamins and minerals. When cow's milk is eliminated from your diet, your first concern (and rightly so) might be how to get enough calcium and vitamin D. Added calcium and vitamins in some of the enriched versions of these rice milks give them a vitamin profile similar to that of cow's milk.

HEMP MILK: When I suggest to food-allergic families that they try hemp milk, I often get a funny look, and a question like, "What? Hemp? Isn't hemp the same thing as marijuana?" The answer is no; while both marijuana and hemp are from the same plant genus (*Cannabis*), marijuana and hemp come from different varieties, with some significant differences. The leaves of the marijuana plant contain tetrahydrocannabinol (THC), a psychoactive ingredient. But hemp has a very different profile—low in THC and high in cannabidiol (CBD), an antipsychoactive ingredient. Furthermore, hemp milk is made from the seeds of the plant, which contain no THC.

So, why the confusion? The United States Drug Enforcement Agency doesn't distinguish between varieties of the *Cannabis* plant. When the Controlled Substances Act of 1970 made it illegal to grow marijuana, growing hemp in the United States was also banned. But hemp is grown (legally) in Canada and most industrialized nations, and it is legal to purchase hemp in the United States. Organizations (including the North American Industrial Hemp Council and Vote Hemp) are working to legalize the production of hemp in the United States. Interestingly, despite the controversy and confusion surrounding it, hemp could be considered a wonder crop: It is an extremely hardy plant, requiring no pesticides or fertilizer and very little water to thrive, and hemp seeds offer terrific nutritional benefits, as you will soon see. I am optimistic that we may see hemp farming legalized in the United States within the next few years; every two years since 2007, Representative Ron Paul has introduced or reintroduced the Industrial Hemp Farming Act,[14] which would amend the Controlled Substances Act to exclude industrial hemp from the definition of marijuana.

While hemp is sometimes called a nut and has a rich nutty taste, it's not a nut; hemp is a seed. Best of all, the seeds have not been known to produce allergic reactions, and the milk formulas are free of all common allergens. Under the brand name Tempt, Living Harvest Foods offers original (plain), vanilla, chocolate, and unsweetened varieties of hemp milk. Manitoba Harvest also offers hemp milk under the brand name Hemp Bliss. Similar to Living Harvest, it comes in original, vanilla, chocolate, and unsweetened varieties. The vanilla and chocolate varieties take on those flavors. These two brands are dedicated to hemp products, making them an ideal choice for those concerned about cross-contamination.

Imagine Foods, which makes the Rice Dream milks discussed earlier, also markets hemp milk under the brand name Hemp Dream. Pacific Natural Foods offers hemp milk in original and vanilla flavors. Manitoba Harvest is a Canadian company, while Living Harvest, Imagine Foods, and Pacific Natural Foods are based in the United States and import hemp seeds from Canada.

One of the reasons hemp milk is a favorite in my family is its nutritional content. Hemp milk is a great source of protein. Because it is a natural source of calcium and vitamins, including vitamin D, it is an ideal alternative to cow's milk. And it's a great natural source of omega-3 and omega-6 fatty acids—something none of the other non-dairy milks can claim. Ninety-two percent of the fat content in Tempt hemp milk is omega essential fatty acids and one serving provides 50 percent of your estimated daily value of omega-3 EFAs. Until recently, hemp milk was much more expensive that other non-dairy milks, but costs have come down in the past couple of years.

If you flipped ahead and took a look at the recipes I have created for you, you will have seen that hemp milk is one of my favorites for baking. I love the richness of the milk, and find that the taste complements most baked goods. While I favor original hemp milk for most recipes, I usually choose chocolate hemp milk for chocolate baking recipes.

COCONUT MILK: As discussed earlier (and despite its misleading name), coconut is not a nut (see page 10), and most who are allergic to tree nuts will not need to avoid it. (Always check with your doctor, however.) Furthermore, coconuts are rarely processed in the same facilities as milk or soy products are, and coconut is naturally gluten-free. That makes coconut milk another fabulous option for replacing cow's milk when baking.

There are two different types of coconut milk that you should be aware of. The first is the traditional coconut milk that has been on the grocery store shelves for years. This milk usually comes in a 13- to 14-ounce can, and is often found in the Asian foods or specialty foods section of the store. It is used frequently in Southeast Asian cuisine, but if you're not a fan of Thai food you may not be familiar with it. Coconut milk in the can is as close to pure coconut milk as you can get; ingredients usually include coconut milk, water, and guar gum. This is very rich milk, and has the fat content to prove it; one cup of coconut milk can contain as much as 42 grams of fat—yikes! But one small can of coconut milk goes a long way. High-quality coconut milk will have a layer of cream on top; I suggest skimming off the cream and reserving it for making Whipped Coconut Cream (page 44). What's left can be mixed with water (1 to 1) to make a lighter version of coconut milk. If you choose to use the coconut milk in its richest form, be sure to mix it well.

There are also "light" versions of coconut milk in the can that more closely resemble the "coconut milk beverages" that have recently hit the grocery store shelves. These lighter beverages start with the same coconut milk you find in the can, with added water, sweeteners, and vitamins. They also contain considerably less fat—approximately 5 grams per cup. One such beverage is Turtle Mountain So Delicious Coconut Milk Beverage; it's dairy-free and comes in original, unsweetened, and vanilla flavors in refrigerated containers, and more varieties (including chocolate) in shelf-stable containers. The latter can usually be found next to the hemp milk and rice milk. Both types of coconut milk are great options for baking.

OAT MILK: As discussed earlier, while oats are gluten-free (and oats are not wheat), the processes used to manufacture oats lend themselves to cross-contamination (see page 8). Oats are frequently manufactured on the same equipment and in the same facilities as wheat. Although gluten-free oats can now be found on the market, as of the writing of this book, there is no widely available gluten-free oat milk. If someone in your family is allergic to wheat or is gluten-intolerant, then oat milk is not the right choice for you today, but I am confident that we will see gluten-free oat milk for sale over time.

Oat milk has a full body and a thick appearance, and is a little bit sweet. Unlike rice milk, which is white in color, oat milk has a bit of a tan or beige hue to it. The same is true for hemp milk, but don't worry; these milks simply take on the natural color of the grains or seeds used to produce them.

Pacific Natural Foods' oat milk is widely available in stores in the United States, in both plain and vanilla varieties. Like rice milk, oat milk is high in carbohydrates, but is also a good source of protein. Like Rice Dream, Pacific Foods' product is fortified with calcium and vitamins to mimic the nutritional qualities of cow's milk.

You may find great uses for all of these milks, or you may choose to stock your pantry with just a couple of favorites. In either case, I recommend trying a few different options to see what works for your family. Because they don't spoil quickly when unopened, it's practical to keep a variety of non-dairy milks on hand. Also keep in mind that all of these milks have a tendency to separate. Always shake them well before using.

When I'm creating recipes, I usually opt for hemp milk or coconut milk beverage. While each has a unique taste, I find that can work to my advantage. I love the taste of coconut paired with banana (see Banana Bread, page 94), or hemp paired with chocolate (see Triple-Play Chocolate Cake, page 198). If you prefer a milder taste, you may be more comfortable with rice milk. Feel free to substitute any milk that is safe for your family for the milks used in the recipes in this book. While your choice of milk will change the flavor of your baked goods, it will have little impact on the texture of your muffins or cakes.

There's one more option we should discuss for replacing cow's milk:

Whipped Coconut Cream

MAKES ABOUT 1½ CUPS OF WHIPPED CREAM

1 (14-ounce) can whole-fat coconut milk, refrigerated overnight
¼ cup confectioners' sugar

Drain the coconut milk from the bottom of the can (the cream will have risen to the top). Save the coconut milk in an airtight container in the refrigerator for a later baking project. Scoop the cream into a chilled mixing bowl. Use the whipping attachment on your mixer, and mix on low for about 10 seconds to soften the cream. Turn the mixer up to high, and whip for about 20 seconds, until the cream is fluffy. Add the confectioners' sugar and whip for about 20 seconds longer. Refrigerate and use within 24 hours.

Try this whipped cream with Eggless Chocolate Mousse (page 204).

Traditional sour cream and yogurt are similar in that they are both fermented versions of cow's cream or milk, with the sour cream having a higher fat content. When yogurt or sour cream is used in a baking recipe, it is usually to provide some thickness (as well as nutrients) to the product. The best non-dairy non-soy yogurt I have found is once again So Delicious, from Turtle Mountain; this company's plain (no flavor added) yogurt can be substituted 1 to 1 in recipes calling for dairy yogurt. Coconut milk yogurt can also be used to replace sour cream, but if you want to keep the same consistency, mix 1 part coconut cream (the skimmed-off cream from a can of coconut milk) to 3 parts coconut yogurt.

Another option to replace either yogurt or sour cream in recipes is a blend of non-dairy milk with applesauce. (See page 59 for more on applesauce and how to make your own.) I like to mix 1 part original hemp milk with 1 part unsweetened applesauce. The result is thickened milk with a denser consistency than the milk alone.

About oils

Nearly all traditional baking recipes use some type of fat, and most of the time those fats will be in the form of oil, butter, or margarine. Let's talk about oils first. As I mentioned in chapter 1, highly refined oils are exempt from food-allergen labeling laws (see page 11). Oils derived from common food allergens include nut oils and soybean oil. The key question is, *are they safe to consume if you have a food allergy?*

Whipped Coconut Cream

Most food allergies are to the proteins in the food. Refined oils have been processed so that impurities (including the protein) have been removed and just the fat remains. Reactions to the non-protein components in food are more commonly associated with intolerances (e.g., lactose intolerance to milk). However, if you are concerned or your doctor has told you to avoid a particular oil, then you must avoid that oil. Choose an appropriate substitute from the options below. While oils do provide taste, any oil can be substituted 1 to 1 in recipes.

What about peanut oil? The Food Allergy and Anaphylaxis Network (FAAN) notes that studies have shown that most allergic individuals can safely eat (highly refined) peanut oil,[15] and a 2008 study published in the *Journal of Agriculture and Food Chemistry*[16] supports that. No proteins were detected in the refined oils they studied (including soy and peanut oil). The researchers did find protein content in some of the unrefined oils. Nevertheless, peanut oil remains controversial—I believe that is because allergic reactions to peanut tend to be severe and not all peanut oils are highly refined. For that reason, I recommend avoiding peanut oil if you have a peanut allergy. In my own home (with allergies to peanut and soy) we avoid peanut oil, but have deemed soybean oil okay when it's included in a list of product ingredients.

When baking, the best choice, of course, is to choose an oil that doesn't require you to question whether there's a chance of an allergic reaction. My favorites, which you will see used in my recipes, include:

GRAPESEED OIL: Grapeseed oil does indeed come from grapes; it's a by-product of the winemaking process. While it's not great for cooking due to a low smoke point, it has a nice light taste, and complements most baked goods.

SUNFLOWER OIL: Extracted from the sunflower, this oil has a slightly nutty taste.

SAFFLOWER OIL: Safflower oil comes from the safflower plant, and is essentially flavorless.

HEMP SEED OIL: From my favorite crop—hemp, of course. This oil with a nutty taste has the added benefit of being a great source of omega 3 and 6, but it is harder to find, and can be pricey. If you can get your hands on some, I recommend trying it as a substitute in any of the recipes.

All four of these oils are low in saturated fat and trans fat. All of these oils are great choices when baking.

One more healthy oil is occasionally used in the recipes in this book: olive oil, which, of course, comes from olives. In baking, I reserve this oil for use with some breads, where the taste of the oil will provide a benefit. If you are avoiding saturated fats, substitute one of the four previously mentioned oils.

You may notice that my recipes do not use canola oil. Canola oil, also known as rapeseed oil (not to be confused with grapeseed oil), comes from a pretty yellow flowering plant called rapeseed. Most canola oil comes from crops that have been grown in the northern United States and Canada from genetically modified seeds. It is simply my choice to use non-GMO products when I can. If you prefer canola oil, however, it can be substituted 1 to 1 in any of these recipes.

Another consideration when choosing oil is the method used to extract the oil from the seed, flower, or fruit. If you are using oil from a food source that could be an allergen (such as soy), you already know that you must choose a highly refined oil, but many methods are used to refine the oil. It's common to find oils that have been chemically extracted, using a solvent such as hexane, which is evaporated during the cleaning process prior to packaging for sale. Many companies are now turning to expeller pressing—extracting the oil mechanically, using a machine press—to make their oil products. The yield from expeller-pressed oils is lower, making these oils more expensive for you and me. However, these highly refined oils are considered high quality, and I opt for them when I can.

While there are no standards in the United States around the use of the following term, oils that are labeled "cold-pressed" are most likely unrefined oils.

I also use coconut oil and palm oil when baking, most frequently in place of butter or shortening. Which brings us to the next topic.

Butter, margarine, and shortening

Butter, butter, butter. It's not just Julia Child who favored butter in her cookies; top bakers across the world use butter liberally, especially in crusts and doughs. Because of its appealing taste and ability to be cut into flour (see page 129), butter does the job extremely well, but it is a solid form of milk and clearly not an option for the milk-allergic. Replacing butter is one of the most difficult tasks for an allergen-free baker, second only to replacing eggs. The most important factor to consider when replacing butter is form; the challenge is to find a product that is solid when chilled (and remains solid at room temperature), and tastes great. Butter substitutes will not taste like butter any more than milk substitutes taste like cow's milk, but the right choice can definitely enhance the flavor of your pie crust. Shortening is what we will turn to most often to replace butter.

What exactly is *shortening*? The term is used to describe any combination of fats or oils used to make a crust or dough. The generic term includes margarine, but most margarines include milk products (e.g., whey and buttermilk), so let's turn our focus to oil-based shortenings. When using a single oil, you can pick the one that's right for you. When choosing a shortening to replace butter you're often buying packaged products that use a combination of oils, and one of the most common oils in non-dairy shortening is soybean oil. If you and your doctor agree that soybean oil is safe for you, you will have more options to choose from. If it's not for you, don't fret—there are still great products that you can use. Note that the first two options below contain soybean oil:

EARTH BALANCE NATURAL SHORTENING: This shortening is vegan, made from expeller-pressed non-GMO oils, and comes in stick form. It is a blend of palm fruit, soybean, canola, and olive oils. After trying many options for replacing butter, this is my top choice for baking; it holds its form even in warm temperatures, making it a perfect choice for cutting into dough. Note that Earth Balance makes a variety of shortenings. Don't confuse this product with Earth Balance Natural Buttery Sticks; the buttery sticks contain soy protein, and are not acceptable for the soy-allergic.

CRISCO ALL-VEGETABLE SHORTENING: Yes, this is the stuff in the blue can that you may have remembered your parents or grandparents using (and yes, it is still available at the grocery store). It's made from soybean and palm oils and is another choice to replace butter.

SPECTRUM ORGANIC ALL VEGETABLE SHORTENING: While the name of this product would lead you to believe that it's a combination of oils, this shortening contains only one ingredient—palm oil. Palm oil (sometimes referred to as palm fruit oil) comes from the fruit of the palm tree. This product is unusual because it's one of the few shortenings sold in a tub that truly remains solid. Palm oil needs very high temperatures (around 95°F) to melt, which is one reason why it's included in so many margarines, and why it's a good choice for replacing butter or other shortening when baking. A frosting made with palm oil will not need to be refrigerated, and (short of the warmest climates and record-breaking temperature days) a cake frosted with a palm oil–based frosting will be able to sit out at the family picnic. If you require a shortening without soybean oil, this is a great choice.

EARTH BALANCE SOY FREE NATURAL BUTTERY SPREAD: While I am not a fan of most products labeled "spreads," this is one I wanted to mention because it contains no soy fats (oils), in addition to no soy proteins. This product contains palm fruit, canola, safflower, and olive oils. It also contains a number of other ingredients, including pea protein (an uncommon allergen), and flavor derived from corn (another potential allergen). Some allergen-free bakers tout this as a soy-free alternative to the Earth Balance Natural Buttery Sticks, but I find that it softens quickly, making it difficult to work with when preparing crusts and doughs. If you choose to use this product (or need to, so as to avoid soybean oil), I recommend keeping it refrigerated as long as possible, and freeze (rather than refrigerate) your dough before rolling it out.

COCONUT OIL: I have been using many of the products in this book for ten years or more, but coconut oil is a recent discovery for me, and I am fascinated by it. As more coconut products have appeared on the market catering to the vegan community, those of us in the allergen-free community have benefited as well. In the past two years I have experimented with coconut oil, and have been delighted with the results. Unlike the shortenings we have discussed so far, which are mostly tasteless, unrefined coconut oil has a distinctive odor and flavor that lets you know it is coconut. Refined coconut oils are sometimes considered odorless or unscented; in my experience there is no such thing as a truly unscented coconut oil, but the highly refined versions will have a milder taste than the unrefined ones do. Both can work equally well when baking. The reason you can use coconut oil as a shortening is that it remains solid to 76°F. If you live in Arizona, your coconut oil may always be liquid. In the northeastern United States, where I live, my coconut oil is solid most of the year. If coconut oil melts, refrigerate it to bring it back to a solid. If you're making pies on a warm day, keep the coconut oil in the fridge until you are ready to use it, and double the chilling time before rolling out your crust.

Making the most of shortening

Notice that I have made a distinction between shortening and oil based on the form the product holds at room temperature: Oils are liquids at room temperature, whereas shortenings are solids. When you choose oil or shortening, consider what you plan to use the product for. If you intend to melt shortening to make cupcakes, you are using it as an oil. When you use palm or coconut oil to make cookies, you are using it as a shortening; the same recipe made with liquid oil will result in dough that doesn't hold together. When modifying recipes, you may replace oil with a melted shortening, but not vice versa.

In my recipes, I most frequently use Earth Balance Natural Shortening and coconut oil where butter would be used in traditional recipes.

I have highlighted just a few products here, but there are dozens of shortenings you can choose from. These can be substituted 1 to 1 in recipes that call for shortening. As you evaluate new options, keep these guidelines in mind:

* Choose a shortening that remains solid at room temperature. To test, simply scoop out a tablespoon or two of shortening and let it sit in a small bowl for 3 to 4 hours at room temperature. The products that start to look watery or glossy around the edges will break down as you are working with them. This will result in cookies that spread too soon and burn around the edges, or a pie crust that can't be rolled because it won't hold its shape. The products that hold their form (even when softened) are the ones that will be the easiest to work with.
* Check all of the ingredients on the labels to ensure that there are no proteins that your family members are allergic to. Work with your doctor to determine whether soybean oil and/or coconut oil are safe options for your family.
* If non–chemically processed ingredients are important to you, look for the words *expeller-pressed* to describe the oils contained in your shortening.

In place of ice cream

Although you won't use them directly in baking, it's good to know that non-dairy frozen desserts are available from many of the non-dairy milk manufacturers, in the frozen food section. Two that food-allergy families may like are Living Harvest Foods Tempt frozen desserts made with hemp milk, and So Delicious frozen desserts made with coconut milk. If you need an alternative to ice cream to serve with Vanilla Pound Cake (page 108), try So Delicious brand Cookie Dough (yes, the cookie dough is gluten-free!) or Cherry Amaretto frozen dessert. Tempt Chocolate Fudge Frozen Dessert served with Chocolate Glaze (page 177) makes a great summer afternoon treat, whether or not you have food allergies.

Key Lessons

✓ There are many non-dairy (soy-free and nut-free) milks to choose from, including rice, hemp, and coconut milk. Each has a unique taste and can be used 1 to 1 to replace cow's milk in recipes.

✓ Milk products include butter, cream, cheese, cream cheese, yogurt, sour cream, ice cream, and most margarines.

✓ The term *dairy* is sometimes (mistakenly) thought to include eggs. Conversely, not everyone recognizes that cheese and butter are made from milk. Special attention is required when describing milk and egg allergies.

✓ It is the protein in food that triggers food allergies; work with your doctor to determine whether highly refined oils based on soy or nuts are safe for your family.

✓ Check the ingredients carefully on shortening labels to ensure they are safe for your family.

✓ You can never be too clear or ask too many questions about ingredients, whether purchasing a product at the grocery store, eating at a friend's house, or dining out.

✓ When replacing butter, choose a shortening or oil that remains solid at room temperature.

Glazing Chocolate Croissants (page 175)

4

Baking Without Eggs

IF BAKING WITHOUT WHEAT, milk, and but-

ter is a puzzle (and I do believe it is), then baking

without wheat, milk, butter, and eggs is a four-

dimensional puzzle. Replacing wheat is initially

tough, because non-gluten grains behave differ-

ently than gluten grains, but once you understand

the rules and try a few baking projects, you'll get

the hang of it. Replacing milk is relatively straight-

forward once you understand the non-dairy op-

tions you have. Likewise, replacing butter becomes

easier once you understand the rules. Eggs—or the

lack of eggs—on the other hand, are much more

difficult to compensate for. There's a reason why I titled this chapter "Baking Without Eggs" rather than "Replacing Eggs"—no ingredient (that I have found yet) can do exactly what an egg does. Eggs truly are incredible, despite being inedible by many with food allergies.

Between 1 and 2 percent of the population is allergic to eggs, and egg is the second-most-common food allergen in children (milk being the most common). Egg is also the last ingredient that commercial bakers choose to go without. Mass-produced gluten-free and dairy-free products frequently include egg or egg protein. Most bakeries—even many that cater to gluten-free and food-allergic families—still use eggs; check and double-check if you buy your baked goods over the counter. And of course, egg protein, egg whites, albumin, dried eggs, powdered eggs, egg wash, eggnog, hydrolyzed egg protein—they're all egg, and must be avoided by those allergic to eggs. Egg Beaters, or other scrambled egg products that you find in the refrigerated section of the grocery store, are made from eggs; they are also off limits for those allergic to eggs. While it is usually the egg whites that cause food allergies (the yolks are primarily fat), it is virtually impossible to separate an egg without leaving traces of the egg white; therefore, egg-allergic individuals must also avoid egg yolks.

Mayonnaise is typically made from eggs. Some mayonnaise substitutes on the market are made from soy—but these are not an option if you are also allergic to soy. Mayonnaise is less of an issue when baking, but you will need something to replace it when you make a sandwich using my recipe for Basic Sandwich Bread (page 161). Earth Balance recently introduced a line of dressing and sandwich spreads called Mindful Mayo, based on oils and containing no egg, dairy, or soy. It was first introduced at Whole Foods Market and is slowly making its way into the refrigerated section of health food stores. Some of the formulas contain mustard and/or pea proteins (less common allergens). Of course, for the non-allergic there's always mustard, but you might want to try a hummus spread, or my son's favorite—mashed avocados. Also, keep in mind that salad dressings and sauces often contain egg or egg protein. Like the other top food allergens, eggs must be clearly called out on food labels in the United States. Always check.

There are a few things you won't be able to do with allergen-free egg substitutes. You won't be able to make a fried, scrambled, poached, or over-easy egg. You won't be able to make a traditional omelet or frittata. Allergen-free egg substitutes will not work in a dish where the egg is the center of attention without dramatically changing the profile of the dish. Likewise, you won't be able to use allergen-free egg substitutes to make meringue, a whipped egg white topping. What you can do—yes, even without eggs—is create great baked goods, and I'll show you how in this chapter. Meanwhile, if you're lucky enough to be able to eat eggs, go ahead and add them back in. In the recipes in part 2, I have noted the equivalent number of eggs where I have used alternatives. (See appendix B, page 257, for more information on substitutions.)

Why traditional bakers use eggs

Before we explore how to bake without eggs, let's take a look at what the egg does in a traditional baked goods recipe. The egg is a multitasker—it plays many roles. To understand how to replace eggs effectively, you need to understand what functions they provide and determine which of those roles is most important for the item you are making. This is where all the puzzle pieces have to come together.

Leavening is the characteristic we associate most often with eggs in baking. Eggs will help your cake rise and your pastries to become fluffy. When egg proteins are heated, their motion causes them to bond (to each other and to the ingredients they are mixed with) and helps the food to lift and expand. If you bake an egg (see the following experiment) it will nearly double in size. But eggs do more than help food rise; they also act as a thickening agent. When you crack open an egg it appears to be liquid, but that's a bit deceiving. Egg solidifies at 150°F —even over low heat on a stove it will change state and become a solid. As you think about replacing eggs in traditional recipes, it's important to think of them as a solid even though you will typically add the egg in with the wet ingredients; this mind-set affects the proportion of liquid to dry ingredients when baking.

Egg is also unusual in its ability to hold other ingredients together; it binds other solids. This is a characteristic that is especially helpful as you are working with dough. Texture is another characteristic to think about when you choose an egg replacement. The smoothness of the cake and the fullness that you taste—these are provided (in part) by the egg in traditional recipes.

What I miss the most in baking without eggs is the protein that the egg provides. One egg contains approximately 6 grams of protein. Many gluten-free bakers compensate for the protein they lost when they eliminated wheat by adding eggs (which also helps with leavening), but allergen-free bakers need other options. These include packaged egg replacers, gel made from flaxseeds, and fruit purees. Before we discuss these in detail, I've devised an experiment for you to try, to demonstrate what each of these egg substitutes can do:

THE BEHAVIOR OF EGG AND ALLERGEN-FREE EGG SUBSTITUTES WHEN BAKING

Preparation: Preheat the oven to 350°F (the most common baking temperature). In each of four ramekins, prepare the equivalent of one egg:

1. One egg, scrambled with a fork*
2. Flaxseed gel: 1 tablespoon flaxseed meal mixed with 3 tablespoons warm water, left to sit for 8 minutes prior to baking
3. Fruit puree: ¼ cup applesauce (use applesauce that is just apples and water)
4. Packaged egg replacer: 1½ teaspoons Ener-G Egg Replacer mixed with 2 tablespoons warm water, left to sit for 3 minutes prior to baking

Do not add any additional ingredients to any of the ramekins.

Bake: Place the ramekins on a baking sheet, and bake at 350°F for 20 minutes.

Observe: Each of these products behaves differently.

1. The egg will solidify and double in size and then fall back to about 1.5 times its size prior to baking. Imagine that if the egg were mixed with flour and liquids, it would have the ability to expand the flour, providing what is commonly known in baking as rise. Note that only the real egg is completely solid after baking.
2. The flaxseed gel will thicken and become sticky. If you run a fork through it, you will see that it is pliable. While it hasn't increased visibly in volume, it is tacky and has texture. It thickens, but does not become a solid.
3. The applesauce will have no visible change in state. Other than being warmed with a bit of the moisture evaporated, it doesn't change.
4. The packaged egg replacer will increase in volume to about 1.5 times its original size, and will then fall back after cooling. This mixture is very sticky, with an almost glue-like consistency. Of all of the non-egg options, this is the only one that shows properties of leavening.

*Note: If you are the family member allergic to eggs or you have eliminated eggs from your home, you may choose to do this experiment with all options except the traditional egg.

As you can see, none of the products we refer to as egg substitutes do everything that an egg can do, but they each provide some of the same properties as an egg. This is clearly a case where one size doesn't fit all. While you will see charts elsewhere that show you how to substitute for egg, what the charts leave out is an explanation of how these products behave; they are interchangeable only to a certain degree. In practice you will see that some options work much better than others, depending on what you are baking. Now that you have a sense of what you can work with and what each egg substitute can do, let's take a look at each of them in closer detail.

Flaxseed gel

Flax is a flowering plant. The fibers of the plant are used to make linen fabric, but it's the seeds we're interested in. The plant bears a fruit that contains tiny seeds. Flaxseeds (and flaxseed oils) are often talked about as healthy foods, and with 9 grams of omega fatty acids, 12 grams of fiber, and 11 grams of protein in ¼ cup of flaxseeds, you can see why. This is just one of the reasons that flaxseed gel is my favorite egg substitute to work with; the other reason is that I am fascinated each and every time I see what these seeds can do.

Flaxseed gel is made by mixing ground flaxseeds or flaxseed meal with warm water. The nature of the seeds makes them capable of absorbing the moisture and thickening into a gel in a way that other seeds (like hemp seeds or sunflower seeds) cannot. If you can find them, chia seeds have the same property as flaxseeds and can also be made into a gel for replacing egg.

I sometimes refer to flaxseed gel as "flaxseed goop" because it is very gloppy and goopy. When mixed properly, flaxseed gel has the consistency

flaxseed meal

whole flaxseeds

flaxseed gel

of an egg prior to baking—it can slide through your fingers and feels a little bit like the green slime you played with when you were a kid.

There are many different types of flaxseeds, but most are classified as either brown or golden. I prefer to work with golden flaxseeds. While they are slightly more expensive, you will be able to consistently find high-quality golden flaxseeds and the lighter color won't affect the color of your baked goods as much as the brown flaxseeds would. Flaxseed gel made with brown flaxseed meal will leave little brown specks in your muffins, but they taste good and are a viable choice, as are chia seeds.

Flaxseed gel can be made in two ways—either by grinding your own flaxseeds, or by using pre-ground flaxseed meal. I prefer to grind my own. While flaxseed meal is still a whole food, once the seeds are ground, the meal will spoil more quickly. You can keep flaxseed meal in the refrigerator for up to 3 months, while whole flaxseeds will stay fresh for a year or more—their shell protects them. Here's the quick and easy method to make flaxseed gel:

HOW TO MAKE FLAXSEED GEL

This formula makes approximately ¼ cup of flaxseed gel; that's how much you will use to substitute for one egg.

1. Place 1 tablespoon of ground flaxseed meal in a small mixing bowl.

2. Add 3 tablespoons of warm (not hot) water.

3. Use a tiny whisk or fork to whisk together the water and flaxseeds.

4. Let it sit for 8 to 10 minutes. The mixture will thicken.

5. Whisk again to fully incorporate the water.

6. Add the flaxseed gel to the wet ingredients for your recipe.

If you are grinding your own flaxseeds, and I recommend you do, you will find that 1 tablespoon of flaxseeds makes about 1½ tablespoons of flaxseed meal; it fluffs up during grinding, after the seeds are cracked open. To compensate, use a "short" tablespoon of flaxseeds (about three quarters full) when grinding to make one flaxseed egg (or simply measure after grinding). See page 73 to find out more about seed grinders.

If you're doing a lot of baking, I recommend mixing up batches of flaxseed gel in advance. Use the same ratio—1 tablespoon of flaxseed meal to 3 tablespoons of warm water—to make as many "eggs" as you need. Prepared flaxseed gel will keep in the refrigerator for up to a week. When you are ready to bake, measure ¼ cup of flaxseed gel to equal one egg. Bring the flaxseed gel to room temperature before using it (as you would with an egg).

To make chia seed gel, follow the procedure above, but use only ½ tablespoon of chia seeds to 3 tablespoons of warm water to achieve the proper consistency. Chia seed gel can be made with either whole chia seeds or ground chia seeds, whereas flax seeds need to be ground before they can be digested.

I mentioned earlier that this egg substitute most closely mimics the consistency of an egg prior to baking. Also like an egg, flaxseed gel has the ability to hold other ingredients together; while it doesn't solidify, it does have a tackiness that helps baked goods form. That's a property that will come in handy when you prepare batters and doughs.

Applesauce and other fruit purees

Applesauce is about as close as you can come to a superfood for baking. Besides the obvious virtues of being a whole food, all natural, gluten-free, and rarely a cause of food allergies, it's packed with vitamin C and fiber. It's no wonder applesauce is one of the first solid foods many of us feed our children. Even though I have chosen to write about applesauce in a chapter about replacing eggs, applesauce could be considered the "universal replacer"; it can be used in place of sugar or other sweeteners, or—in some cases—to replace a portion of the fat.

When choosing applesauce to replace egg, the measurement is simple: ¼ cup of applesauce should be substituted for one egg. This amount gives a volume that is very similar to the egg, making it easy to replace in batters. The applesauce should be added in with the wet ingredients, and the resulting batter should be very similar in consistency to the same batter made with an egg. Because the real egg will solidify quickly and the moisture in the applesauce will need time to evaporate, the same batch of brownies made with applesauce will take a few minutes longer to bake than if it were made with egg. The inverse is also true—if you choose to use traditional eggs in any of the recipes in this book, reduce the baking time by a few minutes to compensate.

If you want to reduce the sugar in a recipe, try replacing up to ½ cup of sugar with an equal amount of applesauce. Likewise, if you want to reduce the fat, up to ½ cup of fat (oils only—not shortening) can be replaced with applesauce. But stick to just one of these applesauce substitutes at a time. For example, if you are using applesauce in place of eggs, do not also use it to replace the oil—too much of a good thing can turn out badly. Also, if you choose to use applesauce in place of sugar or fat, do so only in batters; doughs and yeast breads have different requirements, which we'll explore in "The Allergen-Free Baking Lab."

Applesauce is nothing more than apples and water (and sometimes a preservative). It's a fruit puree. Many of the commercially prepared applesauces sold in grocery stores are sweetened (often with high-fructose corn syrup), but I suggest you use the unsweetened varieties. These are sometimes labeled "natural" or "unsweetened." Some also have added flavors (such as cinnamon) or are blended with other fruits. All of these choices will work, and can be found easily and inexpensively. Or—you can try making your own.

Applesauce is as easy to make as mashed potatoes—and the process is surprisingly similar. The advantage of making your own (besides another use for those baskets of fall apples) is that you can control the ingredients. My version is unsweetened, and contains no added preservatives.

Unsweetened Applesauce

This recipe works best with sweet apples (Red Delicious, Fuji, or Gala all work well) or a combination of apples. Because this recipe contains no preservatives, it will only keep in the refrigerator for about a week. Freeze what you don't plan to use. Adding 1½ teaspoons of fresh lemon juice to the blender with the apples will prolong its shelf life. You can scale the recipe up (just double, triple, etc.) for big batches. For a sweetened version, add 2 tablespoons of sugar while blending.

MAKES ABOUT 1½ CUPS OF APPLESAUCE
(THE EQUIVALENT OF 6 EGGS)

4 cups peeled, cored, and chopped apples (about 4 medium-large apples)
About ¾ cup water

Place the chopped apples in a medium saucepan and pour the water over them, just enough to cover. Boil for 10 to 15 minutes, until you can easily insert a fork through the apples. Drain. Place the apples in a blender or food processor and blend until smooth. Let the applesauce cool and then refrigerate it.

As noted earlier, applesauce is simply a fruit puree. Any other fruit puree can provide the same function as applesauce does—pears, bananas, and peaches (any soft fruit that you might find in a baby food jar) all behave comparably to applesauce in baked goods. Keep in mind that fruit

Unsweetened Applesauce

purees do add taste. I recently made Double Chocolate Muffins (page 197) with a mango puree in place of my usual ½ cup of applesauce. The muffins baked perfectly, but they did have a hint of a mango taste. Applesauce lends a more neutral taste.

Remember that fruit puree is used primarily to provide texture; it will not provide any leavening. That's where packaged egg replacers—or chemical egg replacers—come in.

Packaged egg replacers

Yes, I just referred to these as chemical egg replacers. Is that a bad thing? Absolutely not! Remember organic chemistry? Everything we eat is made up of organic compounds. In the case of packaged egg replacers, organic compounds are combined to create what is known as an egg replacer. While these are processed foods (and they provide virtually no nutritional value), this is one scenario where you should give yourself a pass and embrace them. If you can't see clearly, you wear eyeglasses, right? If you can't bake with eggs, an assist with leavening is in order.

The term *egg replacers* is actually a misnomer—I like to think of them as super-duper baking powders. A typical baking powder contains a leavening agent (e.g., sodium bicarbonate), an acid, and a starch. Now, let's take a look at the ingredients in a packaged egg replacer: starches, leavening agents (e.g., calcium carbonate), an acid, and gums. They have very similar profiles, the egg replacer having more starch and the added benefit of gums.

If you had a recipe that was devised to leverage egg replacer, you could actually add the product directly to your dry ingredients, just like you do with baking soda, baking powder, and xanthan gum. But because the product is marketed as a substitute, the package directions suggest that you combine it with water. This is a good idea because it allows you to use the product as a liquid (like an egg prior to baking), and it ensures that the gums are thoroughly incorporated (without lumps) in your baked goods. See page 26 for more on gums.

Most egg replacers are simple to prepare and instructions vary by product. I have called for Ener-G Egg Replacer in many of my recipes, because it is easy to find, easy to use, and it contains none of the top eight allergens or gluten. With this product, 1½ teaspoons of egg replacer should be combined with 2 tablespoons of warm water to replace one egg. Make sure you use warm (not hot) water, and whisk the ingredients together with a tiny whisk or fork in a ramekin or small mixing bowl. Let it sit for 3 minutes before re-whisking and adding it to your wet ingredients. You will see that the mixture thickens a bit as it sits, giving it a nearly egg-like consistency. In volume, this mixture will measure less than a medium egg. That's okay. Remember that an egg solidifies during baking—resist the impulse to add more liquid.

Ener-G Egg Replacer contains potato starch, tapioca flour, calcium lactate, calcium carbonate, citric acid, and gums. Another similar egg replacer is Orgran No Egg Natural Egg Replacer; this product contains potato starch, tapioca flour, calcium carbonate, citric acid, and vegetable gum. The gums in these products are very similar to xanthan gum and will become thick and gluey (see my experiment on page 26). In addition to the leavening function, packaged egg replacers provide a stickiness that helps to hold dry ingredients (and especially gluten-free flours) together. This makes them a shoo-in as my preferred choice for an egg substitute in yeast breads.

Other products on the market perform a similar function to packaged egg replacers, but are marketed as (and more aptly named) gluten substitutes, or cake enhancers. Orgran offers Gluten Free Gluten Substitute (GfG) that is made with rice flour, pea extract, maize (corn) starch, and gums. King Arthur Flour offers Gluten Free Cake Enhancer (that is not just for cakes) made from rice starch and fatty acids. Both of these products are formulated so they can be mixed in with the dry ingredients. If you need to avoid xanthan gum, choose one of these instead, but prepare them as you would an egg replacer (mixing with warm water).

As you look for chemical egg replacer products at the grocery store, be aware that there are some egg-free variations that contain other common food allergens. One of these is Bob's Red Mill Vegetarian Egg Replacer, made with wheat and soy proteins. Read the labels and check for other allergens that your family needs to avoid before purchasing an egg replacer.

If none of the packaged egg replacers work for you, or you just prefer to make your own, it's very easy to do:

MIX YOUR OWN EGG REPLACER

Combine 1 teaspoon of corn starch (or tapioca starch) with ½ teaspoon of baking powder and ⅛ teaspoon of xanthan gum (or guar gum). Whisk these ingredients together well in a small bowl. Add 2 tablespoons of warm (not hot) water. Whisk together until well blended. Let it sit for 3 minutes, then re-whisk and add the mixture to the wet ingredients for your recipe.

Once you prepare an egg replacer, be sure to use it promptly; it will lose its effectiveness if it sits too long.

Other options

Not every recipe for baked goods needs an egg. That's right, I said it. Sometimes, the best option is to just leave out the egg. I almost never add an egg to a pie crust, for example. I don't need the leavening and I can keep the dough together with water and shortening. Adding an egg replacer is unnecessary in that situation. If you omit the egg replacer from a cake, you may have some loss of texture, but the cake will still form (assuming you used enough baking powder for leavening). You can forgo the egg if the other ingredients in your recipe are able to do the job without it.

Gluten-free recipes often need more baking powder and/or baking soda than do their wheat counterparts. Later on, you will see that I recommend adding additional baking powder and/or baking soda to compensate for the loss of gluten in the flour (see page 96). The same concept applies to replacing the eggs. Baking powder and baking soda are simply leavening agents, and (as noted earlier) baking powder is a key ingredient in packaged egg replacers. With some recipes, you may be able to achieve what you need by simply adding that extra baking powder. This approach will be most effective with baked goods made from batters—including cakes, muffins, and quick breads.

Keep in mind that yeast is also a leavening agent. When you are working with yeast, you may find that simply increasing the amount of yeast you use is enough to compensate for the lack of an egg.

Two options that home bakers don't think of as readily when they need to substitute for eggs are vinegar and carbonated water. One tablespoon of vinegar (including apple cider vinegar, brown rice vinegar, or white vinegar) may be able to take the place of an egg; I find that this works best in recipes that are already acidic, such as Basic Chocolate Cupcakes (page 195). The vinegar combines with the sodium bicarbonate in baking soda or baking powder, giving off a bubbly gas that provides lift. Carbonated water doesn't need another chemical to react with; the carbonation performs the trick all by itself. Replace up to 1 cup of water (or milk) with carbonated water. This works best when the milk is not required for taste. Note that these options provide leavening, but do not mimic the texture or binding capabilities of an egg.

Choosing an egg substitute

Remember that puzzle we were solving? Selecting which ingredient to use in place of the eggs is often the most critical decision when baking allergen-free. It's not just about replacing individual ingredients; it's about how they interact. My thought process in choosing what to use instead of an egg starts with identifying what role the egg would have played in that recipe, had I been able to use it.

When texture is my primary concern—this would be the case when making cakes, muffins, or cookies—I will choose a fruit puree or flaxseed gel. I may also add baking powder to compensate for the loss of leavening ingredients. If I want the stickiness and hold of an egg (perhaps in a cookie or pie crust), then flaxseed gel is the best option. This option is also the one that most closely resembles the consistency of an egg—which means that a batter will look and feel the same (before baking) as if I used an egg laid by a chicken. If I really need the leavening capabilities of an egg, then a packaged egg replacer (e.g., Ener-G Egg Replacer or one that I have mixed on my own) is the best choice. Whereas yeast provides its own leavening capabilities, if I need to add an "egg" to a yeast recipe, I nearly always choose a packaged egg replacer. (See appendix B on page 257 for more on which options to use when adapting traditional recipes.)

Ask yourself, "What do I need the egg to do in this recipe?" and then choose accordingly.

Key Lessons

✓ Eggs play many roles in baking, including leavening, binding, providing texture, and providing taste. No single egg substitute provides all of these qualities.

✓ Traditional eggs will solidify during baking; egg substitutes will not.

✓ Experiment with different egg substitutes to understand how they behave in your favorite recipes.

✓ The only egg replacers with properties of leavening are packaged egg replacers, which can be likened to enhanced baking powder.

✓ Flaxseed gel comes the closest to mimicking the consistency of an egg prior to baking.

✓ Applesauce and other fruit purees can be used to replace eggs, oil, or sugar—but don't substitute fruit for more than one of those ingredients in a single recipe.

✓ You may also substitute vinegar for eggs in recipes that are already acidic.

Making Cinnamon Raisin Bread (page 185)

5

The Allergen–Free Baker's Pantry

I FIND THAT IT really helps to have the right tool for the job. In this chapter I will introduce you to baking tools that you may have not used in the past, such as a bench knife or a probe thermometer. You can certainly start baking without them, but over time you may want to consider purchasing them. I keep only the essentials in my kitchen, but every tool I have gets a lot of use.

My pantry is one deep cupboard. With the exception of the overflow to the dining room as I prepared recipes for this book, my flours, sweeteners, flax-seeds, shortenings, and milk substitutes are all stored in that cupboard, my refrigerator, or my freezer. What you won't find in my pantry is anything made with soy protein, wheat, or gluten. I have eliminated boxes of cereals, cookies, and other packaged foods that are filled with those food allergens—and you might be surprised how much space was freed up for all the new foods my family can safely eat.

I confess that I do keep cow's milk and cheese in the refrigerator, for those in the family who can tolerate milk. The cheese products are isolated from everything else—they have their own special drawer—which brings us again to the topic of contamination, this time to the kind that occurs not in the factory but in the home.

Avoiding contamination

No food allergy book would be complete without a discussion about contamination. Contamination occurs when there is cross-contact between allergen-free food and food allergens. Sometimes called cross-contamination, both terms mean the same thing: that an ingredient, meal, or dish that was intended to be allergen-free unintentionally contains traces of a food that you may be allergic to. The emphasis here is on the word *unintentional*. You may have prepared a sauce containing no food allergens, and then your spouse stirred the pot with a spoon that had been in contact with milk. The sauce is now contaminated with milk.

There are many ways that contamination can occur. Here are just a few examples:

* A plastic storage container that was used to hold peanuts wasn't washed thoroughly before your son's favorite allergen-free snack was put in the same container.
* Just a few crumbs left on a cutting board after a sandwich was made with wheat bread caused chaos when the same cutting board was used to make a sandwich for your wheat-allergic daughter.
* You layered a slice of cheese on a burger, and didn't wash your hands before handling the dish for your milk-allergic child's dinner.
* The same spoon that was used to scoop out salsa was dipped into the cheese bowl, and then returned to the salsa, ruining taco night for your milk-allergic guests.

You can see how easy it is for food to become contaminated, even when everyone knows the rules. I wash my hands a lot when I am in the kitchen, and I have an eagle eye for crumbs left on the counter. Determining the food safety procedures to follow in your home is just as important as planning the fire escape route.

Extra caution is required when eating away from home. In my experience, most friends and family members have the best intentions and do try to accommodate food allergies, but they often lack the vigilance to ensure that small traces of food allergens don't make their way into a meal. Sometimes, a simple error in judgment can lead to a serious mistake. At a recent family event, my mother decided to throw cheese on the salad at the last minute, thinking it would make the salad more interesting. She was well versed in my son's food allergies, but in that moment, my milk-allergic son's well-meaning grandmother simply forgot that cheese was milk. She suggested that Patrick could pick the cheese out of his salad, but if you've been paying attention you know that wasn't an option—no salad for him that night.

Likewise, restaurant staff can easily make mistakes. In my experience, most restaurant workers truly want to serve you a safe meal; problems occur due to lack of understanding and awareness. Notably, Massachusetts was the first state to enact food allergy legislation for restaurants, requiring training and menu notices. I grew up in Massachusetts, and I love going out to eat when I visit. The increased awareness has led to more menu options and greater attention to detail by restaurant staff. While more restaurants are taking food allergies and restrictions seriously, offering special menus, and training their staff to avoid cross-contamination, the more you know about the ingredients in the food you are ordering and how the chef prepares the dish, the better off you will be. While this book is focused on baking at home, there are an increasing number of resources available for the food-allergic family eating out. See appendix E (page 267) for more information. Meanwhile, let's get back to your kitchen.

The simplest way to avoid contamination at home is to eliminate all of your family's food allergens, but that may not be practical. Some of you may be juggling multiple conflicting food allergies, or family members may not be willing to live without a particular food—and I must point out that eating allergen-free can be expensive (more on that later). While this is by no means a comprehensive list, here are some tips to help avoid contamination and keep your family safe:

※ **KEEP THE COUNTERS CLEAN.** I don't care how messy your bathroom is, but I strongly urge you to keep the kitchen clean. I wipe down my counters frequently, and I'm a big fan of paper towels. While I do realize that the use of paper towels is not the best choice to save the environment, be aware that sponges and kitchen towels are prime sources of cross-contamination. If you wipe down the counter with a dishrag, be careful not to use it again after cleaning up a milk spill. If you haven't eliminated food allergens from your home and you choose the kitchen towel over paper towels, be sure to change them frequently.

✳ **PREPARE THE ALLERGEN-FREE DISH FIRST.** I cook and bake to the least common denominator—I try to make food that everyone at the table can eat. I frankly never had the time to prepare two separate meals, and I didn't want my food-allergic child to feel left out or deprived. You may choose a different approach. I know many families that prepare separate meals for their food-allergic family member, and in some cases (where one child can only have rice and the other can only have corn) it's a necessity. If you are preparing separate meals, prepare the allergen-free dish (or dishes) first. This minimizes the possibility that you will use a contaminated serving utensil or transfer food from your hands.

✳ **USE UTENSILS AND PANS THAT ARE EITHER DEDICATED FOR ALLERGEN-FREE USE OR MADE FROM MATERIALS THAT ARE EASY TO CLEAN.** Certain items in your kitchen are especially prone to contamination. These include graters, cutting boards, pans with creases (including some expensive ones), cooling racks, strainers and colanders, sifters, grinders, blenders, and food processors. Anything with a crack or crevice where small particles can hide, or made from porous materials such as wood, should either be avoided when baking allergen-free, or dedicated for allergen-free use. For example, don't use the same Microplane grater for zesting lemons as you did for grating Parmesan cheese last night. Materials that work well when avoiding food allergens include high-density dishwasher-safe plastics (for bowls and cutting boards), stainless steel, glass, and stoneware.

✳ **USE THE DISHWASHER.** There is simply no better way to clean and sanitize your baking dishes and tools. When I am spending a busy baking day in the kitchen, I may run my dishwasher two or three times. On a typical day though, a single run of the dishwasher is usually sufficient. Make sure all of your baking tools are dishwasher safe, and wash them after every use.

✳ **WASH YOUR HANDS.** And insist that family members wash their hands. We've all been trained to wash our hands frequently to avoid colds and the flu in the winter, and the same concept applies to food allergens. A toddler who eats a slice of pizza and doesn't wash his hands can contaminate the toys in the family room—the same toys your food-allergic daughter plays with.

The tools you need

When my son was diagnosed with food allergies, in addition to weeding out food allergens from my pantry, I had to reassess all of the pans, baking dishes, and baking tools in my kitchen. Tempting as it might be, most of us can't afford to throw out everything in our kitchen and start from scratch. Initially, I designated a few baking dishes just for allergen-free baking, and kept them in a separate cabinet. You may want to do the same. Over time I transformed my kitchen so that every baking tool I use is for allergen-free use only. Again, materials that work well for allergen-free baking are those that can be easily thrown in the dishwasher, don't have gaps where small food particles can hide, and are made from nonporous materials such as glass, stainless steel, stoneware, and hard plastics.

After examining your own kitchen and eliminating the items that are unsuitable, you may find that you need to add a few items. You don't need to spend a fortune. Unless you're planning to be the next Martha Stewart, keep in mind that your baking dishes don't have to match. The exception to this is cake pans, which really need to be the same size and material to ensure that your cake layers will stack properly. Look for baking dishes at yard sales (make sure they can be sanitized in your dishwasher) and on clearance at your favorite home goods store. I visit my local Pier 1 store regularly, and head to the clearance section; you'll be amazed at the bargains you can find when there is only one left. Make a budget and prioritize. Here are a few items that I suggest every allergen-free baker have in the kitchen:

KITCHENAID STAND MIXER: Luckily, I don't live in an area that is prone to natural disasters, but if we did have to evacuate, this is the one item from my kitchen that I would take with me. I'm not going to say you must buy one—I baked for years using only a hand mixer—but I am strongly suggesting that you consider it. Yes, they are expensive; this is the one true luxury item on this list. Having a great stand mixer will free up your hands while you're mixing batters, save you time, make baking a lot more fun, and likely be the last mixer you buy. More important, the KitchenAid mixer is very easy to clean; the stainless-steel bowl and beater blade can go right into the dishwasher. While I don't usually subscribe to the concept of appliances as gifts, this is one you'll be very happy that Santa brought you.

SEED GRINDER: I never had a reason to own a seed grinder until I needed to make flaxseed gel as a replacement for eggs. While you can use flaxseed meal to make flaxseed gel, I prefer grinding my own; this allows me to use high-quality flaxseeds, and unlike flaxseed meal, whole flaxseeds are unlikely to go bad if kept refrigerated. Seed grinders are widely available at kitchen stores and online. I purchased my Cuisinart model for less than $20 and I use it exclusively for grinding flaxseeds. I don't recommend grinding flaxseeds in your food processor or blender unless you have designated those tools for allergen-free use only. If a seed grinder doesn't fit in your budget, opt for flaxseed meal.

KITCHEN SCALE: Some gluten-free flours are very heavy, whereas others are very light, and almost all gluten-free flour blends weigh more than wheat flour (see page 32). To ensure consistency and good baking results, you need to take the weight of your flour into account as you bake allergen-free. The simplest way to do that is to use a basic kitchen scale. I use an Escali scale, which runs about $25. Alternatively, see page 33 to learn how to adjust for the gluten-free flour blends I recommend.

MINI WHISKS: In addition to one large whisk for baking on the stovetop, I recommend having a couple of tiny whisks on hand. These will be indispensable when you are mixing egg replacer or flaxseed gel. You can pick these up at the grocery store for a couple of dollars apiece.

BENCH KNIFE: This is sometimes referred to as a bench, pastry, or dough scraper. I was introduced to a bench knife when I took my first baking class. Prior to that I made do with regular knives and spatulas. I didn't know what I was missing until I used the right tool for the job. A bench knife is simply a flat blade with a large, flat surface and sharp scraping edge. You can find an inexpensive bench knife for less than $10. Be sure to choose one with a stainless-steel blade and a plastic handle so that it can go into the dishwasher.

PASTRY CUTTER: A pastry cutter is a great tool to have in your kitchen if you plan to be making a lot of cookies or pies. It's used to "cut" (rather than blend) fat into flour (see page 129). While a pastry cutter will make the job easier, an alternative is a pastry fork—a very wide-pronged heavy-duty, stainless-steel fork. I think both choices work equally well. And if you have neither a pastry cutter nor a pastry fork, use your hands.

PARCHMENT PAPER: You will use parchment paper for lining cookie sheets and rolling out dough. Parchment paper comes in rolls (the most cost effective) and in pre-cut sheets. If you have a cookie sheet designated for allergen-free use only, it's less critical to use parchment paper, but it does make clean up much easier. Do not substitute wax paper for parchment paper. Parchment paper is made to withstand temperatures up to 450°F, while wax paper is not.

ROLLING PIN: Throw out your old wooden rolling pin (or set it aside for traditional baking only). A good rolling pin can make all the difference when you're making crusts. I have a large silicone rolling pin, but my favorite is a mini silicone rolling pin. I find myself reaching for the smaller pin, which is intended to be used with smaller pastries, even when I'm preparing larger crusts and flatbreads—it's just so easy to use.

ASSORTED BOWLS: As you work your way through the recipes in this book, you will find that having an assortment of bowls on hand will make the job much easier. Surely you already have many of these bowls in your kitchen, but you may need to evaluate what you have. The bowls I use frequently when baking include:

* Small glass bowls—for mixing egg replacers and making flaxseed gel
* Small mini prep bowls or ramekins— for organizing ingredients as you prepare for baking
* Nesting melamine bowls (1½-, 2-, and 3-quart)—for blending together dry ingredients, mixing wet ingredients, whisking batters, and more
* A large stainless-steel bowl for preparing doughs and mixing flour blends

These, plus a large stainless-steel bowl or the stainless-steel bowl of your stand mixer, should be enough to get you started. Be sure to choose materials that are easy to clean and dishwasher safe.

ASSORTED BAKING DISHES: My favorite baking dishes are non-stick stainless steel and stoneware. If you are baking for the first time, or you are inspecting your current collection of bakeware to assess whether it can be safely used without cross-contamination consider this list of must-haves:

- ✳ Large baking sheet or cookie sheet (preferably with edges)—also to be used for baking scones, doughnuts, and rolls. This doubles as a pizza tin.
- ✳ 9- or 10-inch pie plate—for pies, of course!
- ✳ 8- or 9-inch square baking dish—my 9-inch square stoneware baking dish is the most used baking dish in my kitchen. I use it for brownies, cakes, breads, coffee cake, and more.
- ✳ 9 by 5-inch loaf pan—for quick breads, pound cake, and yeast breads
- ✳ 12-cup muffin tin—for muffins and cupcakes
- ✳ Two matching 8- or 9-inch round cake tins—a must if you want to make layer cakes

If you have the pans listed above (plus a medium saucepan for baking on the stovetop), you will be able to make every recipe in this book (with some ingenuity). If you want to add a few more specialty pieces, I would suggest:

- ✳ 9 by 13-inch baking dish—for making sheet cakes and larger batches of brownies
- ✳ Doughnut pan—for baked doughnuts and bagels with a smooth edge
- ✳ 24-cup mini-muffin pan—for mini-cupcakes as well as mini-muffins
- ✳ Baguette pan—while it's possible to make free-form baguettes, it's easier with a baguette pan
- ✳ Gluten-free loaf pan—a specialty item, but one to consider if you'll be making your own allergen-free and gluten-free bread. This 9 by 4 by 4-inch pan is a bit narrower and taller than a traditional loaf pan, and really does help bread rise. This is for use with yeast breads; use your loaf pan for quick breads.

COOLING RACK: Especially when you are working with gluten-free flour, it's important that you remove your baked goods from their vessels shortly after removing them from the oven. A simple nonstick cooling rack will do the job. Cooling racks tend to have small crevices where food particles can hide. If you are also baking with wheat and other food allergens, I recommend that you designate one cooling rack for your allergen-free baking projects, to avoid contamination (see page 68).

MEASURING CUPS AND SPOONS: There are two types of measuring cups. Measuring cups intended for wet ingredients are usually made from glass (so you can see from the outside as you are measuring) and have the lines below the top of the cup (to avoid spillage). Dry measuring cups are typically plastic or stainless steel, and the measurement goes to the very top of the cup. Either type can be used for both wet and dry ingredients, but I do prefer using dry measuring cups for flour and sugar; I find that the dry cups can be used to scoop out the required amounts without compacting the flour. You will also need a full set of measuring spoons. If you can find an inexpensive set of measuring spoons with a ½ tablespoon included, do buy that one; the ½ tablespoon can be used whenever 1½ teaspoons are called for and will come in handy when using egg replacer. Don't try to use the "teaspoons" in your flatware set for measuring; they are often larger than a true teaspoon.

PROBE THERMOMETER: It's nearly impossible to ensure that yeast breads are not underbaked or overbaked unless you have a probe thermometer. You may use the same thermometer you use to check the turkey, as long it goes up to 220°F. If you're up for it, though, I'd suggest springing for a digital probe thermometer that can be left in the oven while baking. For less than $20 you can pick up a really nice model, some of which can be programmed and include a timer. In addition to using it to check for doneness, I use my probe thermometer to check the temperature of my proofing zone (see page 158).

PASTRY MAT, PASTRY BOARD, OR ANOTHER SMOOTH PREP SURFACE: When you're working with thick batters, doughs, and yeast breads, it's important to have a smooth surface that your dough won't stick to. Some pastry mats have imprinted circles that designate the diameter of a crust; this is really helpful when you need to make your pie crust 11 inches in diameter to fit your 9-inch pan. You can find these for less than $10. My favorite rolling surface is a marble pastry board. Marble remains cool and is a great surface for rolling refrigerated dough, but it's a bit pricey and not for everyone. A less expensive alternative is granite, which also works very nicely. If you have a marble or granite counter, even better—just make sure the surface is cleaned well before you start rolling. If none of these options are available to you, wax paper is the next best thing. Avoid using wood or any other porous material as your prep surface, to minimize the possibility of contamination.

Stocking the shelves

For a while, your shopping list may sound as if it's written in a foreign language. You may find your head spinning trying to recall whether it was the garbanzo bean flour or the sorghum flour that your family liked best in the dinner rolls. At times you may be overwhelmed by the many options in the specialty foods section of the store, and at other times you'll be pulling your hair out trying to find the right ingredient to make one of the recipes in this book. You want to find the right items to fill your pantry with, and avoid wasting money on things you don't need.

Most modern grocery stores have a section or an aisle designated for many of the ingredients you need, and you will find other ingredients in the traditional baking section. Plan a little extra time for your first few shopping trips, and be prepared to read labels. To keep things simple, I have organized this list for you in two categories—items to keep stocked in your pantry at all times (because you will be using them a lot), and items to buy as you need them (because they are used less frequently, in just a few recipes, spoil quickly, and/or are optional). In the cases where I have designated a brand name, it is because I prefer the product for allergen-free baking or it's an item (e.g., shortening) that comes in many formulations and the product name mentioned is the only one (or one of just a few) that does not contain the top eight food allergens. Be sure to read every label and choose only products that are safe for your family. (See page 6 for more on reading labels.) Store them in dedicated containers to avoid cross-contamination.

What to keep stocked at all times

GLUTEN-FREE FLOUR BLENDS: I recommend keeping one multigrain and one white gluten-free flour blend in your pantry at all times. With these flours you should be good to go for all of the recipes in this book. If you don't have one of the single-grain flours that follow, you can adapt the recipe to use just a multigrain flour blend. See page 28 for a complete description of the flour blends I recommend.

SINGLE-GRAIN FLOURS: In some recipes I recommend combining a featured flour with a flour blend. These include oat, buckwheat, millet, and garbanzo (also known as chickpea) flours. When buying oat flour, make sure you opt for one that is labeled gluten-free. An alternative to garbanzo bean flour is garfava flour (a garbanzo/fava bean blend).

food stores, or the gluten-free/allergen-free section of your grocery store. See page 62 for more on egg replacers and how to use them.

APPLESAUCE: Applesauce is on my short list of all-time favorite ingredients for baking allergen-free. This is such a simple yet versatile product. Applesauce can be used as an egg replacer, as a substitute for oil, and as a sweetener. I always have four or five jars of it in my pantry. Opt for unsweetened (for sure) and organic (if you can swing the cost), or make your own (see page 60).

APPLE CIDER VINEGAR: If I had to pick just one vinegar for baking, it would be apple cider vinegar. Like applesauce, the taste works well with most baked goods. Rice vinegar is also used in a few recipes, but apple cider vinegar can be substituted. (Balsamic vinegars are not suitable for baking.)

LEMON AND/OR LIME JUICE: There are times when an acidic reaction will be needed, and those recipes will use a small amount of fresh lemon or lime juice. These fruit juices are also used in pie fillings. You can make do with one or the other, except when you are making an item that is specifically lemon (e.g., the Lemon Tart on page 148) or lime. If you have a juicer (and a little bit of time) you may choose to juice your own fruits; otherwise choose one of these juices to put on your grocery list. It should be 100 percent juice. A few recipes also call for orange juice. If you're like me, you already have orange juice in your refrigerator, or if you have the time, you can squeeze your own.

EARTH BALANCE NATURAL SHORTENING: This stick-style product is found in the refrigerated section of your health food store (do not confuse this with the company's similarly packaged Natural Buttery Sticks). The brand matters: Most margarines and shortening contain milk and/or soy proteins. You will use this frequently, so stock up. I usually buy four or five packages at a time. This product is a blend of oils, including soybean oil (see page 11); if soybean oil is a concern, forgo this item and choose coconut oil or palm oil instead.

COCONUT OIL AND/OR PALM OIL: Two oils I really like baking with, that behave like shortening (see page 50 for more on that topic), are coconut oil and palm oil. These can be difficult to find, and (especially coconut oil) can vary tremendously in quality and taste. Spectrum Organic makes a shortening that is 100% organic palm oil, which I have used with great results. Two coconut oil brands that I use are Kelapo and Tropical Traditions. Look for these online, or opt for the Nutiva or Spectrum brands at your local store.

GRAPESEED, SUNFLOWER, AND/OR SAFFLOWER OIL: In addition to shortening, another fat you will use frequently is oil. While melted shortening can sometimes be used instead, most recipes that call for oil will work best when an oil is used. You can get by with just one of these oils. Many people have a taste preference, but each of these has a relatively mild taste, and work equally well when baking. See page 44 for more on oils.

HEMP MILK: Many of my recipes use hemp milk. I choose original (or original unsweetened) for most recipes where I need a non-dairy milk and chocolate (or chocolate unsweetened) for chocolate recipes. You may also want to try vanilla (or vanilla unsweetened) hemp milk for a richer taste. If you prefer, rice milk can be substituted. These milks are usually found in the specialty or natural food section of your grocery store. Especially if you are also drinking hemp milk and using it on your cereal, it will go fast. See page 38 for more on hemp milk.

COCONUT MILK (OR COCONUT MILK BEVERAGE): Whether you opt for the very rich coconut milk found in a can or one of the newer coconut milk beverages found in the aseptic boxed containers or the dairy case, I recommend having coconut milk available for your allergen-free baking. Unless you need to avoid coconut, choose one of these products. If you like whipped cream, opt for the canned version, and skim the cream off the top. See page 40 for more on coconut milk.

VANILLA EXTRACT: Vanilla extract is a common ingredient found in the traditional baking aisle. It is used in nearly all of the recipes in this book. Only a small amount is needed for each recipe. When you're ready to experiment, other flavored extracts, including orange and lemon, are great to add to your pantry and lend a nice taste to frostings and glazes.

CINNAMON: Another common baking ingredient, ground cinnamon brings flavor to your baked goods. A little bit goes a long way.

Buy as you need it

INDIVIDUAL FLOURS AND GRAINS—If you choose to mix your own gluten-free flour blend (see page 29), you will most likely need brown rice flour and potato starch (not potato flour), in addition to the tapioca starch mentioned earlier. Other flours you may want to experiment with or add to a flour blend include sweet rice flour, amaranth, quinoa, sorghum, and teff. In addition, brown rice will be needed for Brown Rice Pudding (page 216); this is the same rice you would serve at dinner.

RICE MILK: While I don't often turn to rice milk for my recipes, I do use it occasionally, and it can be substituted for hemp and/or coconut milk, if that is your preference. See page 37 for more on rice milk.

CORNMEAL: This is an optional ingredient used for dusting the crusts of baguettes and English muffins, but it will make those baked goods look and taste more authentic. See page 20 for more on cornmeal.

QUICK-COOKING GLUTEN-FREE OATS: These will be used in cookies and bars. If you bake these recipes frequently, you may want to move this item to the "keep stocked at all times" list. Opt for gluten-free oats, to ensure no cross-contamination with wheat.

CEREALS: A couple of recipes in chapter 11 require a crisped rice cereal. A gluten-free and allergen-free version of crisped rice cereal is Erewhon Crispy Brown Rice Gluten Free cereal. The same company makes a fabulous corn flake cereal. If you are using these as breakfast cereals, go ahead and stock them; otherwise, buy them as you need them.

SWEETENERS: Two sweeteners used less frequently in my recipes are Sucanat and maple syrup. Raw sugar or light brown sugar can be substituted for Sucanat (see page 143 to learn more about Sucanat).

FRUIT: Fruit is used in many recipes, including tarts, pies, crumbles, and jams. I tend to choose my baking projects based on what fruit is in season—in summer, it's berry tarts and blueberry muffins; in the fall, it's apple pie and cranberry bread. When I have a hankering for blueberry muffins in the winter, I use frozen fruit from the grocery store or fruit that I have frozen from the season's harvest. When buying frozen fruit, look for whole unsweetened options. I also buy fruit (especially berries) organic, whenever I can. There is no reason why allergen-free foods need to be organic; it's simply my personal preference. I find that my family's already sensitive gastro-intestinal systems thrive better on organic foods. Cost may be a consideration for you here.

SEEDS: Sunflower seeds are a fantastic replacement for peanuts. In fact, "nut" butters made from sunflower seeds, which can be found off the shelf at the grocery store, are becoming the standard peanut butter replacement for food-allergic families as well as those with children in peanut-free classrooms. Likewise, hemp seeds are terrific in trail mixes and in recipes like the Rocky Oat Bars (page 211).

VEGETABLES: You may be wondering why vegetables are on a list of baking ingredients. A few of the recipes in this book use zucchini, carrots, jalapeño peppers, and sweet potatoes. These are best when fresh ingredients are used; buy them as you need them.

OLIVE OIL: In addition to the oils mentioned earlier, I like to keep light olive oil in my pantry. While olive oil has too strong a presence for cakes and cookies, it works extremely well with some yeast breads and pizza dough. That said, any of the other recommended oils can be substituted for olive oil in my recipes.

SO DELICIOUS COCONUT MILK CREAMER: This new product is a fabulous thick milk that I use in Creamy Coconut Frosting (page 109). Like the coconut milk beverage mentioned above, this creamer is a fortified version of coconut milk. You may use this infrequently, and you can always opt for a non-dairy milk in its place.

GLUTEN-FREE BAKING MIXES: In chapter 12, I will show you how to use gluten-free baking mixes (with allergen-free substitutions) to make some super-easy baked goods. It's unlikely that you will make them all next week, so buy them as you need them. If you've been longing for some simple, mix-in-one-bowl brownies, then you may want to stock up on Pamela's Products Chocolate Brownie Mix, or if buckwheat pancakes get you excited, you'll want to keep Orgran Buckwheat Pancake Mix in your pantry. I recommend trying the baking mixes and then buying the ones you like best in bulk. Check the labels and only buy baking mixes that will work for your particular food allergens. See page 223 for more information on gluten-free baking mixes and brands.

Buying allergen-free products

Now that you have your shopping list, let's talk about where to buy these products. While gluten-free and allergen-free foods are becoming more available in mainstream stores, some items can still be hard to find. If you can't find a store in your area that sells what you need, you will be able to find it online. Don't be afraid to purchase food through the mail. With the exception of chocolate (which many manufacturers will not ship from late spring to early fall to avoid melting), food can be delivered to you safely, and it's often less expensive to buy that way.

Once you start buying allergen-free and gluten-free products, you will undoubtedly notice that your grocery bills have gone up. While baking your own allergen-free bread will be cheaper than buying allergen-free bread off the shelf, the ingredients you will be using are still more expensive than their traditional counterparts. That is the reality that we food-allergy families have to deal with. We can't just buy the cereal or cookies that are on sale this week; we need very specific ingredients that we can trust. I'm confident that as more large food vendors recognize that there is a growing market for allergen-free food, the prices will come down. In the meantime, we need to feed our families, and most of the food vendors that cater to our needs are small businesses that need to turn a profit. I, for one, am very grateful for them.

So what can you do about keeping costs down? I've given you a lot of suggestions on brands to consider buying throughout this book, but always check to make sure they are safe for *your* family. Once you have tried a few products and know what your family likes best, you'll want to look for the best bargains. Here are a few tricks that have worked for me:

* **ASK YOUR STORE TO BUY FOR YOU IN BULK.** Many stores will give a 10 to 15 percent discount on foods bought by the case. If you have a favorite non-dairy milk or gluten-free baking mix, this is often the cheapest way to go. Keep in mind that many of these foods will stay shelf-stable for months.

* **REGISTER AT COMPANY WEBSITES.** Almost all of the food manufacturers referenced in this book have an online presence. Signing up for their newsletters is one of the best ways to receive coupons, discounts, and special offers, in addition to learning about new products. For example, Jules Gluten Free regularly runs specials for large purchases. Also look for loyalty programs; for example, with King Arthur Flour's current loyalty program, I receive a $25 gift card for every $250 I spend.

* **USE SUBSCRIPTION SERVICES THAT PROVIDE A DISCOUNT IF YOU BUY IN BULK.** One example of this is Amazon.com's "Subscribe & Save" program. This type of service can help you manage costs, while ensuring that you don't run out of a product. Just be sure to manage your subscriptions and delay or cancel products as needed.

Organizing your kitchen for safety

My son was ten years old when his food allergies were diagnosed. I was working full-time outside of the home. Patrick and his older brother were home alone after school. If you have boys, you know that when they reach the age of ten they are growing fast. On top of that, my boys were playing sports and needed lots of extra calories. They were hungry. An afternoon snack was important. Patrick was used to grabbing cookies, cereal, snack bars, and yogurt—whatever he wanted—from the pantry or refrigerator after school. Clearly, I needed a system to ensure that he knew what was safe and what was off limits for him.

Initially I didn't eliminate wheat from my home; some family members were not quite on board with eating wheat-free, and I was still in the process of searching for and testing the best allergen-free foods. So I reorganized my pantry. I cleared an entire shelf and designated it "Patrick-safe," labeling it so everyone in the family knew that these were foods that Patrick could eat and everyone else shouldn't eat. I purchased storage containers and designated them for allergen-free foods. When I bought an allergen-free treat, it was for Patrick only. This system worked well for us because my boys were responsible, and my son had no inclination to cheat on his diet—he had been miserable for so long that he was highly motivated to avoid his food allergens.

Over time, the balance has shifted so that nearly everything in my kitchen is allergen-free. If I buy wheat rolls for hamburgers because we're having a cookout, the wheat ingredients go in a special corner in the kitchen (and don't stay around for very long). Because milk is the allergen that my son reacts to most severely, the refrigerator is my biggest area of concern. Most of us only have one refrigerator, making it impossible to designate that space allergen-free. I have one drawer designated for cheese—whether it's slices of American cheese or tubs of cream cheese, anything with milk it in get stored in that drawer, always well wrapped. Sandwich meats are in a separate drawer, isolated from the cheese. Cow's milk is on the left side of the refrigerator; hemp milk is on the right.

The method you choose for organizing your own kitchen may depend on the specific allergens in your family, the severity of the allergies, and the age of your food-allergic family members. For small children, some families use a food-allergy version of the "yuck" stickers (typically used for cleaning materials) on any package that contains an allergen. Others teach their children not to eat anything unless a parent has approved it. As your children get older, you will want to teach them about reading labels and choosing their own safe products. You may need to invent your own system to put your mind at ease. Whatever approach you use, it is vital to think about eliminating any possibility of accidentally eating a food allergen.

Key Lessons

✓ Having the right tools and products for the job will make baking easier and a lot more fun!

✓ Contamination can happen inside the home as well as outside. Take steps to avoid it, including selecting the right tools and organizing for safety.

✓ Choose utensils, tools, and baking dishes that can be washed easily. If possible, avoid using the same baking dishes and tools for traditional baking and allergen-free baking.

✓ The dishwasher is one of the best ways to sanitize tools and dishes. Likewise, using paper towels instead of cloth ones can help reduce cross-contamination.

✓ Keep costs down by buying in bulk and taking advantage of loyalty programs.

✓ Always check to make sure the products you buy are safe for *your* family.

PART

2

the
Allergen–Free
Baking Lab

Blueberry Muffins (page 93)

6

Get Started with Simple Batters:

Cakes, Muffins and Quick Breads in a Snap

THE EASIEST AND MOST forgiving baked
goods to make are muffins, quick breads, and cakes.
All of these are made with simple batters and contain a higher proportion of wet to dry ingredients
than do other baked goods. They need to be made
in structured baking dishes (e.g., cake pans, muffin
tins, or bread pans) so they can hold a shape. This
is a great place to start when you're learning to
bake allergen-free because you can make mistakes
and still have a great finished product. You will also
be able to correct as you go. If your batter is too

thick before baking, add more water or non-dairy milk. If your batter is too thin, bake it a little longer, to allow the excess moisture to evaporate.

When working with *batters* (both here and later on with thick batters), always bring the ingredients to room temperature before using them. This could mean taking your non-dairy milk, shortening, applesauce, and flours out of the refrigerator an hour or two before you start baking. Note that different rules may apply when working with *doughs* and *yeast* (see pages 129 and 151), where some ingredients will need to be cold and others warm.

Unless a recipe directs you to do otherwise, always use the center rack of the oven and place the baking dish in the center of the rack. This allows for the most even distribution of heat, and should eliminate the need to rotate the pan halfway through baking.

Moisture is also an important factor when working with batters. Because simple batters are made in pans or baking dishes with sides, it's important not to let them sit too long once you remove them from the oven. While you can get away with letting traditional muffins stay in the pan for a couple of hours after baking, their gluten-free cousins will begin to get soggy if they sit for too long. After you let them cool for fifteen to twenty minutes, promptly remove them from their tins, and always use a cooling rack.

In addition to being the easiest to make, muffins, quick breads, and cakes can be some of the most versatile and flexible baked goods. Muffins can be breakfast or a snack, or thrown in a lunch box for dessert. Quick breads can be sliced and used as an alternative to yeast bread. Cake batters can be used to make loaves, double layer cakes, sheet cakes, cupcakes, or even mini-cupcakes. Play with ingredients and have some fun with these recipes!

Mixing Ingredients

WHEN I FIRST started baking I had a bad habit of trying to use as few dishes as possible, leaving less of a mess to clean up later. Regardless of which ingredients the recipe said to mix together first, I just threw them all in the same bowl. Most of the time it worked. But this is a very bad practice, and one that I want to break you of (even if you're mess-phobic like me). When working with gluten-free and allergen-free batters, you want to stack the deck in your favor. The technique that follows will help you do that. Typically, when you see a recipe for a batter, you will see instructions in this order:

1. Mix the dry ingredients together and set them aside.
2. Blend together the wet ingredients using your mixer (or by hand).
3. Slowly add the dry ingredients to the wet ingredients.

There are a couple of very good reasons for using this method, especially in allergen-free baking. You will usually be using xanthan gum in your batters (either in your flour blend or as an added ingredient). As soon as xanthan gum touches a liquid, it starts to gum up. Clumps of xanthan gum can create a gluey lump. Gums should be very well blended with the rest of the dry ingredients before mixing them with the wet ingredients (see page 26 for more on how to use gums), and your batter should go into the oven quickly once mixed.

Another reason to add the dry ingredients to the wet ingredients last is to get the most benefit out of your baking powder and baking soda. They will start to react very quickly once they find liquid (see page 96), and let's face it; we need all the lift we can get when baking without eggs and wheat!

As you get ready to start baking, note that all of the recipes in this chapter can easily be prepared in multiple forms. A recipe that makes one quick bread (in a 9 by 5-inch pan) is the equivalent of twelve muffins made in a standard muffin tin, or twenty-four mini-muffins. The smaller the size of the finished product, the less time it will need to bake. For example, if a quick bread takes fifty minutes to bake, muffins from the same recipe may take twenty-two minutes, and mini-muffins may take only ten minutes.

Blueberry Muffins

Blueberry Muffins

I sometimes dream about blueberry muffins that came from a department store in Rhode Island, where I spent my early childhood. Those luscious muffins had enormous tops covered with sugar that crunched when you bit into them, but the large juicy blueberries inside were what truly made them special.

I think blueberries are one of nature's finest fruits, full of antioxidants and bursting with flavor. It's no wonder that blueberry muffins are a classic, found in virtually every bakery and on every breakfast menu. These muffins are fabulous when blueberries are in season, but also work quite well with frozen blueberries. The raw sugar is what gives these muffins a crunchy top.

{ MAKES 9 TO 12 MUFFINS }

2 cups gluten-free flour blend

½ teaspoon xanthan gum (leave out if your flour blend contains xanthan gum)

½ cup granulated sugar

4 teaspoons baking powder

1 teaspoon salt

8 tablespoons (1 stick) Earth Balance Natural Shortening, melted (see tip)

½ cup flaxseed gel (equal to 2 eggs)

1 cup original hemp milk

1 teaspoon vanilla extract

¾ cup blueberries (see tip)

¼ cup raw sugar

1. Preheat the oven to 350°F. Spray a muffin tin with cooking oil.
2. Mix the flour, xanthan gum (if needed), granulated sugar, baking powder, and salt together in a medium bowl. Set it aside.
3. Combine the melted shortening, flaxseed gel, hemp milk, and vanilla together in a large bowl, with a mixer on medium-low speed, about 1 minute.
4. Gradually add the flour mixture to the wet ingredients. Blend on medium-high speed, about 2 minutes, until the batter is smooth.
5. Mix in the blueberries by hand. Spoon the batter evenly into the cups of the muffin tin.
6. Sprinkle about ¾ teaspoon of the raw sugar on top of each muffin.
7. Bake at 350°F for 28 to 32 minutes.

TIPS

∗ Be careful not to overheat the shortening when melting it in the microwave. Microwave it for 30 seconds, then for 10-second spurts until the shortening is just liquefied.

∗ If using frozen blueberries, thaw them for a couple of hours and drain before using.

Banana Bread

Bananas, oat flour, and coconut milk work extremely well together, as you will see with this banana bread. It makes a great breakfast and is just sweet enough to be considered dessert—it can even be frosted with Creamy Coconut Frosting (page 109), if you choose. Try these as muffins or mini-muffins for a great alternative to cupcakes for classroom treats.

{ MAKES 1 LOAF, 12 SERVINGS }

1 cup gluten-free oat flour

1 cup gluten-free flour blend

½ teaspoon xanthan gum (reduce to ¼ teaspoon if your flour blend contains xanthan gum)

½ cup Sucanat (see tip)

2 teaspoons baking powder

¼ teaspoon salt

3 teaspoons Ener-G Egg Replacer mixed with 4 tablespoons warm water (equal to 2 eggs)

¼ cup sunflower oil

¾ cup coconut milk beverage (see tip)

1 teaspoon vanilla extract

¾ cup mashed bananas (about 2 medium or 3 small bananas)

1. Preheat the oven to 350°F. Spray a 9 by 5-inch loaf pan with cooking oil.
2. Mix together the flours, xanthan gum, Sucanat, baking powder, and salt in a medium bowl. Set it aside.
3. Blend the egg replacer mixture, oil, coconut milk, and vanilla in a large bowl, with a mixer on medium speed, about 1 minute.
4. Add the mashed bananas. Blend on low speed, about 2 minutes. The mixture will be lumpy.
5. Gradually add the flour mixture to the wet ingredients. Blend completely on medium speed, allowing small chunks of bananas to remain. Pour the batter into the loaf pan.
6. Bake at 350°F for 45 to 55 minutes.

TIPS

❋ Light brown sugar can be substituted for Sucanat.

❋ If you need to avoid coconut due to an allergy, any dairy-free milk (e.g., rice or hemp) can be substituted.

❋ Never throw your bananas away. When they are about to become overripe, place them in the freezer in their skins (making sure the skins are intact). The skins will turn brown in the freezer, but that's okay. When you are ready to use them for baking, let them thaw, then slice the skins open and the banana mush will slide right out. Bananas will keep in the freezer for four to six months. As an alternative, you can skin the bananas before freezing them; in that case, place them in an airtight freezer-safe container.

❋ If you choose to make these as mini-muffins, reduce the baking time to 22 to 25 minutes.

Cinnamon Raisin Whole-Grain Muffins

This recipe is for everyone who longs for the taste of cinnamon and raisins, but wants quicker results than the Cinnamon Rolls (page 181) and Cinnamon Raisin Bread (page 185). I like to make these muffins with a multigrain flour blend.

{ MAKES 9 TO 12 MUFFINS }

2 cups multigrain gluten-free flour blend

½ teaspoon xanthan gum (leave out if your flour blend contains xanthan gum)

1 tablespoon cinnamon

4 teaspoons baking powder

1 teaspoon salt

½ cup grapeseed oil

½ cup flaxseed gel (equal to 2 eggs)

1 cup original hemp milk

1 teaspoon vanilla extract

½ cup honey (see tip)

1 cup raisins (see tip)

1. Preheat the oven to 350°F. Spray a muffin tin with cooking oil.
2. Mix together the flour, xanthan gum (if needed), cinnamon, baking powder, and salt in a medium bowl. Set it aside.
3. Blend the oil, flaxseed gel, hemp milk, vanilla, and honey in a large bowl, with a mixer on medium speed, about 2 minutes.
4. Gradually add the flour mixture to the wet ingredients. Blend completely on medium speed, until the batter is smooth.
5. Mix in the raisins by hand. Spoon the batter evenly into the cups of the muffin tin.
6. Bake at 350°F for 25 to 28 minutes.

TIPS

✳ Agave nectar can be substituted for honey.

✳ Raisins bake best when they are plump and juicy. If need be, soak them in warm water for 20 minutes, and then drain before using them in your recipe.

Using Baking Soda and Baking Powder

THE BAKING SODA and baking powder you will use in your allergen-free baking are exactly the same as what traditional bakers use. As always, you must read the product labels (see page 6), but these products do not typically contain any of the top eight food allergens and are naturally gluten-free.

What changes when you bake allergen-free is the level of importance of these products. You no longer have the gluten in flour to help your cakes and muffins expand, providing that fluffy quality we love, and you no longer have eggs to boost the leavening action. When you're baking with traditional ingredients, you might even be able to leave out the baking soda or baking powder completely, and no one will be the wiser. Not so when baking allergen-free. So let's take a look at what these products are, what they do, and how to choose which to use.

Baking soda is a very simple product—it is one ingredient, sodium bicarbonate. Baking soda releases tiny gas bubbles that help batters expand. The catch is that baking soda needs an acid to react with to do its magic. That acid could be vinegar (of any type), an acidic juice (e.g., fresh orange or lemon juice), or even chocolate (which, yes, is acidic). The downside to baking soda is that it reacts very quickly and it reacts only once. Similar to how a bottle of soda fizzes when you open it, once the gas is released, the baking soda has done its job for the day. When baking soda is your only leavening agent, you will want to get your baked goods into the oven quickly after the dry and wet ingredients are mixed.

Baking powder combines sodium bicarbonate (baking soda) with additional ingredients, usually an acid and a starch. Because the acid is built right in, baking powder only needs liquid to react. You will want to choose a double-acting baking powder, the kind most commonly found at the grocery store. Double-acting baking powders provide the same initial release of gas that you see with baking soda, but they also give off a second reaction during the baking process, when temperatures rise.

It's common to see higher amounts of baking powder used in allergen-free recipes than in traditional recipes, to compensate for the lack of other leavening ingredients. A cake that may have used 2 tea-

spoons of baking powder when made with wheat and eggs may need 3 or 4 teaspoons when made without them.

It's also common to see allergen-free recipes that call for both products. I don't often use baking soda alone, as I find that the second reaction in the oven is key in many recipes, but it can be advantageous when making a highly acidic recipe (e.g., the Cranberry Bread on page 98). When in doubt, choose baking powder. It can be substituted for baking soda, but you will need to double or triple the amount called for. For example, if the recipe calls for 1 teaspoon of baking soda and 1 teaspoon of baking powder, use 3 teaspoons of baking powder alone. See appendix C (page 259) to learn how to adapt traditional recipes.

If you find that your muffins don't rise, first test your baking soda and baking powder for freshness before deciding to add more:

TESTING BAKING SODA

Combine 1 tablespoon of vinegar (any type) with 1 teaspoon of baking soda. If your baking soda is still fresh, you will see an immediate fizzing reaction.

TESTING BAKING POWDER

Combine 1 tablespoon of warm tap water with 1 teaspoon of baking powder. If your baking powder is still fresh, you will see an immediate bubbling/foaming reaction.

Both products should last for eight to twelve months after opening, and should not be used after the expiration date.

Be aware that while most baking powders do not contain any of the top eight allergens, most do contain corn starch, and the corn-allergic will need to find an alternative. Two options for corn-free baking powder are Hain's Featherweight Baking Powder (which uses potato starch in place of corn starch) and New England Cupboard's completely starch-free version of its Bakewell Cream leavening agent.

Cranberry Bread

When I drive to Cape Cod to visit family, I drive past miles of bright red cranberry bogs, and I am always fascinated by the marshy wetlands where these fabulous berries grow on their vines. The cranberry is native to North America, and a major fruit crop for the United States and Canada. It's no wonder that it's such a staple for our holiday meals. I usually make a couple of extra loaves of this Cranberry Bread to freeze and enjoy during the winter.

Notice that there is no egg substitute in this recipe. The orange juice combines with the baking soda to provide leavening (see page 53 for more on egg substitutes).

{ MAKES 1 LOAF, 12 SERVINGS }

1 cup gluten-free oat flour (see note)

1¼ cups gluten-free flour blend

½ teaspoon xanthan gum (reduce to ¼ teaspoon if your flour blend contains xanthan gum)

1 teaspoon baking soda

2 teaspoons baking powder

1 teaspoon salt

2 tablespoons Earth Balance Natural Shortening, melted

¾ cup honey (see note)

1 cup orange juice

1 cup fresh cranberries, chopped (keep them a bit chunky)

1. Preheat the oven to 350°F. Spray a 9 by 5-inch loaf pan with cooking oil.
2. Mix together the flours, xanthan gum, baking soda, baking powder, and salt in a medium bowl. Set it aside.
3. Combine the melted shortening, honey, and orange juice in a large bowl, with a mixer on medium speed, about 2 minutes.
4. Add the cranberries and mix for 1 minute longer.
5. Gradually add the flour mixture to the wet ingredients. Blend on medium speed, about 2 minutes, until all ingredients are combined.
6. Pour the batter into the loaf pan.
7. Bake at 350°F for 40 to 50 minutes.

TIPS

* Gluten-free oat flours are becoming more readily available. As an alternative you can make your own by grinding gluten-free quick-cooking oats to a fine powder, using a food processor or high-speed blender.
* Try this recipe with cranberry honey, if you can find it. I buy mine on Cape Cod, but it can also be found online.
* Stock up on cranberries in the fall, while they are in season. I recommend chopping the cranberries first, then freezing them in plastic freezer bags.

Apple Cinnamon Breakfast Cake

Not quite a muffin, not quite a pie, not quite a cake. Here's an easy one-dish recipe for breakfast that even includes a serving of fruit.

This is another recipe that uses baking soda for leavening, along with a small amount of baking powder. The baking soda is effective because of the apple cider vinegar. This is also an example of a recipe that uses only apple cider vinegar as the replacement for eggs. You'll see how great this works!

{ MAKES 12 TO 16 SERVINGS }

3 medium apples, peeled, cored, and diced (about 2 cups)

1½ teaspoons fresh lime juice

¾ cup light brown sugar

1 teaspoon cinnamon

1½ cups gluten-free flour blend

¼ teaspoon xanthan gum (leave out if your flour blend contains xanthan gum)

1½ teaspoons baking soda

1 teaspoon baking powder

½ teaspoon salt

1 cup original hemp milk

2 tablespoons apple cider vinegar

⅓ cup grapeseed oil (see tip)

1. Preheat the oven to 350°F. Spray a 9-inch square baking dish with cooking oil.

2. Toss together the apples, lime juice, ½ cup of the brown sugar, and the cinnamon in a medium bowl. Set it aside.

3. Mix together the flour, xanthan gum (if needed), baking soda, baking powder, salt, and the remaining ¼ cup of brown sugar in a medium bowl. Set it aside.

4. Combine the hemp milk, vinegar, and oil in a large bowl, with a mixer on medium speed, about 1 minute.

5. Gradually add the flour mixture, blending on medium speed until all the ingredients are combined and the batter is smooth.

6. Pour the batter into the baking dish, spreading it to the edges.

7. Spoon the apple mixture on top of the batter. The apples will sink into the batter, but shouldn't be covered. The cake will form around the apples as it bakes.

8. Bake at 350°F for 35 to 40 minutes, until a toothpick inserted in the center comes out clean.

TIPS

* Use a 9-inch round pie plate and serve this as an alternative to apple pie for dessert. Make it à la mode by adding a scoop of non-dairy ice cream (see page 50).
* I like the flavor that grapeseed oil brings to this recipe, but you can easily substitute another favorite oil with great results. (See page 44 for more on oils.)
* Refrigerate the leftovers (as you would with a fruit pie). Warm them in the microwave before serving.

CRASH COURSE

When Is It Done?

AT A RECENT family gathering, my niece Anna prepared a fabulous gluten-free dish. When I asked how long it needed to stay in the oven she replied, "Until it's done." Of course, what I really wanted to know was how long it needed to be in the oven—ten minutes? twenty-five? an hour?

Experienced cooks can tell when their food is ready by just looking at it, as can experienced bakers. But a baker who is just starting out, or one who has spent his or her entire life baking with wheat, butter, and eggs, may have difficulty eyeballing when a cake is ready to come out of the oven. To further complicate matters, the look of a product can vary dramatically depending on which flour you use. Gluten-free and wheat-free flours can range from pure white to muddy brown in color. Some bread crusts made with these flours don't brown as typical wheat flours do, and the outer surface of your finished product may look very different from what you are used to. And such factors as altitude and the types of pans you choose will make a difference in how long your baked goods need to stay in the oven. The same recipe baked in a 9-inch square stainless-steel pan will generally require less time than one baked in a stoneware pan of the same size—but just by a minute or two.

So how *do* you know when it's done? The best method for determining whether your baked goods made from batters are done is to test with a toothpick. You can't always rely on the "spring" method (pressing lightly in the center to see if it springs back) for allergen-free cakes and quick breads, the way you can with wheat recipes. With a gluten-free product, you may have a harder crust or you may create a crater that won't spring back.

Choose a toothpick that hasn't been coated with oils or colored with dyes. When your timer goes off, test for doneness by inserting the toothpick into the middle section of your baked goods (the thickest part). Insert the toothpick about an inch deep and pull it right back out. If it's wet or feels mushy as you insert, you need to bake the item longer. As soon as the toothpick comes out clean, you may want to bake for only one to two minutes longer—any longer than that and you risk burning your muffins!

How long should you set your timer for? Many recipes provide a time range (e.g., 20 to 24 minutes). Ovens vary in terms of how well they cook, and 350°F in one oven may actually be a few degrees hotter

or cooler than in another. I recommend always setting the timer for three to five fewer minutes than the lowest suggested time (three for faster-baking items such as muffins and five for longer-baking items such as quick breads). Test when the timer goes off and then add more time based on the results of your toothpick test.

If you find that your baked goods always need to stay in the oven longer than the recommended time, try increasing the temperature you bake at (in ten-degree increments) until you are in the right range. Once you've made the same recipe (with the exact same ingredients) a few times, you can forgo the testing and rely on your experience. I encourage you to keep notes as you bake, rather than relying on memory.

Zucchini Bread

Zucchini Bread

Often when people think of zucchini bread they also think of chocolate. Although I am a fan of chocolate zucchini bread, chocolate does mask the taste of zucchini in a quick bread or muffin. My version of zucchini bread can best be described as vanilla zucchini bread, allowing the zucchini flavor to shine.

Because the zucchini adds some weight to the bread, I have chosen Ener-G Egg Replacer as the egg substitute here. The additional leavening agents in this egg replacer help to keep the bread light. The added fiber from the zucchini makes this a great way to start your day. Try it with Strawberry Jam (page 219).

{ MAKES 1 LOAF, 12 SERVINGS }

2 cups gluten-free flour blend (see tip)

½ teaspoon xanthan gum (leave out if your flour blend contains xanthan gum)

¾ cup sugar

3 teaspoons baking powder

1 teaspoon salt

½ teaspoon cinnamon

3 teaspoons Ener-G Egg Replacer mixed with 4 tablespoons warm water (equal to 2 eggs)

½ cup grapeseed oil

¾ cup original hemp milk

1½ teaspoons vanilla extract

1½ cups zucchini, shredded (1 medium to large zucchini) (see tip)

1. Preheat the oven to 350°F. Spray a 9 by 5-inch loaf pan with cooking oil.
2. Mix together the flour, xanthan gum (if needed), sugar, baking powder, salt, and cinnamon in a medium bowl. Set it aside.
3. Blend together the egg replacer mixture, oil, hemp milk, and vanilla in a large bowl, with a mixer on medium speed, about 1 minute.
4. Gradually add the flour mixture, blending on medium speed until the batter is smooth.
5. Add the zucchini and mix for an additional 2 minutes, until combined.
6. Pour the batter into the loaf pan.
7. Bake at 350°F for 50 to 55 minutes.

TIPS

* This bread tastes great with a multigrain flour blend.
* Leftover zucchini can be shredded and frozen in an airtight container until you are ready to use it.

* VARIATION:

CARROT BREAD: Substitute peeled, shredded carrots for the zucchini and nutmeg for the cinnamon, in equal amounts. Follow the directions above.

Coffee Cake with Streusel Topping

Did you know that most coffee cakes don't contain coffee? They get their name because they are intended to be served with coffee, which makes them the perfect treat for breakfast. My favorite part of a coffee cake is always the streusel topping—just enough sugar to wake you up.

The technique used here to create the streusel topping is one that will be used frequently when making cookie dough and pie crusts.

{ MAKES 12 TO 16 SERVINGS }

FOR THE CAKE:

- 2 cups gluten-free flour blend
- ½ teaspoon xanthan gum (leave out if your flour blend contains xanthan gum)
- 3 teaspoons baking powder
- ½ teaspoon salt
- 4 tablespoons (½ stick) Earth Balance Natural Shortening, softened (see tip)
- ½ cup granulated sugar
- 3 teaspoons Ener-G Egg Replacer mixed with 4 tablespoons warm water (equal to 2 eggs)
- ½ cup unsweetened applesauce
- 1 cup coconut milk beverage (see tip)
- 1 teaspoon vanilla extract

FOR THE STREUSEL TOPPING:

- ⅔ cup gluten-free oat flour
- ¾ cup light brown sugar
- 3 tablespoons Earth Balance Natural Shortening, cold

1. Preheat the oven to 350°F. Spray a 9-inch square baking dish with cooking oil.

PREPARE THE CAKE BATTER:

2. Mix together the flour, xanthan gum (if needed), baking powder, and salt in a medium bowl. Set it aside.

3. Cream together the shortening and granulated sugar in a large bowl, with a mixer on medium speed, for about 5 minutes, until a textured paste forms. Scrape down the sides of the mixing bowl as needed.

4. Add the egg replacer mixture, applesauce, coconut milk, and vanilla to the creamed sugar. Blend with a mixer on medium-low speed for 2 to 3 minutes.

5. Gradually add the flour mixture and blend on medium speed, about 2 minutes.

6. Pour the batter into the baking dish, spreading it to the sides of the pan.

PREPARE THE STREUSEL TOPPING:

7. In a large mixing bowl, combine the oat flour and brown sugar, using a pastry cutter or pastry fork.

8. Cut the shortening into tablespoon-sized pieces. Use the pastry cutter to work the shortening into the flour.

9. Crumble the streusel topping over the batter.

10. Bake at 350°F for 32 to 36 minutes.

TIPS

* Note that the shortening for the cake is used at room temperature, whereas the shortening for the topping is used cold. Plan to let just the 4 tablespoons sit out to soften and leave the remainder in the fridge until you need it for the streusel.
* If you need to avoid coconut due to an allergy, substitute hemp milk or rice milk for the coconut milk.

Coffee Cake with Streusel Topping

About Creaming

EVERY NOW AND then you'll come across a recipe that directs you to cream the shortening and sugar until it's smooth and fluffy. You might be tempted to skip this step in favor of just throwing all the ingredients in the bowl together. Instead of winging it, let's take a look at what creaming is all about, and how you can use it to your advantage.

Creaming is used to make batters lighter. It's all about the chemical reaction of the sugar with the fat. Traditional creaming methods use butter as the fat, cream it with the sugar, and then incorporate eggs. You will be use shortening instead of butter and you won't be adding eggs, but you will still be able to achieve a fluffier cake than without creaming.

Creaming only works with the right ingredients. First, you must use a strong shortening—one that is still solid after warming to room temperature, and not breaking down around the edges (see page 48). My favorite allergen-free choice for this is Earth Balance Natural Shortening. Oils will not work, and even coconut oil breaks down as you beat it. And you must use a crystal form of sugar; granulated cane sugar works best (see "Sweetening Options," page 140). Creaming will not work with honey, agave nectar, or any liquid sweetener. The sugar must be in crystal form to cut its way into the fat. As you beat the shortening and sugar together, tiny air bubbles will form. Those fat-coated air bubbles will expand as you bake, helping the cake to rise. If you do this correctly, you will be able to feel the graininess of the sugar in the creamed shortening mixture as you scrape down the sides of your bowl. It will appear fluffy but grainy.

Before you start, make sure all the ingredients are at room temperature. Here are the steps to follow:

1. Place the shortening in the mixing bowl and soften it with a mixer fitted with the beater blade, on medium speed, for no longer than 1 minute. If your shortening was already at room temperature, this step may take as little as 20 seconds. You want the shortening to be light and fluffy. Too much friction will cause it break down too much.

2. Add the sugar to the mixing bowl. Beat on medium speed for 3 to 5 minutes. You are beating the sugar into the fat. It's usually better to cream a little bit too long than too short. More beating creates more air pockets. You can't speed the process up by beating on high speed—medium is just the right speed for those air bubbles to form.

3. Continue with blending in the wet ingredients, then the dry ingredients. Notice that when you blend in the wet ingredients (and even after you incorporate the dry ingredients), the mixture will not be completely smooth like most batters. This is okay. The shortening-coated sugar is ready to do its job in the oven.

Use a stand mixer or a hand mixer for creaming. You won't be able to beat fast enough to create air bubbles beating by hand.

Vanilla Pound Cake

Have you ever wondered what makes a pound cake a pound cake? The classic version is made with one pound each of flour, fat (butter, oil, or shortening), eggs, and sugar. My allergen-free version uses both applesauce and flaxseed gel in place of eggs, but I chose to make it light, with only half the fat and sugar of the classic version.

This makes a great sliced cake, but it can also be prepared as a traditional cake or cupcakes. The very first time I made this, my son told me that I had "hit it out of the park." I hope your family loves it too!

{ MAKES 1 LOAF, 12 SERVINGS }

1¾ cups gluten-free flour blend

¾ teaspoon xanthan gum (leave out if your flour blend contains xanthan gum)

3 teaspoons baking powder

½ teaspoon salt

1 cup light brown sugar

8 tablespoons (1 stick) Earth Balance Natural Shortening, softened

½ cup original hemp milk

½ cup unsweetened applesauce (equal to 2 eggs)

½ cup flaxseed gel (equal to 2 eggs)

2 teaspoons vanilla extract

1. Preheat the oven to 350°F. Spray a 9 by 5-inch loaf pan with cooking oil.
2. Mix together the flour, xanthan gum (if needed), baking powder, and salt in a medium bowl. Set it aside.
3. Cream together the brown sugar and shortening in a large bowl, with a mixer on medium speed, for 5 minutes. (See page 106 to learn about creaming.)
4. Add the hemp milk, applesauce, flaxseed gel, and vanilla to the creamed mixture. Mix on medium speed for 2 minutes.
5. Gradually add the flour mixture, blending on medium speed, about 2 minutes.
6. Pour the batter into the prepared loaf pan.
7. Bake at 350°F for 45 to 55 minutes.

TIPS

❊ To make a two-layer cake in 9-inch round pans, double the recipe and reduce the baking time to 25 to 28 minutes.

❊ Frost with the Creamy Vanilla Frosting that follows, if desired.

Creamy Vanilla Frosting

Most creamy frostings are made with—you guessed it—milk-based cream. Here I offer you two easy recipes for vanilla frosting made without traditional cream. The first is made without any milk at all, and is perfect on chocolate cake.

The variation uses just enough coconut oil and coconut cream to keep the frosting light without over-powering the taste. Use it as a topping for Vanilla Pound Cake (page 108), or any of the cakes found in this book. I love it on Carrot Cake (page 233).

{ MAKES ENOUGH TO FROST 1 DOUBLE-LAYER CAKE }

3 cups confectioners' sugar

¼ teaspoon salt

12 tablespoons (1½ sticks) Earth Balance Natural Shortening, softened (see tip)

1 tablespoon vanilla extract

2 to 4 tablespoons water (as needed)

1. Blend together the confectioners' sugar, salt, and shortening in a large bowl, with a mixer on low speed, until well blended (about 5 minutes).
2. Add the vanilla and 2 tablespoons of water. Mix on medium-low speed for 2 to 4 minutes.
3. Add up to an additional 2 tablespoons of water, ½ tablespoon at a time, until the frosting is creamy enough to spread.

TIPS

* Reduce the shortening to as little as 10 tablespoons (1 stick + 2 tablespoons) for a lighter frosting.
* Be sure to start with the shortening at room temperature.
* Refrigerate leftover frosting. When you're ready to use it again, let it soften at room temperature before frosting your cake or cupcakes.

✳ VARIATION:

CREAMY COCONUT FROSTING: Use 6 tablespoons of softened shortening and 6 tablespoons of room-temperature coconut oil instead of the 12 tablespoons of shortening. Reduce the vanilla extract to 1½ teaspoons, and use 3 tablespoons of coconut milk creamer or coconut cream instead of the water.

Making Sweet Potato Dinner Rolls (page 122)

7

Next Batter Up:
Scones, Doughnuts and Other Yeast-Free Standbys

DOUGHNUTS AND SCONES DIDN'T enter my at-home baking repertoire until I started baking gluten-free and allergen-free. There was no need to make my own. It was easy enough to run out to Dunkin' Donuts or a local bakery if I needed some of these fancier baked goods. But that isn't an option anymore, and sometimes a simple muffin or a quick bread just doesn't cut it. Think about Sunday brunch, or bridal showers, or a long overdue reunion with your best friend from high school. That's where thick batters come in. Using thick batters, you can create treats of every size and shape. You aren't limited by the size of the pan—often you won't need more than a cookie sheet and parchment paper. Better yet, working with thick batters can be a lot of fun. What you create is limited only by your imagination, and it's a great opportunity to include the kids.

Are you ready? Let's find out more.

About Thick Batters

THE TECHNIQUES YOU will use to make baked goods from thick batters are very similar to those used for muffins and cakes. What differs is the consistency of the batter. Instead of mixtures that can be poured into a pan, the batters you'll be making in this chapter hold together in mushy balls. They aren't quite as thick as the dough you will use for yeast breads, but they don't contain as much liquid as did the baked goods in chapter 6. Here you will use a different proportion of wet to dry ingredients, with less of the liquids. The thicker consistency allows you to mold and sculpt the batter into shapes that will stay put while baking. This opens up a world of possibilities, including scones, doughnuts, and rolls of all shapes and sizes. Yes, you have permission to play with your food!

As with simple batters, the technique used most often to form thick batters is to mix the dry ingredients, mix the wet ingredients, then add the dry to the wet. You may find it necessary to scrape down the sides of your mixing bowl with a spatula during the mixing process to ensure that your batter is well blended. When you choose to use a formed pan (such as a doughnut or scone pan), be sure to transfer the baked goods from the pan to a cooling rack within ten to fifteen minutes of removing them from the oven. If you are using a baking sheet, while less critical, it's still best to cool them on a rack, so air can circulate beneath them.

Keep in mind that when you work with thicker consistencies, it's a little bit harder to adjust as you go. Baking too long may result in scones that you can skip across the lake. On the other hand, if you don't bake them long enough, they will be heavy enough to sink straight to the bottom! For that reason, I recommend substituting ingredients and adjusting proportions in small increments.

Blueberry Scones

It is believed that scones originated in Scotland, and made their way to England and the rest of Europe from there. Surprisingly, the first scones were made from oats, without leavening ingredients. Yes, they were gluten-free and wheat-free! Because they were unleavened, they were quite flat. With the leavening options we have today, we can make our scones a little bit lighter and more cake-like.

Today, most of us think of scones as an alternative to muffins. In Europe they are a standard with afternoon tea, and I can't think of a better low-sugar treat. Scones might best be described as biscuit-like quick breads, not as sweet as cakes or cookies. They are typically shaped into triangles, but can be made in almost any shape. If you're pressed for time (or you just don't want to get your hands dirty), try making them in your muffin pan and let them take on whatever organic form they choose.

Staying true to tradition, I have chosen to use oat flour in this recipe, combining it with a gluten-free flour blend.

{ MAKES 8 SCONES }

1¼ cups gluten-free oat flour

1 cup gluten-free flour blend

½ teaspoon xanthan gum (reduce to ¼ teaspoon if your flour blend contains xanthan gum)

3 teaspoons baking powder

1 teaspoon baking soda

½ teaspoon salt

½ cup light brown sugar

½ cup flaxseed gel (equal to 2 eggs)

¼ cup sunflower oil

½ cup original (or original unsweetened) hemp milk

1 tablespoon fresh lemon juice

2 tablespoons water (as needed)

1 cup blueberries (see tip)

1. Preheat the oven to 350°F. Line a baking sheet with parchment paper.

2. Mix together the flours, xanthan gum, baking powder, baking soda, salt, and brown sugar in a medium bowl. Set it aside.

3. Combine the flaxseed gel, oil, hemp milk, and lemon juice in a large bowl, with a mixer on medium speed, about 2 minutes.

4. Gradually add the flour mixture to the wet ingredients. Blend completely on medium-low speed, about 5 minutes.

5. Add water, ½ tablespoon at a time, if needed (up to 2 tablespoons), until a wet, pasty batter forms.

6. Fold in the blueberries by hand.

7. Form the scones (see page 115) and arrange them on the lined baking sheet with space in between.

8. Bake at 350°F for 20 to 24 minutes, until lightly browned.

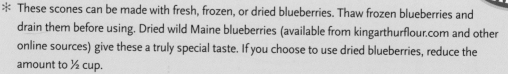

TIPS

✳ These scones can be made with fresh, frozen, or dried blueberries. Thaw frozen blueberries and drain them before using. Dried wild Maine blueberries (available from kingarthurflour.com and other online sources) give these a truly special taste. If you choose to use dried blueberries, reduce the amount to ½ cup.

✳ If you don't have blueberries on hand, try this recipe with raisins or other berries. If your raisins are dry, I recommend soaking them in water to plump them up and draining them before using.

How to Form Scones

REMEMBER HOW MUCH fun you used to have with Play-Doh, or Silly Putty, or that green slimy stuff that felt cold and gooey in your hands? Baking gives you a chance to have that same kind of fun in your own kitchen. While it's possible to form scones with gloves on (go for it if you don't want to get your hands dirty), using naked hands allows you to feel the consistency of the batter and helps you shape the scones properly. Be sure to take off any rings and bracelets, and wash your hands thoroughly before you start.

Sure, it's possible to make scones using a scone pan, but they're expensive and take up valuable space in your cabinet. If you don't have a scone pan, all you need is a baking sheet lined with parchment paper, a smooth preparation surface, your own hands, a bench knife, and a little bit of warm water.

Once the batter is ready, it will be a loose ball. If you can pick it up with your hands, but it slowly slimes through your fingers, you have the right consistency. You will need a smooth surface to prepare the scones on. This could be a pastry board (these can be pricey and come in luxury surfaces like marble and granite), a nonstick pastry mat, a smooth cutting board (avoid wood), or wax paper. For simplicity, I will refer to this as the pastry board. Follow these steps to form your scones:

1. Line a baking sheet or cookie sheet with parchment paper.
2. Spread a few drops of warm water on the pastry board.
3. Using a spatula or a spoon, loosen the batter from the sides of the mixing bowl.
4. Wet your hands with a little bit of warm water. Lift the batter ball from your mixing bowl and place it in the center of the pastry board.
5. Flatten the top of the ball using your wet fingers, keeping the round shape but letting it spread about 9 inches in diameter and about an inch thick.
6. Run the bench knife under warm water and use it to slice the batter into eight pieces (as you would a pizza). If you don't have a bench knife, a standard flat-edged knife will do.
7. Use a bench knife or spatula to move the scones and place them on the lined cookie sheet, leaving space between the scones for baking.

Your scones are now ready to go into the oven. If the scones lose their shape when you move them, use wet fingers and your knife to reshape them. This technique can be used to form any shape you desire from a loose batter, including Baked Doughnuts (page 119) and Sweet Potato Dinner Rolls (page 122).

Scones bake quickly because of their large surface area. The best way to test for doneness is to tap lightly on the top of a scone. The surface should be thin but hard. If the top of the scone doesn't indent, they are ready to come out of the oven. Don't worry; they will soften a bit as they cool.

Cranberry Orange Scones

Cranberry Orange Scones

I can't think of two fruit flavors that go together better than cranberry and orange. It's the perfect blend of flavors from different corners of the United States. Whether it's a punch made with cranberry and orange juices, a relish, or these scones, you just can't miss when you mix these flavors.

Notice that in this recipe I have chosen honey as the sweetener. The gumminess of this sugar (in its prebaked state) helps hold the pastry together and allows you to shape it with your hands.

{ MAKES 8 SCONES }

2 cups gluten-free flour blend

½ teaspoon xanthan gum (leave out if your flour blend contains xanthan gum)

1 teaspoon salt

2 teaspoons baking soda

2 teaspoons baking powder

¼ cup unsweetened applesauce (equal to 1 egg)

¼ cup grapeseed oil

¼ cup honey

½ cup fresh orange juice

1½ teaspoons orange zest

1 cup roughly chopped cranberries

1. Preheat the oven to 350°F. Line a baking sheet with parchment paper.
2. Mix together the flour, xanthan gum (if needed), salt, baking soda, and baking powder in a medium bowl. Set it aside.
3. Combine the applesauce, oil, honey, orange juice, and orange zest in a large bowl, with a mixer on medium speed, about 2 minutes.
4. Gradually add the flour mixture to the wet ingredients. Blend completely on medium-low speed, about 5 minutes.
5. Add the cranberries and blend for 30 seconds longer.
6. Form the scones (see page 115) and arrange them on the lined baking sheet with space in between.
7. Bake at 350°F for 16 to 18 minutes, until lightly browned.

TIPS

* These scones are easy to make. If you have time to make breakfast tomorrow morning, take the applesauce and orange juice that you will need out of the refrigerator before bedtime. Serve these warm for breakfast or pop them in a lunch box for a special treat. They take less than 30 minutes to make, including baking time.

Baked Doughnuts

I have a confession to make. There was a time when I would serve my family store-bought chocolate frosted doughnuts for breakfast—almost every day. I cringe when I think about it now. Nevertheless, when I eliminated wheat, milk, and eggs from my family's diet, doughnuts were one of the treats I missed most. I needed to create an allergen-free doughnut, but I didn't want it to be the high-calorie, high-sugar doughnut of my past. I also wanted my doughnut recipe to be quick and easy. That meant it had to be yeast-free and had to be baked rather than fried.

This basic baked doughnut recipe is most like an old-fashioned doughnut. It can be eaten plain, or topped with just about anything you want. Have fun with toppings; let the kids each decorate their own, or create a topping bar (as you would for ice-cream sundaes).

If you have time, these can be made in less than 30 minutes in the morning. Just remember to take the refrigerated ingredients out the night before.

{ MAKES 8 TO 10 DOUGHNUTS }

2½ cups gluten-free flour blend

½ teaspoon xanthan gum (leave out if your flour blend contains xanthan gum)

½ cup light brown sugar

4 teaspoons baking powder

½ teaspoon salt

½ cup original hemp milk

½ cup unsweetened applesauce (equal to 2 eggs)

1 tablespoon grapeseed oil

½ teaspoon vanilla extract

1. Preheat the oven to 350°F. Line a baking sheet with parchment paper, or spray a doughnut pan with cooking oil.
2. Mix together the flour, xanthan gum (if needed), brown sugar, baking powder, and salt in a medium bowl. Set it aside.
3. Combine the hemp milk, applesauce, oil, and vanilla in a large bowl, with a mixer on medium speed, about 1 minute.
4. Gradually add the flour mixture to the wet ingredients. Blend completely, about 5 minutes on medium speed, until a wet ball forms.
5. Transfer the dough to a smooth prep surface and separate the dough into 8 to 10 balls.
6. Wet your hands. Roll a ball back and forth between your hands to lengthen it into a cylindrical shape about 6 inches long.
7. Form the cylinder into a doughnut on your prepared baking sheet or in your doughnut pan. Use a few drops of water to glue the ends of the doughnut together. Use wet fingers to smooth the sides and top of the doughnuts.
8. Repeat this process for the remaining doughnuts.
9. Bake at 350°F for 15 to 18 minutes, until lightly browned.

(continued)

Baked Doughnuts

* These doughnuts will have a heartier taste when made with a multigrain flour blend.
* As an alternative to doughnuts, try forming crullers. After rolling the dough into a cylinder, twist it on your baking sheet to create the traditional cruller shape.
* A doughnut pan will help give the doughnuts a smooth shape. Whether you use a pan or a baking sheet you will get the same great taste.
* With the exception of Sugar-Crusted Doughnuts (see below), the toppings should be added when you are ready to serve. Undecorated doughnuts will keep for up to a week, and can easily be frozen.

* VARIATIONS:

GLAZED DOUGHNUTS: Prepare Vanilla Glaze (page 184). Drizzle the glaze onto cooled doughnuts.

CHOCOLATE-FROSTED DOUGHNUTS: Prepare Chocolate Glaze (page 177). Drizzle the glaze onto cooled doughnuts.

SUGAR-CRUSTED DOUGHNUTS: Before baking, sprinkle about ½ teaspoon of raw sugar over the top of each doughnut.

POWDERED DOUGHNUTS: Spread ¼ cup of confectioners' sugar on a plate. Dip the tops of the baked doughnuts into the sugar, and then serve. This works best when the doughnuts are slightly cooled.

Sweet Potato Dinner Rolls

Every year as Thanksgiving approaches, my family begins the debate about whether I should prepare mashed potatoes or sweet potatoes. In the end, I usually just make both. When it comes to rolls, however, everyone agrees that these sweet potato rolls are the way to go. Although most of the roll and bread recipes are in chapter 9 because they require yeast, this one is simpler, yeast-free, and can be prepared using the same techniques as scones and other thick batters.

Notice that there is no standard egg replacer in this recipe. The sweet potato provides the same effect that a fruit puree would (see page 59), acting as the replacement for eggs, providing both taste and texture, and the starch in the potato will help to keep the rolls together.

{ MAKES 8 TO 10 ROLLS }

1 cup mashed sweet potatoes (about 2 medium potatoes)

⅔ cup millet flour

1⅓ cups gluten-free flour blend

¼ teaspoon xanthan gum (leave out if your flour blend contains xanthan gum)

3 teaspoons baking powder

1 teaspoon salt

8 tablespoons (1 stick) Earth Balance Natural Shortening, softened

⅔ cup original hemp milk

Up to 3 tablespoons water (as needed)

Up to 2 tablespoons additional flour for dusting

1. Bake the potatoes (either in a microwave or traditional oven), until a fork inserted goes in easily. After the potatoes cool, cut them open and scoop out the meat. Set it aside.

2. Preheat the oven to 375°F. Line a baking sheet with parchment paper.

3. Mix together the flours, xanthan gum (if needed), baking powder, and salt in a medium bowl. Set it aside.

4. Combine the shortening and hemp milk

in a large bowl, with a mixer on medium speed, about 3 minutes.

5. Add the sweet potato meat. Mix for 2 to 3 minutes more on medium speed, until smooth.

6. Gradually add the flour mixture to the wet ingredients. Blend completely, about 5 minutes on medium speed.

7. Add water, ½ tablespoon at a time, until a wet ball forms.

8. Dust a smooth prep surface with a light coating of flour.

9. Scoop the dough onto the prep surface. Use a bench knife to separate the dough into 8 to 10 balls.

10. Roll each section of dough between your hands to form a smooth ball. Place the formed rolls on the prepared baking sheet and gently flatten the tops.

11. Bake at 375°F for 20 to 24 minutes, until lightly browned. If you want both sides evenly browned, flip the rolls halfway through baking.

TIPS

* These rolls can be made into a variety of shapes, including flat-topped rolls and rounded rolls. They can be made into English muffin shapes, or sliced in half and used as rolls for burgers or sandwiches.
* The process for forming these rolls is the same as I described for scones and doughnuts (see page 115), with the added trick of using flour for dusting. You will use dry hands, rather than wet, to form the shapes here. When dusted, the rolls will have a traditional bakery look; however, dusting is not required to achieve a great taste. Feel free to form the rolls with wet hands for a smoother finish.

Oatmeal Raisin Cookies

This recipe is a classic—in an allergen-free version. While most of the cookies in this book can be found in the next chapter, I have included this recipe here because the techniques used to create these cookies more closely resemble those you use for a batter.

{ MAKES APPROXIMATELY 24 COOKIES }

¾ cup gluten-free flour blend (see tip)

1½ cups gluten-free quick-cooking oats (see tip)

¼ teaspoon salt

1 teaspoon baking powder

½ teaspoon cinnamon

8 tablespoons (1 stick) Earth Balance Natural Shortening, softened

½ cup raw sugar (see tip)

½ cup flaxseed gel (equal to 2 eggs)

2 tablespoons water

¾ cup raisins (see tip)

1. Preheat the oven to 350°F. Line a cookie sheet with parchment paper.
2. Combine the flour, oats, salt, baking powder, and cinnamon in a medium bowl. Set it aside.
3. Cream together the shortening and raw sugar in a large bowl, with a mixer on medium speed for about 5 minutes, until a textured paste forms. Scrape down the sides of the mixing bowl as needed. (See page 106 to learn about creaming.)
4. Add the flaxseed gel and water. Blend with a mixer on medium-low speed, about 1 minute.
5. Gradually add the flour mixture and blend on medium speed, about 2 minutes. The batter will be thick.
6. Stir in the raisins by hand.
7. Use a large spoon and damp hands to form cookies. Place them on the prepared baking sheet, leaving space in between.
8. Bake at 350°F for 12 to 15 minutes, until the tops are lightly browned.

TIPS

* While it's okay to select a gluten-free flour blend that contains xanthan gum, notice that there is no xanthan gum used in this recipe.
* This recipe makes a soft cookie. For a crunchier cookie, substitute gluten-free old-fashioned rolled oats for the quick-cooking oats.
* You may substitute granulated cane sugar for raw sugar (see "Sweetening Options," page 140).
* Try these with dried cranberries instead of raisins, or leave out the fruit entirely for a simple oatmeal cookie.

Poured Pizza Crust

I was inspired to create this pizza crust after attending a gluten-free baking class at the Culinary Institute of America. I had tried packaged gluten-free pizza mixes with allergen-free substitutions, and I wasn't completely happy with any of them. Most of them used yeast and required a rise cycle. They took too long to prepare and were just a little too hard to sink your teeth into.

The pizza crust we made in Chef Coppedge's class also used yeast and still required some rising time, but he did something I had never seen before: He taught us how to form individual pizza slices, using a pastry bag to spread the dough on a baking sheet. What a novel idea! There was no need for a rolling pin and no mess in transferring the crust to the pizza tin.

But I wanted an even simpler pizza crust—one that was shaped like a pizza, didn't require yeast, and had no rising time—so I developed this one. After all, Friday night pizza should be quick and fuss-free!

{ MAKES 1 LARGE PIZZA CRUST, 8 SERVINGS }

1¾ cups gluten-free flour mix

¼ teaspoon xanthan gum (leave out if your flour blend contains xanthan gum)

1 teaspoon salt

1 teaspoon baking soda

4 tablespoons (½ stick) Earth Balance Natural Shortening, melted

1 cup original hemp milk

1 tablespoon rice vinegar

Your choice of toppings (see suggestions)

1. Preheat the oven to 350°F. Coat a pizza tin with olive oil.
2. Combine the flour, xanthan gum (if needed), salt, and baking soda in a medium bowl. Set it aside.
3. Combine the shortening, hemp milk, and vinegar in a large bowl, with a mixer on medium-low speed, for 1 minute.
4. Add the flour mixture to the wet ingredients and blend for 2 to 3 minutes on medium speed.
5. Pour the batter into the pizza tin. Use a spatula (or the back of a soup spoon) to spread the batter evenly to the edges.
6. Bake at 350°F for 15 minutes.
7. Remove the partially baked crust from the oven. Use a spatula to gently flip the crust over so that the browned side is now the top. Add desired toppings.
8. Bake for 12 to 18 minutes more until the toppings are done.

TIPS

＊ Because this is a batter, this recipe works best if you use a pizza tin with a little bit of an edge— ½ inch will do. If you don't have a pizza tin, a large cookie sheet or baking sheet with an edge will work.

＊ While not required, flipping the crust after it is partially baked will allow the crust to bake more evenly and leave it slightly crispy on both sides.

＊ Try making personal pizzas in round cake pans, and let the kids choose their own toppings.

✳ TOPPING SUGGESTIONS:

Keep in mind that it's not a requirement to have cheese on your pizza. Nor is there a requirement to use tomato sauce, or any of the other traditional ingredients. While there are some cheese substitutes available on the market, a pizza with tomato sauce, veggies, and meats can be very satisfying. You can customize toppings to suit your family's particular food restrictions. Here are a few to try:

PEPPERONI: This is the classic pizza, without the cheese. Layer tomato sauce, Italian spices, and pepperoni. If you feel the need for a cheese substitute, add Daiya Mozzarella Style Shreds.

GREEK PIZZA: Layer sliced tomato, spinach, and olives. Drizzle olive oil mixed with basil over the top.

VEGGIE PIZZA: Layer chopped onions, green peppers, red peppers, and mushrooms over a thin layer of tomato sauce. Add a non-dairy cheese option, if desired.

SALAD PIZZA: Prepare your favorite salad and serve it over the pizza crust. For this pizza, don't bake the toppings. Add the toppings after the crust is fully baked.

Making Chocolate Chip Cookies (page 132)

8

No Butter, No Problem:

Perfect Allergen-Free Cookies, Tarts and Pies Every Time

A FRIEND RECENTLY HAD a craving for chocolate chip cookies, but was tired from a long day at work. On her way home she stopped at the grocery store and picked up a roll of Nestlé Toll House cookie dough from the refrigerated section. When she got home, she and her boys sliced them up and popped them into the oven. It doesn't get more convenient than that. We've all been there, taking the shortcut so we can optimize family time. I've done it too—for years the only pie crust I used was the Pillsbury roll-out crust from the refrigerated section—and yes, it was easy and convenient.

When you're eating allergen-free, most prepackaged products are no longer an option, but you may be surprised at how simple it is to prepare your own allergen-free dough and use it later. Baking doesn't have to be time-consuming. I was intimidated by having to create my own crusts, until I understood that all I needed was flour, shortening, and little bit of cold water to create one.

If you mix up big batches of cookie dough, you can refrigerate or freeze what you haven't used. Dough will keep for weeks in the refrigerator and for up to twelve months in the freezer. The next time you need a special treat, you'll be ready to bake just as few or many as you desire, and you'll have them in minutes. If you like pies, mix up batches of pie crust dough and store them in the refrigerator or freezer. This can bring your time in the kitchen down to forty-five minutes or less when you're ready to start baking.

About Gluten–Free Doughs and Crusts

WHEN WORKING WITH batters, you will get the best results when the ingredients are at room temperature. This "neutral" temperature ensures that the ingredients don't react too soon, but are ready to react as soon as they find the oven heat. When working with doughs and crusts, notice that many of the ingredients will be used cold. This is deliberate. The shortening should be cold when you cut it into the flour for a crust, and cold water will keep the crust from sticking to the rolling surface. Many recipes, including the ones I have created for you here, require refrigerating the dough prior to scooping cookies or rolling out a pie crust. Why? Spread is a common problem with doughs and crusts, whether or not they are wheat-free. With non-gluten grains, the problem is exacerbated because you no longer have the gluten to help the baked goods hold their shape. Chilling firms up the fat (the shortening), which keeps cookies from spreading too much, and allows pie crusts to hold their own.

One technique you will use when creating doughs is called cutting (sometimes referred to as rubbing). This is a technique in which first the dry ingredients are blended together, then the fat is "cut" into the flour mixture, and lastly, a small amount of cold liquid is added to help the ingredients stick together. This is similar to the technique used to create the streusel topping for Coffee Cake (page 104), and you'll see it used throughout this chapter. To cut the fat into the flour you can use a pastry cutter, a wide-pronged fork (a pastry fork), or your hands. Yes, hands are fantastic tools for baking.

When preparing doughs, you won't be using an electric mixer. If you blend the ingredients with a mixer you will most likely blend them too well; the fat (the shortening) should remain in small pieces in your dough. During the baking process the shortening will melt, giving the cookie or crust a flaky pastry quality. Likewise, resist the urge to blend too well when rubbing. And because you won't be getting these baked goods into the oven right away after mixing, it's important to ensure that the xanthan gum is very well blended into the flour before adding any wet ingredients.

There's one final point I need to make before you start baking cookies: I have called for Earth Balance Natural Shortening in the recipes in this chapter because it performs better than the rest of the pack.

CRASH COURSE

Earth Balance makes a number of shortenings—this one comes in stick form, in a green and pale yellow box. The ingredients include soybean oil, but no soy protein. If you and your doctor have determined that you must avoid soybean oil, substitute Spectrum Organic All Vegetable Shortening or coconut oil. See page 47 for more on shortening options. Whichever you choose, make sure you choose a shortening (rather than an oil) and use it cold; the keys to success when mixing dough are to keep the shortening cold until you are ready to use it and to cut the shortening into tablespoon-sized pieces before you begin working it into the flour.

cutting shortening into flour

forming dough

forming cookie rolls

Sugar Cookies

Remember those rolls of cookie dough that I mentioned earlier? I'm going to show you how you can create your own refrigerated cookie dough, using allergen-free ingredients. While I can't claim that these are low-calorie or sugar-free (they are sugar cookies after all!), the buckwheat flour does add a bit of protein that the originals are lacking.

I sometimes make these as half-and-half batches—½ sugar cookies, and ½ chocolate chip cookies (see the variation below). In my house, that keeps everyone happy. I dare you to tell me that these aren't among the best cookies you've ever had!

{ MAKES 24 TO 36 COOKIES }

½ cup buckwheat flour

¾ cup gluten-free flour blend

¼ teaspoon xanthan gum (leave out if your flour blend contains xanthan gum)

1½ teaspoons baking powder

½ teaspoon salt

½ cup granulated sugar

8 tablespoons (1 stick) Earth Balance Natural Shortening, cold

2 tablespoons unsweetened applesauce, cold (see tip)

1 tablespoon cold water (as needed)

¼ cup raw sugar (for topping)

1. Combine the flours, xanthan gum (if needed), baking powder, salt, and granulated sugar in a large mixing bowl.
2. Cut the shortening into tablespoon-sized pieces and place them on top of the flour mixture. Use a pastry cutter or pastry fork to cut the shortening into the flour mixture.
3. When the flour and shortening are crumbly, add the applesauce and continue cutting with the pastry cutter.
4. Add up to 1 tablespoon of cold water, ½ tablespoon at a time, as needed. Continue cutting until the dough forms.
5. Roll the dough into a long cylinder, about 1½ inches thick. Wrap it in plastic and refrigerate for at least an hour.
6. When you are ready to make the cookies, preheat the oven to 350°F. Line a cookie sheet with parchment paper.
7. Slice the cookies from the roll, about ¼ inch thick. Place the cookies on the cookie sheet, with space in between.
8. Sprinkle raw sugar on top of the cookies and gently press it into the dough.
9. Bake at 350°F for 12 to 14 minutes, until lightly browned.

(continued)

TIPS

✳ The applesauce provides some texture in these cookies, but isn't required. For a crispier cookie, substitute 2 tablespoons of cold water for the applesauce.

✳ These are easy to make in large batches. Keep the rolls of dough in your refrigerator or freezer (just as you would the kind you buy in the refrigerated section of the grocery store).

✳ Use a very sharp, nonstick knife to slice the cookies. If you don't have a nonstick knife, spray a small amount of cooking oil on your blade to make the job easier.

✳ VARIATION:

CHOCOLATE CHIP COOKIES: Prepare the sugar cookies as described on page 131. Prior to rolling the dough into a cylinder (step 5) add ½ cup of allergen-free chocolate chips. Work the chocolate chips into the dough with your hands, roll, wrap, and refrigerate. Leave off the sugar topping. Enjoy Life Mini Chips work extremely well with this recipe (see page 192 for more options).

Chocolate Chip Cookies and Sugar Cookies

Sugar Cookies, Chocolate Chip Cookies, and Chocolate Chunk Cookies (page 138)

Rolling Out a Crust

A S NOTED EARLIER, when working with dough you want the ingredients, especially the fat, to be cold before mixing the dough. Likewise, once the dough is prepared, you want it to be cold before rolling out a crust. A cold dough will ensure that the shortening doesn't spread too much as you're rolling, and it will keep it from sticking too much to the rolling surface. While it's tempting to skip the step where you refrigerate the dough, I don't recommend it; it's much easier to roll out a crust after the dough has been chilled. If you're working from frozen dough, either let it thaw in the refrigerator overnight, or let it thaw at room temperature for a couple of hours. You may need to rework the dough a bit with your hands if you choose the latter option. Now that your dough is nicely chilled, it's time to get the rolling pin out. Now is also the time to preheat the oven and prepare the pan you'll be using for baking.

There are many ways to roll out a pie crust, and most bakers have their favorite technique. What are common among all of them are a nonstick surface and a good rolling pin. I addressed the rolling pin earlier (see page 74), now let's talk about the rolling surface. If you are lucky enough to have a marble counter or slab, that's a great choice; in addition to being a nice smooth surface, marble remains cool. For the rest of us, a nonstick pastry mat is the next best thing. And some bakers simply use two sheets of wax paper and roll their chilled dough between them; after you've rolled out a crust peel back the top layer of wax paper, flip the crust into the pie plate using the bottom sheet of wax paper, and then peel back the second layer of wax paper. Make sure the diameter of your pie crust is 2 inches wider than your pie plate; you need enough crust for the sides of the plate and to crimp the edges.

You might be surprised that it's actually easier to form a gluten-free pie crust than a wheat crust. Yes, this is one area where working with gluten-free flours is an advantage. If a wheat crust cracks or breaks as you're moving it to the pie plate you have to re-roll it (and then attempt to delicately move it again). Gluten-free crusts are easy to repair. If you make a hole, or the crust tears as you move it, simply use your fingers to stick it back together. Add additional dough and a couple drops of cold water, if you need to.

If you have any dough left over from trimming the edges of your crust, store it in the freezer for future use.

Strawberry Tartlets

In the Hudson Valley where my family lives, we belong to a Community Supported Agriculture program called the Poughkeepsie Farm Project. Every week from late spring through fall I look forward to fresh vegetables. But my favorite part of the weekly trip to the farm is the pick-your-own berries. There is absolutely nothing that can compare to juicy ripe strawberries fresh from the field. When I first joined the CSA and saw how many strawberries we would be taking home every week, I knew I had to develop a recipe that would leverage the sweetness of those strawberries but not overpower them.

This tartlet recipe simplifies the concept of a pie, while giving it a natural, rugged feel. It works well with all varieties of strawberries, taking you through the summer. It can also be made with any other berry, or a combination of berries. Have fun with it!

{ MAKES 4 TARTLETS }

FOR THE TARTLETS:

- 1 cup gluten-free flour blend
- ¼ teaspoon xanthan gum (leave out if your flour blend contains xanthan gum)
- ½ teaspoon salt
- 1 tablespoon granulated sugar
- 4 tablespoons (½ stick) Earth Balance Natural Shortening, cold
- 1 tablespoon apple cider vinegar
- 1 to 3 tablespoons cold water (as needed)

FOR THE STRAWBERRY FILLING:

- 1 cup sliced strawberries (see tip)
- 1½ teaspoons fresh lime juice
- 1½ teaspoons tapioca starch
- 1½ teaspoons granulated sugar
- 2 tablespoons raw sugar (optional)

PREPARE THE TARTLET CRUSTS:

1. Combine the flour, xanthan gum (if needed), salt, and granulated sugar in a large mixing bowl.
2. Cut the shortening into tablespoon-sized pieces and place them on top of the flour mixture. Use a pastry cutter or pastry fork to cut the shortening into the flour mixture.
3. When the flour and shortening are crumbly, add the apple cider vinegar and 1 tablespoon of cold water. Continue cutting the ingredients together.

4. Add up to 2 tablespoons additional water, ½ tablespoon at a time, as needed. Continue cutting until the dough forms.
5. Separate the dough and use your hands to create four equal-sized balls. Flatten the balls. Cover with plastic wrap, and refrigerate for at least an hour.
6. When you are ready to roll out the dough, preheat the oven to 350°F. Spray a cookie sheet with cooking oil.

PREPARE THE FILLING:

7. Coat the strawberries with lime juice.
8. Combine the tapioca starch and the granulated sugar. Mix this together with the strawberries, by hand, and then set it aside.

ROLL OUT THE DOUGH AND FORM THE TARTLETS:

9. Place the dough on a smooth prep surface.
10. Using a rolling pin, gently roll each disk into a thin crust, about 6-7 inches round.
11. Use a spatula to gently lift the crusts and place them on the prepared cookie sheet.
12. Scoop the strawberry mixture into the centers of the crusts. Discard any remaining liquid.

(continued)

13. Form the tartlets with your hands by folding the edges of the crusts over the berry filling, leaving the center open. Repair any broken pieces of crust with your fingers and a dab of water, if needed.

14. If a sugar crust is desired, use your fingers to sprinkle raw sugar over the folded crusts.

15. Bake at 350°F for 20 to 25 minutes, until the crusts are lightly browned and the strawberry filling is bubbling.

TIPS

* Slice the strawberries thinly (about ⅛ inch thick) for best results.
* The dough will work best if it's refrigerated for at least an hour prior to rolling it out. It can be made ahead and stored in the fridge overnight, or even frozen. If you are using frozen dough, thaw it in the refrigerator before using it.

Strawberry Tartlets

Chocolate Chunk Cookies

Cookies are so simple, and yet they can be so decadent. What makes a cookie worthy of the name Chocolate Chunk? That would be the mega chocolate chunks that are used in this recipe. Warm, gooey chocolate surrounded by more chocolate—it doesn't get better than that. This is the treat that I would choose at the coffee shop, if they made it in an allergen-free version.

This recipe uses the same technique as the Sugar Cookies (page 131), and it's just as easy to keep in your refrigerator or freezer. Unless you're baking for a big crowd, separate the dough into two parts, and save half for later. You will need to use two baking sheets (or bake two batches) if you make the full recipe.

{ MAKES 24 TO 36 COOKIES }

½ cup buckwheat flour

¾ cup gluten-free flour blend

¼ teaspoon xanthan gum (leave out if your flour blend contains xanthan gum)

½ cup natural unsweetened cocoa powder

1½ teaspoons baking powder

½ teaspoon salt

½ cup sugar

10 tablespoons (1 stick + 2 tablespoons) Earth Balance Natural Shortening, cold

2 tablespoons unsweetened applesauce, cold

1 teaspoon vanilla extract

1 to 2 tablespoons cold water (as needed)

½ cup allergen-free mega chocolate chunks (see tip)

1. Combine the flours, xanthan gum (if needed), cocoa powder, baking powder, salt, and sugar in a large mixing bowl.
2. Cut the shortening into tablespoon-sized pieces and place them on top of the flour mixture. Use a pastry cutter or pastry fork to cut the shortening into the flour mixture.
3. When the mixture is crumbly, add the applesauce and vanilla. Continue cutting with the pastry cutter.
4. Add up to 2 tablespoons of cold water, ½ tablespoon at a time, as needed. Continue cutting until the dough forms.
5. Add the chocolate chunks and work them into the cookie dough with your hands.
6. Roll the dough into a long cylinder, about 1½ inches thick. Wrap it in plastic and refrigerate for at least an hour.
7. When you are ready to make the cookies, preheat the oven to 350°F. Line a cookie sheet with parchment paper.
8. Slice the cookies from the roll, about ½ inch thick, then slice in half. Smooth the edges and place the cookies on the cookie sheet.
9. Bake at 350°F for 12 to 14 minutes, until the edges are just softened.

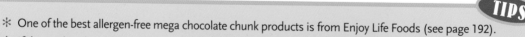

* One of the best allergen-free mega chocolate chunk products is from Enjoy Life Foods (see page 192).
* If the cookie slices fall apart as you are cutting, simply stick them back together again with your hands.
* These cookies get better the longer the dough sits in the refrigerator. I strongly recommend always having a roll of cookie dough (or two) ready to go.

Chocolate Chunk Cookies

Sweetening Options

SUGAR IS SUGAR, right? To a point, that is correct. The crystal form of sugar that we use in baking is almost always sucrose, and usually comes from the sugar cane plant. Chemically, sucrose is a disaccharide (a combination of two sugars), consisting of the monosaccharides (simple sugars) glucose and fructose.

Is sugar bad for you? Keep in mind that sugar is nearly pure carbs and does contribute greatly to the calorie content of your baked goods. One teaspoon of granulated cane sugar is 15 calories. That doesn't sound so bad, but consider that 1 cup of sugar is 770 calories. Yikes! Those calories can sure add up. In many of our recipes we will use ½ cup (sometimes more) of sugar; if that sugar is distributed across eight muffins, about 48 calories per muffin will be from the sugar alone. I'm not suggesting that you forgo the sugar in your baked goods. After all, most of us expect our cookies to be sweet. But, whether it's granulated sugar, confectioners' sugar, brown sugar, or other forms of sugar, you want to make the most of the sugar you do use.

Sugars are also the same in terms of how they behave when heated. When crystal sugar is heated, it liquefies. This is a key concept to understand as you think about the balance of liquids to solids in your recipes. If you reduce the amount of sugar in a recipe, you will be better off adding a little more liquid rather than adding more dry ingredients. Conversely, if you add more sugar, you may need to reduce the liquid in your recipe. Even though you will usually add the sugar to the dry ingredients, except when you are creaming (see page 106), you should think of sugar as a liquid when you think about proportions.

Now that I've let you in on that secret, you can start to imagine how your choice of a sweetener—crystal sugar or an alternative (e.g., honey, pure maple syrup, or agave nectar) can affect your recipes. Any of these work quite well (and can be easily substituted) with simple batters. Thick batters, doughs, and pie crusts will generally be easier to work with and produce a better end result if you choose sugar in crystal form. That's not to say you can't use agave nectar in your scones, but you may need to use a scone pan if you do.

Within the crystal sugar world, there are many options to choose from, and some have specific uses:

✳ **GRANULATED CANE SUGAR:** This is what most of us think of when we think about sugar. It's the sugar you put in your cof-

turbinado/raw sugar

granulated sugar

Sucanat

extra-fine sugar

light brown sugar

confectioners' sugar

fee, and the one you will reach for most often when baking. If you were to pick just one sugar to keep in your pantry, this should be it. Cane sugar plants are actually a form of grass, and all of the crystal sugars discussed here come from these tall fibrous stalks. What differs between the various forms of cane sugar is the level of refinement and processing. The refining process for granulated cane sugar removes nearly all of the molasses, leaving a fine white product. It is virtually tasteless—sweet without flavor. We will discuss working with yeast in detail later

CRASH COURSE

(see page 153), but keep in mind that, while technically any sugar can react with yeast, you will achieve the fastest and most consistent results when using granulated sugar to activate yeast. There are also granulated sugars derived from the beet plant. While it's okay to substitute these, I find that I get the best results with cane sugar.

✳ **EXTRA-FINE CANE SUGAR:** Sometimes referred to as "superfine," "baker's," or "baker's special" sugar, this is finely milled cane sugar. Many bakers prefer this lighter sugar because it can be thoroughly blended with dry ingredients, it absorbs liquid more quickly, and it creates a very smooth texture. It's also more expensive that your typical cane sugar, and harder to find. You can easily substitute baker's sugar for granulated cane sugar, 1 to 1, in your recipes (unless you are creaming). For your everyday baking, granulated cane sugar will do just fine. Unless you own your own bakery or catering business, save the baker's sugar for your grandmother's eightieth birthday cake, or your silver wedding anniversary. It's called special for a reason. If you want to try it and can't find a local source, don't fret—grind your own from granulated cane sugar in a food processor or high-speed blender.

✳ **CONFECTIONERS' SUGAR:** Also referred to as powdered sugar, it is super-finely milled cane sugar—milled down to a powder, hence its name. Confectioners' sugar looks like a very fine snow. This sugar is whiter and lighter than granulated sugar. One cup of granulated sugar weighs approximately 200 grams, whereas one cup of confectioners' sugar weighs 120 grams. You will typically be using large amounts of confectioner's sugar for a frosting recipe (3 cups is common to make enough frosting to cover one cake), but it will absorb moisture very quickly as you add shortening and liquids. I do not recommend substituting cane sugar for confectioners' sugar or vice versa, as your measurements will be way off. In addition to being used for frostings, confectioners' sugar is great for decorating cakes, doughnuts, and other pastries. Those with corn allergies should note that this sugar is often mixed with a small amount of starch (usually corn starch) to prevent clumping. One company that makes a corn-free confectioners' sugar is Miss Roben's.

✳ **BROWN SUGAR:** Whereas white sugars are made by extracting the molasses from the sugar, brown sugars are made by adding

molasses back into the sugar. Light brown sugar usually contains about 3.5 percent molasses, and dark brown sugar has about 6.5 percent. Adding the molasses back changes both the taste and the texture of the sugar. Molasses is thick and syrupy; when added back into cane sugar the result is a wetter (but not liquid) sugar that is just a bit lighter than white sugar, weighing approximately 192 grams per cup. Although most white sugars are consistently tasteless, brown sugars vary quite a bit, with some having a bitter taste. I rarely use dark brown sugar while baking, but light brown sugar is a staple in my pantry and my recipes. For a crumb cake topping or chocolate chip cookies, light brown sugar is the way to go. Store it in an airtight container, as it performs best when soft. When it hardens it will be much more difficult to use. I have seen recommendations to add water to soften brown sugar, but I prefer using a fresh batch. If you need to substitute for brown sugar your best bet is raw sugar.

✳ RAW SUGAR: Also called turbinado sugar and marketed as Sugar in the Raw, this is coarsely grained sugar. It's not really raw—there is processing involved—but it's less processed than all other crystal sugars except Sucanat. As I described brown sugar, you may have been wondering why they bother taking the molasses out of the sugar just to add it back in. That's where raw sugar comes in—it's the form of sugar produced from the first crystallization of the sugar cane. Despite the fact that it's much coarser than white sugar, raw sugar does substitute well for granulated in recipes, but do so sparingly as it's more expensive. Raw sugar's true advantage comes in when you are making a pastry with a sugared topping (e.g., Blueberry Muffins, page 93). When sprinkled on top of pastry, it will hold its form through the baking process, leaving you with a crunchy topping like the kind you would get on many bakery muffins. Yum!

✳ SUCANAT: Sucanat is as natural as crystal sugar gets. It is virtually unprocessed, formed as a result of water evaporating from the sugar cane after it's extracted from the plants. It is coarse, but harder than raw sugar. Sucanat is grainy, and not translucent like raw sugar. It works well as a replacement for granulated sugar, but is best as a replacement for brown sugar in crusts and cookie doughs. It does not work well as a replacement for brown sugar in crumble toppings, or as a substitute for raw sugar when you want a crunchy sugared topping.

CRASH COURSE

Crystal sugars are not the only option for sweetening baked goods. More bakers are turning to other natural sweetening options as they look to reduce the amount of sugar in their diets, or to opt for sweeteners with a lower glycemic index. While it is extensively debated whether these are healthier for you, and there are arguments on all sides, I will simply say that they can be used very effectively when baking. These include:

❋ HONEY: Just like sugar, not all honeys are the same. Honey takes on a very distinctive taste, depending on where the honey is from and what flowers are located near the hive. For example, the cranberry honey I like to use in Cranberry Bread (page 98) comes from Cape Cod, where the honey bees have access to local cranberry bogs. When you find a honey you like, make a note of the brand and type so you can re-create your favorite baked goods. I love to look for local honey sources when I travel. Honey has the same relative sweetness as sugar, and can generally be substituted 1 to 1 for cane sugar. Due to its sticky liquid consistency, I don't recommend using it in crusts, doughs, or yeast breads.

❋ MAPLE SYRUP: Made from the sap of maple trees, pure maple syrup is another natural form of sucrose that can be found locally in many areas. Here in the Northeast, maple syrup is sold by the gallon at roadside farm stands throughout the fall. Both honey and maple syrup remain shelf stable forever—they don't have expiration dates, and they don't go bad. Maple syrup has a strong taste, so choose where you use it. It will change the flavor of your baked goods. For example, if you substitute maple sugar for granulated sugar in Vanilla Pound Cake (page 108), you will have Maple Pound Cake (and feel free to try it!). Like honey, maple syrup works best with simple batters. (Do not substitute pancake syrups; use only 100% pure maple syrup.)

❋ AGAVE NECTAR: Some bakers are turning to agave nectar as a substitute for sugar, honey, or maple syrup, but this sweetener stirs up its own intense debate. Many believe it to be more natural and healthier than crystal forms of sugar. Some even call it a raw food. Still others believe that agave nectar may not be a healthy alternative. So what is agave nectar, exactly? The nectar comes from the cactus-like agave plant that thrives in warm, dry climates. It's a highly processed sweetener—up to 70 percent

fructose. On the flip side, agave nectar is said to have a much lower glycemic index than sugar, and it's very sweet so you can use less of it. I'll leave it to you to decide whether agave nectar is a product you want to use in your baking. It does perform well, especially as a replacement for honey.

✳ **STEVIA:** Stevia is the only sweetener discussed here that is not a sugar; it's an herb. For those who need to eliminate sugar completely from their diet, or for the occasion when your diabetic grandfather is coming for dinner, this is an option worth exploring. The sweetener is extracted from the leaves of the stevia plant (similar to how vanilla or other extracts are made). Stevia is virtually calorie-free. If you choose to use stevia, keep in mind that it is very sweet—just 1 teaspoon of stevia is needed to achieve the same sweetness as 1 cup of sugar. Because stevia is not a sugar, it won't provide the same texture in your baked goods; you will need to add additional liquids or fruit purees if you replace sugar with stevia in your recipes. Please note that allergies to stevia have been reported.

Which sweetener should you use? I am a big fan of the crystal forms of sugar. After years of experimenting with these and the alternatives, my personal preference is cane sugar. Between granulated cane, confectioners', brown, and raw sugar, I can create all of the textures and tastes that I am striving for, from a smooth creamy white frosting to a crunchy sugared crust. While there may be other health reasons to avoid sugar, food allergies are not usually one of them. With the exception of corn starch in some confectioners' sugars, crystal forms of sugar are considered allergen-free. This is one traditional baking product that most of us do not have to substitute for when baking.

While I do offer recipes with all of these choices, feel free to substitute based on your own preference and dietary needs. In the next recipe I have chosen to use Sucanat to give this crust some texture.

Lemon Tart

If he had his druthers, my oldest (non–food-allergic) son would choose cheesecake or lemon meringue pie for dessert. Of course, cheesecake is one of those foods that just wouldn't be the same when made without milk and eggs, and I'm not happy with the options to make meringue without eggs. Sometimes the end result is better if, instead of trying to substitute, you just do without. That's the approach I took with this lemon tart recipe, which comes as close to a lemon meringue pie (without the meringue) as you can get.

{ MAKES ONE 9-INCH TART, 8 TO 12 SERVINGS }

FOR THE TART:

1¼ cups gluten-free flour blend

½ teaspoon xanthan gum (leave out if your flour blend contains xanthan gum)

½ teaspoon salt

¼ cup sugar

8 tablespoons (1 stick) Earth Balance Natural Shortening, cold

2 tablespoons cold water

FOR THE LEMON FILLING:

2 tablespoons corn starch mixed with ¼ cup warm water (see tip)

4½ teaspoons Ener-G Egg Replacer mixed with 6 tablespoons warm water (equal to 3 eggs)

⅔ cup fresh lemon juice

¼ cup original hemp milk

¾ cup sugar

1 teaspoon lemon zest

PREPARE THE TART CRUST:

1. Combine the flour, xanthan gum (if needed), salt, and sugar in a large mixing bowl.

2. Cut the shortening into tablespoon-sized pieces and place them on top of the flour mixture. Use a pastry cutter or pastry fork to cut the shortening into the flour mixture.

3. When the flour and shortening are crumbly, add the cold water. Continue cutting the ingredients together.

4. Use your hands to form the dough into a disk and flatten, keeping the sides rounded. Wrap the dough in plastic and refrigerate for at least an hour.

WHILE THE DOUGH IS CHILLING, PREPARE THE LEMON FILLING:

5. Prepare the corn starch mixture and the egg replacer mixture, and set them aside.

6. In a medium saucepan, whisk together the lemon juice, hemp milk, sugar, and lemon zest. Bring this mixture to a boil over medium-high heat, whisking intermittently.

7. When the mixture reaches a rolling boil, remove the saucepan from the heat. Add the egg replacer mixture and whisk constantly (over no heat) for 1 minute. You will immediately see the liquid rise and start to thicken.

8. Whisk in the corn starch mixture. Return the saucepan to medium-low heat and bring the mixture to a low boil. Whisk frequently for another 5 minutes, until the sauce thickens.

9. Remove the saucepan from the heat, and

allow it to cool. The sauce will thicken further as it cools.

PREPARE THE TART:

10. Preheat the oven to 350°F. Spray a pie plate with cooking oil.
11. Place the dough on a nonstick rolling surface.
12. Use a rolling pin to gently roll the dough into a crust about 10 inches in diameter.
13. Transfer the crust to the pie plate. Use a knife to cut away any loose edges of dough, and repair any broken patches.
14. Bake the unfilled crust at 350°F for 20 minutes.
15. When both the crust and the filling have cooled, spoon the filling into the crust. Refrigerate for at least 4 hours before serving.

TIPS

* If you need to avoid corn, any other starch can be substituted.
* During the first boil, the liquid will be clear. The second boil is reminiscent of a lava lamp, with both large and small bubbles bursting as the mixture boils.
* A quiche dish works extremely well for this tart, giving the edges a true tart effect.
* For a crust-free version, prepare the filling and serve it as lemon mousse. Transfer the mousse to serving dishes before refrigerating.
* Garnish with fresh berries, if desired.

* VARIATION:

KEY LIME TART: Substitute fresh Key lime juice for the lemon juice, and coconut milk beverage for the hemp milk, in equal amounts.

What Is Zest?

EVERY NOW AND then you will come across a recipe, such as the Lemon Tart (page 148), that asks for an ingredient called lemon zest. While it sounds fancy, and you might be wondering what the heck it is, it's actually very straightforward. Lemon zest is the outer layer of lemon skin that has been grated (or super-finely chopped). As the word *zest* implies, it provides an extra pop of citrus flavor, due to the strong aromatic oils in the rind.

The easiest way to make your own lemon zest is using a very fine grater (e.g., a Microplane). Zest should be made from just the outer yellow layer of the lemon only; the white inner layer can be very bitter. One large lemon will yield about 2 teaspoons of lemon zest. If you are buying lemons to make lemon juice, zest the skins before peeling the lemons. Make sure you wash the lemons before zesting. The same process can be used for zesting limes and oranges. If you use the same grater to make zest as you do to grate dairy cheese, be careful to avoid cross-contamination by thoroughly washing the grater prior to using it (see page 68 for more on contamination issues).

Lemon zest can also be purchased off the shelf; note that these packaged products often contain sugar and preservatives.

9

Rise to the Occasion:

Breads, Rolls and Pastries Made with Yeast

YEAST BREADS (WHICH INCLUDE sandwich breads, rolls, and baguettes) made without wheat, milk, soy, and eggs, are among the most difficult foods to find off the shelf. Some of the most highly regarded gluten-free bread manufacturers make breads that are also dairy-free but still contain eggs. In my search for off-the-shelf sandwich bread, the best I have found made without the top eight allergens (including eggs) is from Food for Life; they offer both millet bread and rice bread, available in the frozen foods section. I always keep one of these in my freezer, in case I don't have time to make my own.

CRASH COURSE

vated before you use it. Once activated, it should be added to the bread quickly, to get the best rise. A typical gluten-free recipe that uses active dry yeast will take at least an hour to rise.

Quick-rising yeast also has a few commonly used names. It is sometimes referred to as instant, rapid-rise, or fast-rising yeast. Fleischmann's calls its version RapidRise yeast; another popular brand, Lesaffre Yeast Corporation, simply calls its product Saf-Instant Yeast. If it has the words *fast acting* on the label, you know you've found the right product. Quick-rising yeast is very similar to active dry yeast, but is smaller grained, doesn't need to be activated, and requires less time to rise.

While we won't be using it here, another common yeast I should mention is fresh yeast. It's also known as cake yeast, but has nothing to do with the cakes you bake; it's simply sold in a "cake" of yeast (like a cake of butter). This is live yeast, not dried, and I don't recommend substituting it for active dry or quick-rising yeast.

I use quick-rising yeast in all of the yeast recipes in this book for two reasons: Learning to work with one type of yeast is easier than learning to use multiple types, and quick-rising yeast provides consistent results with the shortest amount of prep time. (See "Using Active Dry Yeast," page 186, to learn how to convert recipes to use active dry instead of quick-rising yeast.) In addition to being able to make bread faster, when you use quick-rising yeast, you can follow the same processes for mixing ingredients that you learned when working with batters (see page 91). Quick-rising yeast needs liquid and sugar to do its job, but that will happen during the mixing process. First, you should mix the dry ingredients (including the yeast) and set them aside. You will then mix the wet ingredients, and add the dry to the wet. In most cases you will then beat the dough for 5 minutes or more. This allows the ingredients to become extremely well blended and pliable. Properly mixed yeast dough will be able to be lifted from the bowl (although it will stick a bit); while I'm not advocating throwing balls in the house, if you were to pat down the dough and throw it across the room like a softball, it would hold together. The exception to this is yeast dough intended to be made in a sided pan, such as Basic Sandwich Bread (see page 161).

The best gluten-free, home-baked yeast breads are ones made with starchy flours—this means you should choose one of the "white" flours I described in chapter 2 (see page 28). If you prefer to use only multigrain flours, reduce the beating time with the stand mixer from the usual 5 minutes to no more than 2 minutes; multigrain flours tend to break down more quickly than starchy flours do.

While ingredients should be at room temperature for mixing batters, and cold for forming doughs, the liquid ingredients for yeast breads should be warm. The optimal temperature for the water or the non-dairy milk you add is 100°F. This will help the yeast do its job. Water and milk can be warmed using the microwave (for about 20 seconds if it's at room temperature before warming, or 45 seconds if cold), or in a small saucepan over low heat. Use your probe thermometer to check. If you overshoot, wait until the temperature drops before adding the non-dairy milk to your mixing bowl.

After mixing the ingredients for yeast breads, and forming them into shape for the recipe you are creating, you will need to let them rise. When using quick-rising yeast, the dough should rise for at least 35 minutes. As a general rule of thumb, the smaller the pastry, the less time needed for rise; a dinner roll may require 35 minutes, while bread may require 45 minutes.

Now, are you ready for a big secret? Gluten-free yeast breads are actually simpler and quicker to make than are yeast breads made with wheat. That's right. I know I told you that making yeast breads without eggs was difficult, and that's still true. But because we're working with gluten-free grains, there is no kneading—none of that pounding or beating the dough to break down the gluten. There's also no need for two rise cycles. Whereas wheat bread may take you upwards of two hours to prepare (and that's before you even put it in the oven), our gluten-free and allergen-free yeast breads (using quick-rising yeast) require only 35 to 45 minutes of rise time. See "Proofing Methods" (page 158) to learn more about the best ways to help your bread rise.

When preparing gluten-free bread, you will still be using the paddle attachment on your mixer, rather than the dough hook. Dough hooks were designed to simulate the hand kneading process. Since there is no gluten to break down in the flour, you can go ahead and put that dough hook away. In fact, when working with yeast doughs, you will want to use a light touch. For example, when preparing Basic Dinner Rolls (page 157) you will need to roll them in your hands; as you do this, you don't want to flatten or compact them. Instead, roll gently to keep them light and fluffy. Even when using a rolling pin (as with the Multipurpose Flatbread, page 167), you are rolling to spread, not flatten; rolling with gentle pressure works best.

How much yeast should you use? A gluten-free bread recipe with 1 ½ to 2 cups of flour will typically require 2¼ teaspoons of yeast. This is precisely how much yeast is contained in the single serving packets, making measuring easy. If you're working with yeast from a jar, you'll need to measure using two scoops with your standard teaspoon and

CRASH COURSE

one scoop with your ¼ teaspoon. Alternatively, if you plan to be working with yeast a lot, a handy tool to have is a yeast measuring spoon, which measures the full 2¼ teaspoons in one scoop.

Now it's time for another science lesson: Sugar and water help yeast to grow; salt inhibits yeast growth. Using too much salt in your bread batter will cause your bread to rise very slowly, and may even cause it not to rise at all. So go easy on the salt. Most of my yeast recipes use just a small amount of salt for flavor. A good rule of thumb is to use no more than ¼ teaspoon of salt per cup of flour. On the other hand, sugar is yeast's best friend. I prefer to use granulated sugar, rather than honey, agave nectar, or other sweeteners, in yeast bread recipes because it performs extremely well. As long as you choose a real sugar (that would be fructose and/or glucose), the yeast will react, but it reacts most quickly with crystal sugar. Stevia will not activate yeast. If you prefer a non-sugar sweetener, you will still need to use at least a teaspoon of sugar to activate the yeast. (See page 140 for a discussion of sweetening options.)

Another element of baking that we must discuss when talking about yeast is temperature. Yeast needs a nice warm climate to grow; bread will rise best in a humid spot that is between 95° and 100°F (see "Proofing Methods," page 158). Likewise, temperature is how you will determine when the bread is done. The toothpick test simply doesn't give you an accurate reading. While the look of baked bread—a nicely browned crust—can sometimes be helpful in determining when it's time to take your bread out of the oven, keep in mind that browning will occur differently, depending on the flour blend you choose. The internal temperature of the bread is the only accurate way to determine whether gluten-free yeast bread is done. This is where the probe thermometer comes in. Your bread is done when the thermometer registers between 200° and 205°F. This is no more complex than measuring the temperature of your turkey or pot roast—just stick the thermometer into the thickest part of the bread, and take a reading. The temperature will go up quickly once the bread reaches 180°F, so watch carefully at that point.

You will also notice that most yeast recipes use a baking temperature that is higher than the usual 350°F for batters and doughs. Most recipes in this chapter use an oven temperature of 375°F for baking.

If you must avoid yeast, due to an illness or dietary restriction, I don't recommend trying to adapt yeast recipes to be yeast-free; they have been specifically designed to take advantage of the fermentation process described here, and sometimes yeast is the only leavening agent in bread recipes. Your best bet in this case would be to focus on quick breads and other yeast-free baked goods.

Basic Dinner Rolls

When eating out allergen-free and gluten-free, the first thing many of us miss is the roll. I am always delighted when I find new options for dining out that cater to food allergies, and more and more restaurants are offering gluten-free bread. It's common enough that I am now on a quest to find the restaurant with the best gluten-free dinner roll.

This recipe is inspired by the rolls made by the Soul Dog Bakery and served at the Artist's Palate restaurant in my hometown of Poughkeepsie, NY. Their version of this roll is gluten-free and dairy-free, but contains eggs. My version is similar to theirs, but of course, also egg-free. Garbanzo bean flour gives this roll a unique flavor.

On the cover of this book, you can see what these rolls look like as they are being made.

{ MAKES 8 ROLLS }

½ cup garbanzo bean flour

1½ cups gluten-free flour blend

½ teaspoon xanthan gum (leave out if your flour blend contains xanthan gum)

2¼ teaspoons quick-rising yeast

¼ teaspoon salt

3 teaspoons baking powder

¼ cup sugar

¼ cup sunflower oil

½ cup warm water

3 teaspoons Ener-G Egg Replacer mixed with 4 tablespoons warm water (equal to 2 eggs)

Up to ¼ cup additional flour for dusting

1. Line a baking sheet with parchment paper.
2. Combine the flours, xanthan gum (if needed), yeast, salt, baking powder, and sugar in a medium bowl. Set it aside.
3. Blend the oil, water, and egg replacer mixture together in a large bowl, using a mixer on medium speed, about 1 minute.
4. Slowly add the dry ingredients to the wet mixture, mixing on medium-low speed, until combined.
5. Beat for 5 minutes on medium-high speed until the dough is pulling away from the sides of the bowl.
6. Spread the dusting flour on a smooth prep surface. Scoop the dough on top of the flour.
7. Use a bench knife or sharp-edged knife to divide the dough into eight equal-sized portions.
8. Roll each portion in the flour to lightly coat. Use your hands to gently roll them into balls (see tip).
9. Arrange the rolls on the lined baking sheet.
10. Proof for 35 to 45 minutes (see "Proofing Methods," page 158).
11. With 5 minutes left to rise, preheat the oven to 375°F.
12. Bake at 375°F for 13 to 16 minutes, until the internal temperature is 200° to 205°F.

TIPS

✳ When rolling the dough in your hands, be careful not to flatten too much; make believe you are rolling an egg in your palms.

Proofing Methods

IN MATHEMATICS, A proof is a convincing demonstration that a particular statement is true. Likewise, in baking, the term *proof* is used to describe the steps taken to demonstrate that the yeast is effective. Proofing the yeast to activate it shows us that the yeast is alive, and proofing the dough is the demonstration that the bread will rise. While the term is used for both steps, it's important not to confuse the two. In the recipes in this book, because quick-rising yeast is used, you won't see steps to activate the yeast; it's not required. What you will see in each recipe in this chapter is a step to proof the work-in-progress baked goods—usually for 35 to 45 minutes. The nice thing about proofing is, once you set it up, you don't need to do much. This is a good time to start the rest of dinner, set the table, or help the kids with their homework.

But first, you do need to make sure your rolls rise, so let's talk about proofing the dough. The key elements of proofing baked goods are temperature and moisture. The yeast that's been added to your bread or rolls is interacting with the sugar and water to multiply. Yeast multiplies best between 100° and 115°F, but the optimal temperature for leavening purposes is between 95° and 100°F; growing too fast will cause cracks and splits in the bread. At temperatures over 120°F the yeast will die, and the bread will flop. The first trick to proofing is to find a place that is warm enough, but not too warm for the bread to rise. The second trick to proofing is moisture. You will get the best results if the spot where you proof the bread is humid. It sounds complicated, but once you find a technique that works for you, you will be able to replicate it for great results, and you'll be able to say, "I made it myself."

When I've taken baking classes, the kitchen always has a proof box—a large sealed refrigerator-sized box with racks to hold baked goods—where the temperature can be set to precisely 98°F. But I don't have one of these at home, and I'm betting you don't either, so let's explore methods that home bakers use:

⁕ A WARMED OVEN: Many recipe developers will write this technique right into their recipes, as it's one of the most commonly used methods. With this technique you will preheat your oven to its lowest temperature (most likely between 170° and

200°F). As soon as the oven reaches this temperature, turn it off and wait. The downside to this technique is that it requires waiting for the oven to heat and cool before you can proof. You need to make sure the temperature drops before you proof, or all of your hard work preparing the dough will be for naught. The trick is to catch it when the oven reaches about 115°F (keeping in mind that it will cool even further). If your probe thermometer is able to stay in the oven, you can use it to watch the temperature of your oven fall. When you reach a low enough temperature, place your dough in the middle of the oven. Place a small bowl with water on a lower rack; the water will keep the dough from drying out. Don't forget to remove the water and dough from the oven before you preheat the oven for baking.

✳ A WARM, HUMID SPOT: This method tends to work best in warmer climates, but could be effective anywhere. Places to explore include the top of a clothes dryer that's just been used, a bathroom where a hot shower has just been taken, or near a warm humidifier (but not right in the spray). It can even be a spot where the sun, or a hot light, warms the counter. This method usually doesn't result in as high a temperature as some of the other methods do, and it may take a little bit longer for your bread to rise.

✳ THE WARMING ZONE ON THE STOVETOP: Many modern stoves with glass tops have a space called the warming zone, intended for keeping a dish warm prior to serving. I have found that this is the perfect spot in my home for proofing, and it is my preferred method. Temperatures may vary on your stove, but if I set my warming zone on low in the summer, or medium-low in the winter, I can keep it between 95° and 100°F. If you choose this method, place your probe thermometer right on the burner. When the temperature is right, place your baking sheet right on top of the burner, and rotate it every five to ten minutes to ensure an even rise. Keep the thermometer on the burner to monitor the temperature. To make sure your baked goods stay moist, spray a sheet of plastic wrap with a few drops of water and place it over your baking project (making sure that the plastic wrap does not touch the burner). A similar technique, for those of you without a warming zone but with a glass-top stove, is to preheat the oven early and then use the entire stovetop as your warming zone.

* A COOLING RACK OVER A BURNER ON LOW: This method is similar to the warming zone method, but is a bit harder to monitor. Here, you will turn a burner on low and place a cooling rack over the burner so you have a raised shelf for your warming zone. If you use this method, make sure you have a cooling rack that can withstand direct heat. As with the warming zone method, you should spray a piece of plastic wrap with a few drops of water and cover your bread (and make sure the plastic wrap doesn't come into contact with the heat). Another way to keep things moist is to turn on the teakettle, on an adjacent burner.

Whichever method you choose, you will need to preheat the oven (usually to 375°F) prior to baking. If you used the oven as your proofing zone, be sure to take your baking project out of the oven before you preheat.

Gluten-free yeast breads and baked goods should expand to about 1.75 times their size during proofing. If your bread hasn't risen adequately after 35 minutes of proofing, proof it for 10 minutes longer. Once you bake a few yeast breads you will notice that there is a sweet spot for the bread's rise; at about 20 minutes it may have risen only slightly and between 30 and 35 minutes you will notice faster rising action. Try to be aware of when your bread has fully risen—that's when it should go into the oven. If you see the dough start to crack or develop tiny holes, you've passed the sweet spot (and want to get it into the oven quickly). Many things can affect how quickly bread rises, including the temperature, humidity, altitude, and even the barometric pressure. Try a few yeast projects and adjust the time needed to proof, based on your conditions. Once your dough has risen and you pop it into the oven, that's about as big as it will get. Although you will still get a small reaction from baking powder and other leavening agents while your bread is in the oven, it's primarily the yeast that you are relying on to expand the bread.

Basic Sandwich Bread

Whereas most yeast breads have a great deal of structure, this bread dough resembles a batter and must be made in a pan. Most of the moisture will evaporate during baking, leaving you with fluffy bread that is perfect for slicing. This is as simple and goof-proof as it gets when making gluten-free yeast bread. This loaf makes a fantastic sliced bread for sunflower butter and jam sandwiches. It's a basic that you'll want to make over and over again.

{ MAKES 1 LOAF, 10 SERVINGS (2 SLICES PER SERVING), OR 12 DINNER MUFFINS }

1½ cups white gluten-free flour blend (see tip)

1 cup multigrain gluten-free flour blend

½ teaspoon xanthan gum (leave out if your flour blends contain xanthan gum, or reduce to ¼ teaspoon if one of the two flour blends contains xanthan gum)

4 teaspoons quick-rising yeast (see tip)

½ teaspoon salt

4 teaspoons baking powder

⅓ cup sugar

⅓ cup grapeseed oil

1 cup warm water

6 teaspoons Ener-G Egg Replacer mixed with 8 tablespoons warm water (equal to 4 eggs)

1. Spray a loaf pan (preferably a 9 by 4-inch gluten-free loaf pan) with cooking oil.

2. Combine the flours, xanthan gum (if needed), yeast, salt, baking powder, and sugar in a medium bowl. Set it aside.

3. Blend the oil, water, and egg replacer mixture together in a large bowl, using a mixer on medium speed, about 1 minute.

4. Slowly add the dry ingredients to the wet mixture, mixing on medium-low speed, until combined.

5. Beat for 2 minutes on medium-high speed until the dough is smooth.

6. Pour the batter into the loaf pan. Do not fill more than half full.

7. Proof for 35 to 45 minutes (see "Proofing Methods," page 158).

8. With 5 minutes left to rise, preheat the oven to 375°F.

9. Bake at 375°F for 40 to 45 minutes, until the internal temperature is 200° to 205°F.

(continued)

TIPS

❊ I like the mix of white and multigrain flour blends in this bread, but a single gluten-free flour blend can be used.

❊ Notice that more yeast is used in this recipe than the standard 2¼ teaspoons. If you are using yeast in a packet, be sure to adjust.

❊ This bread will rise best when a gluten-free loaf pan is used (see page 75). Alternatively, a 9 by 5-inch loaf pan may be used.

❊ This bread is great when spiced up with herbs, seeds, or even dried tomatoes. Have fun experimenting with variations.

❊ Slice the bread before freezing so you can easily remove slices as you need them.

Basic Sandwich Bread

✳ VARIATION:

DINNER MUFFINS: Spray a muffin tin with cooking oil. Follow steps 2 through 5 on page 161. Divide the batter evenly among the muffin cups. They will be about half full. Follow steps 7 and 8. Bake at 375°F for 13 to 16 minutes, until the internal temperature is 200 to 205°F.

Basic Sandwich Bread with sunflower butter and Strawberry Jam (page 219)

Basic Bagels

Eastern European Jews brought bagels to the United States—specifically New York—in the 1880s. My bagels are much simpler to make than the bagels that are proofed for twelve hours and then boiled before baking, as the New Yorkers make them. But these do the trick and pass the test even for true bagel lovers like my husband. While you won't be eating them with lox and cream cheese, they pair perfectly with jam (see page 219), taste great plain, and can even be used for sandwiches.

{ MAKES 10 BAGELS }

2½ cups white gluten-free flour blend

½ teaspoon xanthan gum (leave out if your flour blend contains xanthan gum)

2¼ teaspoons quick-rising yeast

1 tablespoon sugar

3 teaspoons baking powder

½ teaspoon salt

¾ cup warm water

½ cup flaxseed gel (equal to 2 eggs) (see tip)

2 tablespoons grapeseed oil

1 tablespoon light olive oil, optional, for brushing tops

1. Spray a doughnut pan with cooking oil, or line a baking sheet with parchment paper.
2. Combine the flour, xanthan gum (if needed), yeast, sugar, baking powder, and salt in a medium bowl. Set it aside.
3. Blend the water, flaxseed gel, and oil together in a large bowl, using a mixer on medium speed, about 1 minute.
4. Slowly add the dry ingredients to the wet mixture, mixing on medium-low speed, until combined.
5. Beat for 5 minutes on medium-high speed until the dough is pulling away from the sides of the bowl.
6. Scoop the dough onto a smooth prep surface.
7. Use a bench knife or sharp-edged knife to divide the dough into ten equal-sized portions.
8. Use wet hands to gently roll each portion into a long tube with tapered ends.
9. Place the bagels into the prepared doughnut pan or onto the lined baking sheet, laying one tapered end over the other. Use your fingers and a drop of water to glue the ends together.
10. Proof for 35 to 45 minutes (see "Proofing Methods," page 158).
11. With 5 minutes left to rise, preheat the oven to 375°F.
12. Brush the tops with a thin coating of olive oil, if desired. If you are using toppings, the coating is recommended.
13. Bake at 375°F for 12 to 14 minutes, until the internal temperature is 200° to 205°F.

TIPS

✳ The flaxseed gel gives this dough a thicker texture. If you prefer lighter bagels, substitute Ener-G Egg Replacer (see page 62).

✳ VARIATIONS:

MULTIGRAIN BAGELS: Instead of a white flour, use a multigrain flour blend such as King Arthur Flour Gluten Free Whole Grain Flour Blend or Bob's Red Mill Gluten Free All Purpose Baking Flour. Reduce the beating time (step 5) to 2 minutes.

SALTED BAGELS: Top with coarsely ground salt prior to baking.

ONION BAGELS: Top with finely chopped onions prior to baking.

Quick Fixes for Dough

NO MATTER HOW hard you try and how well you follow the instructions, it's bound to happen sometimes—after mixing, your dough just doesn't seem quite right. There's a fine line between dough that is too wet, dough that is too dry, and dough that is just right. If you catch the problem during preparation, it's possible to correct the problem.

Dough that is too dry either will remain crumbly as you mix it, or the ball in the mixing bowl will be too stiff. If no dough at all is sticking to the sides of the mixing bowl after blending, that's a sure-fire sign that your dough needs more moisture. If this is the case, the dough won't rise properly. This is definitely a problem you should fix, and you should fix it while the dough is still in the mixing bowl. Add warm water, ½ tablespoon at a time, until some of the dough is sticking to the sides of the bowl. Blend on medium-low speed, continuing to add very small amounts of water, until you have the right consistency.

I'd rather have dough that's too wet than too dry; it's a bit messier to fix, but too much moisture is easier to compensate for—both with added flour and added baking time. If your dough is too wet it may feel like a thick batter, or will spread when you place it on your preparation surface. You can fix this by adding more flour. For most recipes you will already have a layer of flour below the dough. Sprinkle additional flour on the sides and top of the dough. Use a bench knife to work the flour into the dough, rolling it back and forth, scraping the surface as needed, and folding the flour into the dough. Add more flour, 1 tablespoon at a time, until the dough is easy to work with.

Multipurpose Flatbread

This is one of my favorite recipes. I've always been a lover of wraps, flatbreads, and burritos, and you can use this one recipe to make all of these and more. (Yes, I really did name this multipurpose for a reason.) The recipe can easily be scaled up (double or triple the ingredients), if you find that it's a favorite of yours too. Flatbreads make terrific sandwich wraps, or cut them in half to make a flatbread sandwich. Serve flatbread as hors d'oeuvres with hummus or your favorite allergen-free dip, or cut wedges of flatbread and fill the breadbasket to serve with dinner. Freeze the extras.

Without question, the best flour blend to use with this recipe is Jules Gluten Free All Purpose Flour. (See page 28 for more on the gluten-free flour blends I recommend.)

{ MAKES 8 FLATBREADS }

1½ cups gluten-free flour blend

¼ teaspoon xanthan gum (leave out if your flour blend contains xanthan gum)

2¼ teaspoons quick-rising yeast

1 tablespoon sugar

¼ teaspoon salt

½ cup plus 2 tablespoons warm water

2 tablespoons light olive oil

Up to 2 tablespoons additional warm water (as needed)

Up to 2 tablespoons additional flour for dusting

1. Combine the flour, xanthan gum (if needed), yeast, sugar, and salt in a medium bowl. Set it aside.

2. Blend the water with the oil, using a mixer on medium speed, until combined, about 30 seconds.

3. Slowly add the dry ingredients to the wet mixture, mixing on medium-low speed, until blended.

4. Beat for 5 minutes on medium-high speed until the dough is pulling away from the sides of the bowl. Add up to 2 more tablespoons of warm water, ½ tablespoon at a time, as needed.

5. Scrape down the sides of the bowl, and proof (in the bowl) for 35 to 45 minutes (see "Proofing Methods," page 158).

6. Sprinkle flour on a smooth prep surface. Scoop the dough onto that surface.

7. Use a bench knife or sharp-edged knife to divide the dough into eight equal-sized portions.

8. Use your hands to gently roll each portion into a ball, using additional flour to coat the balls.

9. With a rolling pin, gently roll out each dough ball until they are between 7 and 8 inches in diameter. Be careful not to use too much pressure. They should be thin, but not paper thin.

10. Heat a skillet on medium-high heat. Let it get very hot, and then reduce the heat to medium.

11. Grill the flatbreads, one at a time, for 1 to 2 minutes per side. Light browning will occur and some air pockets may form. Be careful not to overcook the flatbreads. It's better to undercook than to overcook them.

(continued)

* This is where the mini rolling pin I mentioned earlier (see page 74) comes in handy. If you roll the rolling pin over your lightly floured surface it will keep the pin from sticking to the dough.
* Use small sheets of parchment paper to layer the rolled dough and keep it from sticking to your work surface.
* No oil is needed in the pan when grilling the bread.

☀ VARIATIONS:

BURRITOS: Make the recipe as described above. Place the burrito ingredients on the flatbread and roll. Serve immediately, or bake with toppings for 15 minutes at 350°F.

HERBED FLATBREAD: Add 1 teaspoon of chopped fresh parsley and 1 teaspoon of chopped fresh basil to the dry ingredients. Follow the instructions above.

THIN PIZZA CRUST: Follow the instructions above through step 5. Preheat the oven to 375°F. Spray a pizza tin with cooking oil. Lightly coat the dough with flour, then scoop it directly into the center of the pizza tin. Use a rolling pin to roll the dough to the edges of the pan. Note that the crust will shrink about 10 percent while baking. Bake the pizza crust without toppings at 375°F for 10 minutes. Remove the crust from the oven, flip it over with a spatula, and add the toppings for your pizza. Bake for an additional 15 to 20 minutes, until the toppings are done. This recipe is enough to make one large pizza crust.

Millet Baguettes

I have always loved a baguette with a salad, and wanted to create one in an allergen-free version. Since my son's favorite grain is millet, I decided to take advantage of the sweetness of that grain in my baguette. If you haven't tried millet yet, I think you'll find that it works nicely here, with a hint of a corn taste. These baguettes can be made as mini baguettes (as described here), or full-size loaves.

{ MAKES 2 SMALL BAGUETTES, 4 TO 6 SERVINGS }

1 cup millet flour (see tip)

1¼ cups gluten-free flour blend

½ teaspoon xanthan gum (reduce to ¼ teaspoon if your flour blend contains xanthan gum)

2¼ teaspoons quick-rising yeast

1½ tablespoons sugar

¼ teaspoon salt

¾ cup warm water

1 tablespoon light olive oil

2 tablespoons cornmeal (for dusting)

1. Line a baguette pan with aluminum foil. Spray with cooking oil.
2. Combine the flours, xanthan gum, yeast, sugar, and salt in a medium bowl. Set it aside.
3. Blend the water and oil together in a large bowl, using a mixer on medium speed, about 30 seconds.
4. Slowly add the dry ingredients to the wet mixture, mixing on medium-low speed, until combined.
5. Beat for 5 minutes on medium-high speed, until the dough is pulling away from the sides of the bowl.
6. Sprinkle the cornmeal on a smooth prep surface, and scoop the dough on top.
7. Use a bench knife or sharp-edged knife to divide the dough into 2 equal-sized portions.
8. Coat each portion with cornmeal, and use your hands and the bench knife to gently roll each portion into a baguette shape, about 1½ inches in diameter. Try to keep the sides of the baguette as thick as the middle.
9. Lift the baguettes into the prepared baguette pan. Round the edges of the baguettes (using a few drops of warm water, if needed).
10. Proof for 35-45 minutes (see "Proofing Methods," page 158).
11. With 5 minutes left to rise, preheat the oven to 375°F.
12. Bake at 375°F for 22 to 25 minutes, until the internal temperature is 200° to 205°F.

TIPS

* If you need to avoid millet due to a corn allergy, use 2 cups of multigrain gluten-free flour blend. Reduce the beating time (step 5) to 2 minutes. Use additional flour instead of cornmeal.
* If you don't have a baguette pan, there's no need to rush out and buy one. Baguettes can be made on a baking sheet, using some props. A common method is to use dowels and cheesecloth to create a concave (or half-cylinder) holder for the baguettes. I find that two or three sheets of heavy-duty aluminum foil, formed into the shape of a baguette pan, can be strong enough to hold the bread.
* Increase the baking time to approximately 30 minutes if you choose to make one large baguette.

English Muffins with Raspberry Jam (page 219)

English Muffins

As odd as this may sound, some people crave the foods they are allergic to. I can recall the summer that my food-allergic son was eating peanuts by the handful, and another time when he just couldn't seem to get enough butter on his English muffins—we later learned that he was allergic to both peanuts and milk. But even though he won't be slathering them with butter, he can still enjoy these English muffins with our favorite jams (see page 219 for recipes).

English muffins are simply a form of bread; what makes them recognizable is their round shape, the dusting of cornmeal on both sides, and the fact that they are cooked on both sides. Traditionally English muffins are cooked on a griddle (as you would make a pancake), but these muffins are designed to be baked in the oven. If you'd rather make them on the griddle, that's okay too!

Because they're gluten-free, the end result won't have the same nooks and crannies that a wheat muffin would have, but they're just as delicious.

{ MAKES 8 MUFFINS }

2½ cups gluten-free flour blend

½ teaspoon xanthan gum (leave out if your flour blend contains xanthan gum)

2¼ teaspoons yeast

2 tablespoons sugar

½ teaspoon salt

1 teaspoon baking powder

1 tablespoon apple cider vinegar

¾ cup original hemp milk, warmed to 100°F (see tip)

3 tablespoons Earth Balance Natural Shortening, melted

Up to 3 tablespoons warm water (as needed)

¼ cup cornmeal (see tip)

1. Line a baking sheet with parchment paper. If possible, have a second smaller baking sheet (with edges) available, and a second piece of parchment paper.
2. Combine the flour, xanthan gum (if needed), yeast, sugar, salt, and baking powder in a medium bowl. Set it aside.
3. Blend the apple cider vinegar, hemp milk, and shortening together in a large bowl, using a mixer on medium speed, about 1 minute.
4. Slowly add the dry ingredients to the wet mixture, mixing on medium-low speed, until combined.
5. Beat for 5 minutes on medium-high speed, until the dough is pulling away from the sides of the bowl. Add up to 3 tablespoons of warm water, ½ tablespoon at a time, as needed.
6. Sprinkle the cornmeal on a smooth prep surface, and scoop the dough on top of the cornmeal.
7. Use your hands to roll the dough into a log. Use a bench knife or sharp-edged knife to slice the dough into eight equal-sized portions.
8. Gently shape each portion into a disk, and coat both sides with cornmeal.
9. Place the disks on the larger prepared baking sheet. Sprinkle drops of water on the second piece of parchment paper, and place it on top of the disks. Place the second baking sheet (upside down) over the muffins and parchment paper. This second baking sheet keeps the muffins from expanding too high upward, and forces them to expand outward instead.

(continued)

10. Proof for 35 to 45 minutes (see "Proofing Methods," page 158).

11. With 5 minutes left to rise, preheat the oven to 375°F.

12. Bake at 375°F for 10 minutes. Flip the baking sheets over so that the top is now the bottom. Remove the top baking sheet.

13. Bake for 6 to 8 minutes longer, until the internal temperature is 200° to 205°F.

forming muffins

proofing muffins

cooling muffins

TIPS

* The hemp milk can be warmed to 100°F using a microwave (for about 20 seconds if it's at room temperature before warming, or 45 seconds if cold), or in a small saucepan over low heat. Use your probe thermometer to check. If you overshoot, wait until the temperature drops before adding the hemp milk to your mixing bowl.

* Don't skimp on the cornmeal; cornmeal gives English muffins flavor and texture. If you can't use cornmeal due to a corn allergy, substitute flax meal or gluten-free quick-cooking oats.

* If you have English muffin rings, go ahead and use them. Place the disks in the muffin rings prior to laying the second baking sheet over them.

* If you don't have a second baking sheet, flatten the tops of the muffins gently (to help them expand horizontally) before baking, and flip them with a spatula after baking for 10 minutes.

* If you'd like to make these with a griddle on the stovetop, heat a griddle pan and bake them over medium-low heat as you would pancakes, flipping as needed to avoid burning and ensure even baking.

Activating and Testing Yeast

CRASH COURSE

IF YOU CHOOSE to use active dry yeast, rather than quick-rising yeast, you will need to activate it before using it. While it is technically already active, the live yeast cells are encapsulated in dry cells, which need moisture and sugar to wake them up and get them moving. To activate it, place the yeast in a small bowl and add 1 teaspoon of granulated sugar and at least ¼ cup of warm water. Stir the mixture gently, and let it sit for 10 minutes. Now is a good time to check your e-mail or pick up the kid's toys. When you come back, the yeast will be foaming and ready to use. The light brown foam this process creates is not especially appealing, but that's what you want and how you know that your yeast is still good.

One of the advantages of quick-rising yeast is that you don't need to activate it. In fact, it works best if you don't proof it. Unlike active dry yeast, which needs to be woken up slowly before it can do its job, quick-rising yeast is ready to go as soon as it finds sugar and liquid, and it works more quickly, saving you time. This yeast should be added directly to the dry ingredients. Nevertheless, yeast does lose its potency over time, and every few months you should test your quick-rising yeast to make sure it's still got some spunk. To test quick-rising yeast, use the same technique described above for waking up active dry yeast. You should see a near-immediate foaming reaction if your yeast is still able to do its job. Discard the results of this test; once quick-rising yeast is foaming, it won't work as well when you mix it into your dry ingredients.

If either your active dry or quick-rising yeast doesn't foam, it's time to replace it.

Chocolate Croissants

Chocolate Croissants

The French refer to chocolate croissants as pain au chocolat. *Translated literally, this means "chocolate bread," and there's no better place to get it than a street-side café in Paris. Unless of course you need an allergen-free version—in which case you'll want to make your own at home.*

When making a puffed pastry or croissant with traditional ingredients, it's typical to use puff pastry dough. These are unleavened, made with multiple layers of wheat dough, and lots of butter. The technique to make this dough takes advantage of the gluten in the flour, and results in flaking when baked. Since we're baking without gluten, my recipe uses yeast to provide some lift. It won't be as flaky as a croissant made from wheat and butter, but it still gives you that rich, decadent experience you would expect from chocolate bread, and it's lower in fat.

{ MAKES 8 CROISSANTS }

1½ cups gluten-free flour blend

¼ teaspoon xanthan gum (leave out if your flour blend contains xanthan gum)

2¼ teaspoons quick-rising yeast

¼ cup sugar

¼ teaspoon salt

2 teaspoons baking powder

¼ cup grapeseed oil

¼ cup warm water

1½ teaspoons Ener-G Egg Replacer mixed with 2 tablespoons warm water (equal to 1 egg)

1 teaspoon vanilla extract

Up to 3 tablespoons warm water (as needed)

Up to 2 tablespoons additional flour for dusting

¾ cup allergen-free chocolate chips

1. Line a baking sheet with parchment paper.
2. Combine the flours, xanthan gum (if needed), yeast, sugar, salt, and baking powder in a medium bowl. Set it aside.
3. Blend the oil, water, egg replacer mixture, and vanilla together in a large bowl, using a mixer on medium speed, about 1 minute.
4. Slowly add the dry ingredients to the wet mixture, mixing on medium-low speed, until combined.
5. Beat for 5 minutes on medium-high speed, until the dough is pulling away from the sides of the bowl. Add up to 3 tablespoons warm water, ½ tablespoon at a time, as needed.
6. Spread a thin layer of flour on a smooth prep surface. Scoop the dough on top of the flour.
7. Use a bench knife or sharp-edged knife to divide the dough into eight equal-sized cubes.
8. Coat each portion lightly with flour.
9. Use a rolling pin to roll out each cube into a rectangle about 6 inches long and 4 inches wide. Place them on the prepared baking sheet.
10. Place chocolate chips in the center third of each rectangle, and fold the flaps over the chocolate. Place a drop of water under the top flap to help it stay in place, and tuck it under so it stays secure.
11. Proof for 35 to 45 minutes (see "Proofing Methods," page 158).
12. With 5 minutes left to rise, preheat the oven to 350°F.
13. Bake at 350°F for 12 to 16 minutes until the tops are lightly browned and the chocolate is bubbling around the edges.

(continued)

※ Note that the temperature for baking the croissants is 350°F, lower than most yeast bread recipes. You don't want to burn the chocolate by baking it at too high a temperature.

※ Decorate the croissants with the chocolate glaze that follows.

✳ VARIATION:

STRAWBERRY CROISSANTS: Instead of chocolate chips, use approximately ¾ cup of Strawberry Jam (page 219). Follow the directions above. In step 10, use 2 tablespoons of jam in the center of each croissant. This works equally well with any jam.

Chocolate Glaze

The ingredients of this chocolate glaze are similar to my Ganache (page 201), with different proportions. Traditionally both contain cream, but this recipe uses chocolate hemp milk. The trick to a glaze is the consistency; it should be light enough to spread or drizzle easily over croissants, doughnuts, or pastry, but it should also harden shortly after being spread.

This glaze also makes a terrific chocolate sauce for non-dairy ice cream. I love it over So Delicious coconut milk non-dairy frozen desserts (see page 50).

{ MAKES ABOUT 1 CUP OF GLAZE }

1 tablespoon Earth Balance Natural Shortening
2 tablespoons chocolate hemp milk (see tip)
1 cup allergen-free chocolate chips

1. Melt the shortening in a small saucepan over low heat.
2. Add the hemp milk and whisk the ingredients together. Increase the heat to medium. Continue stirring with the whisk.
3. When the mixture is boiling, remove it from the heat.
4. Add the chocolate chips. Use the whisk to stir until the chocolate is completely melted and blended with the shortening and milk. Stir vigorously with the whisk for about 2 minutes longer (over no heat), until the sauce darkens and becomes slightly glossy on top.
5. Let it cool.

TIPS

* While I prefer this recipe with chocolate hemp milk, another non-dairy chocolate milk (e.g., chocolate rice milk) or even original or vanilla-flavored non-dairy milk can be substituted.
* For a lighter chocolate sauce, increase the chocolate hemp milk to 6 tablespoons.
* Refrigerate the leftovers. The glaze will harden. Microwave it for 20 seconds and mix well when you're ready to use the glaze again.

How to Use a Glaze

A GLAZE, SOMETIMES referred to as a drizzle, is usually lighter than a frosting or a ganache. It's meant to decorate your baked goods and provide additional flavor, but not to cover your dessert completely. There is no right way to decorate—that's up to you and your imagination—but here are some means to apply whatever design you choose:

✳ **A SQUEEZE BOTTLE:** These can be found in baking shops and specialty stores, but the easiest thing to do is to repurpose an empty bottle that has been thoroughly washed (preferably in the dishwasher) to avoid possible allergens; agave nectar bottles, honey bottles with squeeze tops, and the bottles you use for mustard and ketchup at picnics all work well, as long as they have small holes. I always prefer to glaze my baked goods just before serving, to prevent sogginess. Using a squeeze bottle makes it easy to store the glaze, and to top the baked goods as I'm ready to serve them. Hold one finger over the opening as you invert the bottle and shake the ingredients down to the edge, position it over your doughnuts or croissants, and decorate.

✳ **A SMALL PLASTIC BAG:** Fill a small plastic bag (a heavy-duty sandwich bag will do) with the glaze. Squeeze the glaze down to one corner of the bag and twist the top. When you're ready to start decorating, use scissors to snip off a tiny bit of the corner. The more you snip, the larger the hole will be, and the faster your glaze will drizzle out.

✳ **DISPOSABLE DECORATING BAGS:** These are the store-bought version of the plastic bag, made for decorating cakes. They come in all sizes. For glazing, smaller bags will work the best. Fill the bag with glaze. Squeeze the glaze to the tip (the bottom) of the bag and twist the top. Use scissors to snip off a tiny bit of the tip, and decorate as you please.

❋ DIPPING: The simplest of all the glazing techniques, this works well when you want to cover the entire top of a pastry or dough- nut with glaze. Pour the glaze into a shallow bowl or dish. Dip the item you wish to glaze upside down into the glaze. After dipping, twist and turn it right side up and you're done!

Glaze is best used when cooled (about an hour after preparing) but not hardened. Likewise, your baked goods should be cooled when you add the glaze. If you're pressed for time, go ahead and use it—just know that it will be more like a sauce than a glaze when used warm (and will be a bit messy).

Crescent Rolls

This recipe uses nearly the same ingredients as Chocolate Croissants (page 175) but instead of filling them with chocolate, these will be shaped into rolls—like the crescent rolls we're all familiar with that come in a tube. Even the gluten-eating members of your family will fight over who gets the last one.

{ MAKES 12 ROLLS }

1½ cups gluten-free flour blend

¼ teaspoon xanthan gum (leave out if your flour blend contains xanthan gum)

2¼ teaspoons quick-rising yeast

¼ cup sugar

¼ teaspoon salt

2 teaspoons baking powder

¼ cup grapeseed oil

¼ cup warm water

1½ teaspoons Ener-G Egg Replacer mixed with 2 tablespoons warm water (equal to 1 egg)

1 teaspoon vanilla extract

Up to 3 tablespoons warm water (as needed)

Up to 2 tablespoons additional flour for dusting

Up to 2 tablespoons light olive oil

1. Line a baking sheet with parchment paper.
2. Combine the flours, xanthan gum (if needed), yeast, sugar, salt, and baking powder in a medium bowl. Set it aside.
3. Blend the oil, water, egg replacer mixture, and vanilla together in a large bowl, using a mixer on medium speed, about 1 minute.
4. Slowly add the dry ingredients to the wet mixture, mixing on medium-low speed, until combined.
5. Beat for 5 minutes on medium-high speed, until the dough is pulling away from the sides of the bowl. Add up to 3 tablespoons warm water, ½ tablespoon at a time, as needed.
6. Spread a thin layer of flour on a smooth prep surface. Scoop the dough on top of the flour.
7. Use a bench knife or sharp-edged knife to separate the dough into six cubed portions.
8. Coat each portion lightly with flour.
9. Use a rolling pin to roll out each cube into a 6-inch square.
10. Use your bench knife to cut each square diagonally into two triangles (you will now have twelve portions).
11. Brush the top of each portion with a thin coating of light olive oil.
12. Starting with the broadest side, roll up the triangles (as you would with the crescent rolls) and pinch the edges inward.
13. Proof for 35 to 45 minutes (see "Proofing Methods," page 158).
14. With 5 minutes left to rise, preheat the oven to 375°F.
15. Bake at 375°F for 10 to 13 minutes, until the tops are lightly browned.

TIPS

❋ You won't be buttering these rolls, but the olive oil inside will keep them moist and tasty.

Cinnamon Rolls

You might be longing for cinnamon rolls like the Pillsbury Cinnamon Rolls that come in the pop-open cylinder. I loved to make them as a kid—they were the perfect breakfast on a weekend morning. Now, with my own allergen-free recipe I can still make cinnamon rolls for my family, with just a little bit more effort—and you can too.

The best cinnamon rolls have a striated effect. The trick to achieving this effect is to hold the cinnamon until after the dough is formed, and then fold it into the dough (see step 8 below).

{ MAKES 8 CINNAMON ROLLS }

¼ cup light brown sugar

2½ teaspoons cinnamon

2¼ cups gluten-free flour blend

½ teaspoon xanthan gum (leave out if your flour blend contains xanthan gum)

2¼ teaspoons quick-rising yeast

¼ cup granulated sugar

¼ teaspoon salt

2 teaspoons baking powder

¾ cup original hemp milk, warmed to 100°F (see tip on page 172)

¼ cup grapeseed oil

3 teaspoons Ener-G Egg Replacer mixed with 4 tablespoons warm water (equal to 2 eggs)

½ teaspoon vanilla extract

Up to ¼ cup additional flour for dusting

1. Spray a medium baking dish with cooking oil.
2. Combine the brown sugar and 1½ teaspoons cinnamon in a small mixing bowl, breaking up any clumps of sugar. Set it aside.
3. Combine the flour, xanthan gum (if needed), yeast, sugar, salt, and baking powder in a medium bowl. Set it aside.
4. Blend the warmed hemp milk, oil, egg replacer mixture, and vanilla together in a large bowl, using a mixer on medium speed, about 30 seconds.
5. Slowly add the dry ingredients to the wet mixture, mixing on medium-low speed, until combined.
6. Beat for 5 minutes on medium-high speed, until the dough is pulling away from the sides of the bowl.
7. Spread a thin layer of flour on a smooth prep surface. Scoop the dough on top of the flour.
8. Use your fingers and bench knife to flatten the dough, about 1 inch thick. Sprinkle the remaining teaspoon of cinnamon on top of the dough. Use your hands to smooth it evenly over the dough. Fold the dough in half (with the cinnamon in the center).
9. Use your fingers to flatten the dough to about 1 inch thick and 6 inches wide.
10. Sprinkle the sugar and cinnamon mixture (from step 1 above) evenly on top of the dough. Use your hands to smooth the topping, leaving about ½ inch at one end uncovered.
11. Roll the dough into a cylinder. At the uncovered edge, use a few drops of water to stick the dough together.
12. Use your bench knife to cut eight ¾-inch slices from the dough, forming the rolls.
13. Arrange the dough in your baking dish, with a small amount of space in between each roll. Scoop up any toppings that may have fallen out, and sprinkle them on top of the rolls.

(continued)

14. Proof for 35 to 45 minutes (see "Proofing Methods," page 158).

15. With 5 minutes left to rise, preheat the oven to 375°F.

16. Bake at 375°F for 15 to 18 minutes until the tops are lightly browned and the cinnamon-sugar centers are bubbling.

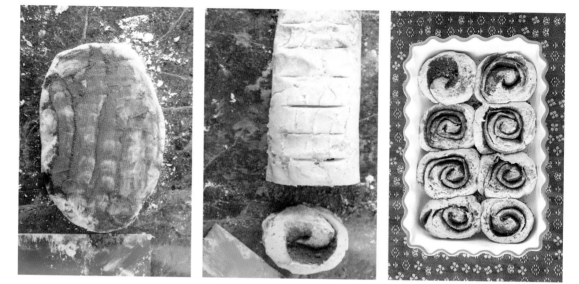

spreading cinnamon   preparing rolls   after proofing

* Top with Vanilla Glaze (page 184), if desired.
* A 7 by 9-inch baking dish (with the rolls arranged in two rows of four), or a 9-inch round cake pan (with the rolls arranged in a circle) works well for making cinnamon rolls.

Cinnamon Rolls

Vanilla Glaze

I love vanilla glaze on doughnuts, but my favorite use for vanilla glaze is on top of cinnamon rolls. A cinnamon roll just wouldn't be a cinnamon roll without the glaze, right?

{ MAKES ABOUT ¾ CUP OF GLAZE }

1½ cups confectioners' sugar

⅛ teaspoon salt

3 tablespoons Earth Balance Natural
Shortening, softened

½ teaspoon vanilla extract

2 tablespoons water

1. In a large mixing bowl, combine the confectioners' sugar, salt, and shortening on low speed, until crumbly.
2. Add the vanilla and water. Mix on medium speed, about 5 minutes longer, until the mixture is smooth and creamy.

TIPS

* Use one of the methods described earlier (see page 178) to decorate your baked goods, or just spread the glaze with a flat knife or spatula for full coverage.
* It's best to frost your baked goods just before serving them.

* VARIATION:

ORANGE GLAZE: Substitute ½ teaspoon of orange extract for the vanilla. Add 1 teaspoon of orange zest (see page 150). Follow the instructions above.

Cinnamon Raisin Bread

This bread uses nearly the same ingredients as the Cinnamon Rolls (page 181), and many of the same methods, but the instructions vary enough that it deserves its own day in the sun. And yes, it's a sunny day every day you make fresh cinnamon bread for breakfast. Although the Cinnamon Rolls and this Cinnamon Raisin Bread are among the most difficult recipes in this book, I think you'll find that you can master them.

{ MAKES 1 LOAF, 12 TO 16 SERVINGS }

2¼ cups gluten-free flour blend

½ teaspoon xanthan gum (leave out if your flour blend contains xanthan gum)

2¼ teaspoons quick-rising yeast

¼ cup sugar

¼ teaspoon salt

2 teaspoons baking powder

¾ cup original hemp milk, warmed to 100°F (see tip on page 172)

¼ cup grapeseed oil

3 teaspoons Ener-G Egg Replacer mixed with 4 tablespoons warm water (equal to 2 eggs)

½ teaspoon vanilla extract

⅓ cup raisins

Up to ¼ cup additional flour for dusting

1½ teaspoons cinnamon

1. Spray a 9 by 4-inch loaf pan with cooking oil.
2. Combine the flour, xanthan gum (if needed), yeast, sugar, salt, and baking powder in a medium bowl. Set it aside.
3. Blend the warmed hemp milk, oil, egg replacer mixture, and vanilla together in a large bowl, using a mixer on medium speed, about 30 seconds.
4. Slowly add the dry ingredients to the wet mixture, mixing on medium-low speed, until combined.
5. Beat for 5 minutes on medium-high speed until the dough is pulling away from the sides of the bowl.
6. Add the raisins to the dough and blend on medium for 30 seconds longer until incorporated.
7. Spread a thin layer of flour on a smooth prep surface. Scoop the dough on top of the flour.
8. Use your fingers and bench knife to flatten the dough, about 1 inch thick and 9 inches wide. Sprinkle the cinnamon on top of the dough, leaving a 1-inch section at the edge uncovered. Use your hands to spread the cinnamon evenly over the dough.
9. Roll the dough into a cylinder. At the uncovered edge, use a few drops of water to stick the dough together.
10. Lift the rolled bread and place it into the loaf pan, with the seam on the bottom.
11. Proof for 35 to 45 minutes (see "Proofing Methods," page 158).
12. With 5 minutes left to rise, preheat the oven to 375°F.
13. Bake at 375°F for 40 to 45 minutes, until the internal temperature is 200° to 205°F.

TIPS

✳ I find that this bread works best with a 9 by 4-inch gluten-free bread pan (see page 75), but a regular 9 by 5-inch loaf pan will certainly work.

Using Active Dry Yeast

YOU WILL NEED to adapt the recipes in this book if you choose to use active dry yeast. Use liquid and sugar from the recipe to activate it, and always activate the yeast first. Here is an example of how to adapt a recipe, using the Basic Dinner Roll recipe (page 157). The items in bold indicate where an adjustment is needed:

USING QUICK-RISING YEAST:	USING ACTIVE DRY YEAST;
INGREDIENTS (IN ORDER USED): ½ cup garbanzo bean flour 1½ cups gluten-free flour blend ½ cup xanthan gum (leave out if your flour blend contains xanthan gum) **2¼ teaspoons quick-rising yeast** ¼ teaspoon salt 3 teaspoons baking powder **¼ cup sugar** ¼ cup sunflower oil **½ cup warm water** 3 teaspoons Ener-G Egg Replacer mixed with 4 tablespoons warm water Up to ¼ cup additional flour for dusting	INGREDIENTS (IN ORDER USED): **2¼ teapoons active dry yeast** **1 teaspoon sugar** **½ cup warm water** ½ cup garbanzo bean flour 1½ cups gluten-free flour blend ½ teaspoon xanthan gum (leave out if your flour blend contains xanthan gum) ¼ teaspoon salt 3 teaspoons baking powder **¼ cup sugar (less 1 teaspoon)** ¼ cup sunflower oil 3 teaspoons Ener-G Egg Replacer mixed with 4 tablespoons warm water Up to ¼ cup additional flour for dusting

Make these changes to the recipe instructions:

1. Prior to any other step, mix the yeast, 1 teaspoon of sugar, and warm water. Set it aside and proof the yeast for 10 minutes.
2. Following proofing, mix the yeast in with the wet ingredients, rather than the dry.
3. Follow the recipe instructions for mixing the remaining ingredients.
4. Double the amount of time required for proofing/rising prior to baking. This will be 1¼ to 1½ hours.

The same method can be used to adapt any recipe. Conversely, if you plan to adapt a recipe that uses active dry yeast to use rapid rise, simply add the yeast to the dry ingredients, add the sugar used for activating the yeast in with the dry ingredients, add the water used for activating the yeast in with the wet ingredients, and let the baked goods rise for half the time suggested.

10

Chocolate 1-2-3:
Tips and Tricks for Cake, Brownies, Mousse and More

IF I HAD MY WAY, chocolate would be a separate food group. I'm kidding, of course, but it's no secret that I love chocolate. I can find a reason to add chocolate chips to almost any recipe, but that's not the only reason why I created a separate chapter of chocolate recipes. Chocolate has its own nuances in baking that are worth some focus and attention.

In many ways, chocolate is like wine—there are many varieties, tastes, smells, textures, and subtleties to explore. If you walk into a shop that specializes in baking products, you will likely find an entire section dedicated to chocolate, with more forms, flavors, and sources than you could imagine. While most of us think of chocolate as a single flavor—and all chocolate does have certain qualities that cause us to recognize it instantly—there are differences in chocolate that start with the cocoa bean itself, just like the differences in wine start with the grape. There are also many brands of processed chocolate, and products with similar names are not always comparable—there's the equivalent of boxed wine (everyday chocolate) and the finest wine (gourmet chocolate).

You've probably heard of cocoa or cacao beans. The *Theobroma cacao* tree, which grows in tropical climates, bears fruit in the form of large pods that contain cacao beans, which are harvested, fermented, and dried before they can be processed into the various forms of chocolate that bakers and confectioners work with. When we see the term *cacao*, many are tempted to correct what we think may be a spelling error, but the spelling is correct. The tree that bears the fruit is accurately called *cacao*, as are the beans within the pods. You will find the use of the terms *cacao powder* or simply *cacao* on some product labels, whereas others use the term *cocoa*. They mean the same thing.

The result of processing whole cacao beans is chocolate liquor (don't worry, there's no alcohol in it). Usually this comes in a molded form—either disks or bars. Cacao is also broken down into two ingredients—cacao butter and cacao powder. The cacao butter is pure fat, while the cacao solids—or cacao powder—are lower in fat. Most of the chocolate available for purchase has had these ingredients extracted from the cacao liquor, and then recombined in various forms. Candy bars, and even some chocolate intended for baking, contain added ingredients, including sugars and sometimes milk. Of course, this step where ingredients are added is what makes chocolate a concern for those with food allergies (see page 8). When I have described chocolate as "allergen-free" in a recipe, I am referring to a product that is chocolate but contains no common food allergens (e.g., milk, nuts) and is free from possible contamination (if that is a concern for you).

Chocolate allergy is rare. Nevertheless, if you need to avoid chocolate, one potential replacement is carob. Carob trees also bear their fruit in pods. Carob beans are legumes that (similar to peas) are harvested from these pods. Carob is naturally sweeter than chocolate and lower in calories. If you choose to use carob in place of chocolate, note that the flavor profile will change dramatically. If you have allergies to legumes, you may need to avoid carob—check with your doctor.

About Chocolate

THERE ARE THREE types of chocolate that you should be familiar with for baking, and all three are used in recipes in this book:

Clockwise from upper left: cocoa powder, assorted chocolate chips, and baking chocolate

UNSWEETENED BAKING CHOCOLATE: Unsweetened baking chocolate is pure chocolate, with no sugars or other ingredients added. While the product you buy may in fact be cacao butter and cacao powder that has been reblended into cacao liquor, you will want to ensure that you use a product that is 100% cacao. This may be stated as "100% cocoa," or "chocolate liquor," or simply "chocolate" as the only ingredient on the label. If you bite into a piece of this chocolate, you will notice a very bitter, acidic taste. While different formulations of baking chocolate will have varying ratios of cacao butter to cacao powder, nearly all of these products have a very high fat content. When baking, think of unsweetened baking chocolate as fat. This means that you may be able to use less of other fats (oils and shortening) when working with baking chocolate.

It can be difficult to find baking chocolate processed in a dedicated facility. If your food allergens dictate avoiding products with warning labels and you are unable to find a source for unsweetened baking chocolate, you may substitute allergen-free chocolate chips for baking chocolate. The result will be a slightly sweeter product.

NATURAL UNSWEETENED COCOA POWDER: This is another form of chocolate that you will find a lot of use for in baking. The baking chocolate we just discussed is chocolate liquor (cacao butter plus cacao powder), whereas cocoa powder contains just the solids (with most of the cacao butter extracted). Once again, the products you choose should be 100% cacao (and again, sometimes labeled "100% cocoa" or "100% chocolate"). I recommend that you always choose unsweetened; the recipes will add sugar and the other ingredients you need to make the chocolate palatable. Avoid chocolate beverage mixes (e.g., hot cocoa mix) that may contain dairy or other allergens.

I also recommend that you choose natural cocoa power. Cocoa powder comes in two different forms—natural and Dutch processed. Natural is as it sounds—unprocessed. But in its natural state, cocoa powder is acidic and bitter. Some cocoa is Dutch processed (sometimes called double Dutch)—treated with alkali to neutralize the acidity with the intent of creating a smoother-tasting chocolate powder. The result is a darker-colored cocoa powder that some argue gives it a deeper chocolate taste. In reality, I find that Dutch-processed cocoa powder has a less-chocolaty taste, and is less consistent to bake

with. If you choose to use Dutch-processed cocoa powder, you may need to adapt some recipes to use baking powder rather than baking soda. Remember that baking soda needs an acid to interact with.

One of my favorite natural unsweetened cocoa powders is Hershey's. I find it to be very reliable and consistent.

CHOCOLATE CHIPS: Many baking recipes use chocolate chips as an ingredient. When you are baking allergen-free, always use semisweet or bittersweet chocolate chips that contain no milk. But even if the label says "dairy-free," this is the type of chocolate where food allergens become even more of a concern. Chocolate chips (and chocolate bars that have added ingredients) are often processed on the same equipment and in the same facilities where candy bars are processed. And many of those candy bars contain milk and nuts. It's unfortunate that so many people prefer milk chocolate—if I had my way, all chocolate would be dark and without nuts, but alas, that's not the case. That means that food-allergy families need to scrutinize the labels on chocolate—especially chocolate that is combined with other ingredients, like the chocolate chips we are talking about now. Pay special attention to products that have been processed in facilities with other food allergens, and choose allergy-safe products accordingly. See page 6 for more on reading labels.

When selecting chocolate chips for use in baking, you should choose a product that is simply chocolate liquor (including cocoa powder and cocoa butter), sugar (or cane juice), and sometimes soy lecithin (more on that later). A product with a small amount of vanilla is also acceptable. Once sugar is added to the cocoa liquor, chocolate becomes highly edible. If you're like me, you may find it hard to keep chocolate chips stocked in your pantry.

Note that although I am discussing chocolate chips here (because they are a very convenient form for baking), the types of chocolate described in this section often come in bar form. Semisweet or bittersweet chocolate bars can be broken up into chunks or melted for use in recipes that call for melted chocolate chips.

The naming conventions for chocolate products are nothing less than confusing. You will find the terms *semisweet*, *bittersweet*, *dark*, and *extra dark* all used to describe chocolate that contains 35% or more cacao (or chocolate liquor). A bittersweet bar or

bag of chips is not always darker, and doesn't always have a higher percentage of cacao than does semisweet. Some manufacturers are voluntarily labeling products with the percentage of chocolate (this could be listed as "% chocolate liquor," "% cocoa," or "% cacao"—they mean the same thing). If a product is not labeled with that percentage, the best way to determine how much chocolate it contains is by looking at the sugar content. Because these bars contain little more than chocolate and sugar, the more sugar, the lower the percentage of chocolate. For example, if a bar is 40% sugar, you can safely assume it is nearly 60% chocolate liquor; conversely, a bar that is 80% cacao will contain only 20% sugar. Most chocolate chips will be on the slightly sweeter side; as long as the product you use is 50% or more chocolate (and contains no milk, butterfat, or other food allergens), you are in good shape.

I should also address the issue of cocoa butter. Its name is unfortunate, as it leads some to question its safety for those with milk allergies. Remember that cocoa butter is pure chocolate. This is not a dairy product; there is no milk in it. Nevertheless, some manufacturers list the ingredient as "non-dairy cocoa butter," as if there were a dairy version of cocoa butter; there is not. Also remember that if a chocolate product contains milk, the word *milk* must be clearly called out in the ingredients list.

The amount of chocolate liquor, the use of the terms *bittersweet* versus *semisweet* versus *dark*, and the confusion over cocoa butter are not the only confusion points when it comes to labeling of chocolate. You will sometimes find a chocolate bar labeled as a baking bar that is actually a semisweet, bittersweet, or dark chocolate bar. The simple check for this is once again the ingredient label. Even if a bar is labeled "baking chocolate," if it contains sugar you should think of it as the same product as the chocolate chips and bars we are discussing here.

Because chocolate chips processed in separate facilities can be hard to find, I want to call out a few brands that I have found to be very high quality and suitable for many with food allergies:

♦ **ENJOY LIFE FOODS** makes chocolate chips in two forms— Mini Chips and the newly introduced Mega Chunks, both labeled "semisweet." The company also makes a dark chocolate bar called Boom Choco Boom. Enjoy Life products are all gluten-free, dairy-free, and free of the top eight food allergens. They are one of the few chocolate products on the

CRASH COURSE

market that do not contain soy lecithin. If soy lecithin is a concern for you, this is your best bet.

✦ **DIVVIES BAKERY** makes a semisweet chocolate chip that comes in the standard chocolate chip size (right in the middle of the two Enjoy Life products). These chocolate chips are dairy-free and nut-free, but do contain soy lecithin.

✦ **HAIN CELESTIAL GROUP** makes a dairy-free chocolate chip under the brand name Chocolate Dream. These semisweet baking chips are also standard-sized like the Divvies chocolate chips, and like the Divvies product they do contain soy lecithin.

As for white chocolate chips, they aren't actually chocolate—they contain no cocoa liquor. Non-dairy white chocolate chips do exist (manufactured by kosher or vegan companies), but may contain soy lecithin and I don't recommend substituting them for chocolate chips.

So why do you need to care about soy lecithin? Soy lecithin is extracted from soybean oil and then added back to many foods (including shortening and chocolate) as an emulsifier or stabilizer. In fact, it's common to see it listed as "soy lecithin (emulsifier)" on food labels. Soy lecithin has no nutritional value; it's simply fat that helps hold the final food product together as a solid.

As I noted earlier (see "Reading Labels," page 6), the FDA requires that soy lecithin be labeled according to the food allergen labeling laws. But as long as the soy lecithin was derived from highly refined soybean oil, there may be little cause for concern, even for those with an allergy to soy protein. The FDA has this to say about the allergic potential of lecithin derived from soy:

As noted, lecithin derived from soy contains very small amounts of soy protein and it is generally used in small amounts, whether for a functional or technical effect in the finished food or as an incidental additive. The proteins in soy lecithin have been found, in some cases, to be soy allergens, and there are a few case reports in the medical literature of allergic reactions to lecithin derived from soy. However, allergy to lecithin derived from soy has been neither definitively established nor definitively negated by oral food challenge studies. Despite its widespread use in the food supply, FDA is aware of only a few allergen-related complaints about FDA-regulated products containing lecithin derived from soy. Also, FDA is aware that some clinicians believe that

foods containing lecithin derived from soy present little or no allergic risk to soy-sensitive consumers, and these physicians do not advise their soy allergic patients to avoid lecithin derived from soy.[17]

Quite simply, this is a gray area that you and your physician should discuss to determine what is right for your family.

Once you find your favorite chocolate products, I suggest you stock up. Chocolate has a very long shelf life. While the manufacturers often label the expiration date as eighteen months after packaging, chocolate can keep much longer if it is stored in a cool, dry spot. Chocolate does have a tendency to separate when it's exposed to very warm or very cold temperatures. When this happens, you will notice a white or gray coating on the chocolate, referred to as bloom. If you are using the chocolate for baking, this is nothing to be concerned about; it can still be melted and used in your recipes. I don't recommend storing chocolate in the refrigerator or freezer. If you are ordering by mail or online, keep in mind that many vendors will not ship chocolate during the warmer months due to the possibility of melting.

Remember that chocolate is a fat. Does that mean you should avoid it? Absolutely not! I would never think of depriving you of chocolate, but it is something to be aware of as you are baking. You may be able to use less of other fats in your chocolate recipes. For example, a cake that requires 8 tablespoons of shortening may only need 6—or even 4—if you are using baking chocolate or chocolate chips.

Another thing to keep in mind about chocolate is that it is acidic. This means that you will see an immediate lift reaction when using baking soda. In some chocolate recipes, baking soda (or baking soda and vinegar) may be the only leavening agents needed, such as in the Basic Chocolate Cupcakes that follow.

Basic Chocolate Cupcakes

Legend has it that during World War II, when eggs and butter were rationed, a version of chocolate cake called Wacky Cake (also known as Crazy Cake or other similar terms) became very popular. Some would argue that the Wacky Cake goes back even further—to the Depression. It got its name because—well, who would have expected that you could make a cake without eggs or dairy? It turns out it was easy and inexpensive. Of course the bakers of the early twentieth century didn't realize it, but they were baking (nearly) allergen-free! It's just one step further to replacing the wheat with gluten-free grains as I did here.

This recipe uses simple ingredients. If your daughter tells you at the last minute that she needs cupcakes for school tomorrow, chances are you'll have everything you need to prepare these. Total time from start to finish is just under half an hour. Double the recipe for a larger batch, or for a double-layer cake.

Notice how the cocoa powder interacts with the baking soda and the vinegar to provide the lift for the cupcakes.

{ MAKES 12 CUPCAKES }

1½ cups gluten-free flour blend

½ teaspoon xanthan gum (leave out if your flour blend contains xanthan gum)

¾ cup sugar

¼ cup unsweetened natural cocoa powder

1½ teaspoons baking soda

½ teaspoon salt

6 tablespoons coconut oil, melted

2 tablespoons apple cider vinegar

1 cup water (see tip)

1 teaspoon vanilla extract

1. Preheat the oven to 350°F. Line a muffin tin with baking cups.
2. Mix the flour, xanthan gum (if needed), sugar, cocoa powder, baking soda, and salt together in a medium bowl, making sure the cocoa is fully incorporated. Set it aside.
3. Combine the coconut oil, vinegar, water, and vanilla together in a large bowl, with a mixer on medium-low speed, about 30 seconds.
4. Gradually add the flour mixture to the wet ingredients. Blend completely.
5. Spoon the batter into the baking cups, filling each cup about ¾ full.
6. Bake at 350°F for 20 to 24 minutes until a toothpick comes out clean.

TIPS

* For a richer taste, try a non-dairy milk instead of water.
* Frost with Creamy Vanilla Frosting (page 109), or serve them unfrosted.
* Be sure to transfer the cupcakes to a cooling rack within 20 minutes of removing them from the oven.

Double Chocolate Muffins

Double Chocolate Muffins

In the last recipe just one type of chocolate was used—cocoa powder. Here, the chocolate taste is provided by unsweetened chocolate, chocolate hemp milk, and the added chocolate chips, resulting in a pastry that is less sweet than the cupcakes—and quite suitable for breakfast.

Note that the two fats—the shortening and the chocolate—are melted together and combined before adding them to the wet ingredients. This ensures that the chocolate spreads evenly in the batter.

{ MAKES 10 TO 12 MUFFINS }

2 cups gluten-free flour blend

½ teaspoon xanthan gum (leave out if your flour blend contains xanthan gum)

½ cup sugar

3 teaspoons baking powder

½ teaspoon salt

½ cup unsweetened allergen-free baking chocolate

8 tablespoons (1 stick) Earth Balance Natural Shortening

½ cup unsweetened applesauce

½ cup flaxseed gel (equal to 2 eggs)

1 cup chocolate hemp milk

1 teaspoon vanilla extract

⅔ cup allergen-free chocolate chips

1. Preheat the oven to 350°F. Spray a muffin tin with cooking oil.
2. Mix the flour, xanthan gum (if needed), sugar, baking powder, and salt together in a medium bowl. Set it aside.
3. Melt the baking chocolate and shortening together in a small bowl. Stir these two ingredients together thoroughly.
4. Combine the applesauce, flaxseed gel, hemp milk, and vanilla together in a large bowl, with a mixer on medium-low speed, about 1 minute.
5. Add the chocolate and shortening mixture and blend for 1 minute more.
6. Gradually add the flour mixture to the wet ingredients. Blend completely.
7. Spoon the batter into the cups of the muffin tin.
8. Bake at 350°F for 30 to 34 minutes, until a toothpick comes out clean.

TIPS

* Melting the chocolate and shortening together can be done either in a small saucepan over low heat, or in a microwave. If you melt them on the stove, be sure to stir constantly to prevent burning. If you melt them in the microwave, do so slowly—10 or 20 seconds at a time, stirring in between—until just melted.
* Allergen-free chocolate chips may be substituted for unsweetened baking chocolate, if necessary (see "About Chocolate," page 189).

Triple-Play Chocolate Cake

What's better than just one or two types of chocolate? You guessed it—three! I love layering the tastes of different types of chocolate together. In this Triple-Play Chocolate Cake I have also combined the textures of flaxseed gel and applesauce to give the cake a rich—almost fudgy—texture. While I haven't skimped on the sugar, using applesauce allowed me to reduce the amount of fat needed in the recipe.

I like this cake best with Creamy Vanilla Frosting (page 109) but for a truly decadent treat, try it with a double recipe of chocolate Ganache (page 201). This is a special-occasion cake. It's sweet, it's moist, and it is most definitely chocolate!

{ MAKES 1 DOUBLE-LAYER CAKE, 12 TO 16 SERVINGS }

2½ cups gluten-free flour blend

½ teaspoon xanthan gum (leave out if your flour blend contains xanthan gum)

1½ cups sugar

½ cup unsweetened natural cocoa powder

4 teaspoons baking powder

1 teaspoon salt

4 tablespoons (½ stick) Earth Balance Natural Shortening

1 cup allergen-free chocolate chips

½ cup unsweetened applesauce

1 cup flaxseed gel (equal to 4 eggs)

2 cups chocolate hemp milk

2 teaspoons vanilla extract

1. Preheat the oven to 350°F. Spray two 8- or 9-inch round cake pans with cooking oil.
2. Mix the flour, xanthan gum (if needed), sugar, cocoa powder, baking powder, and salt together in a medium bowl. Set it aside.
3. Melt the shortening and chocolate chips together in a small bowl. Stir these two ingredients together thoroughly.
4. Combine the applesauce, flaxseed gel, hemp milk, and vanilla together in a large bowl, with a mixer on medium-low speed, about 1 minute.
5. Add the chocolate and shortening mixture and blend for 1 minute more.
6. Gradually add the flour mixture to the wet ingredients. Blend completely.
7. Pour the batter equally into the prepared cake tins.
8. Bake at 350°F for 25 to 30 minutes, until a toothpick comes out clean.

TIPS

* This recipe can easily be used to make a sheet cake. Use a 9 by 13-inch pan, and bake at 350°F for 30 to 35 minutes.
* I make this cake most frequently as a double-layer cake, but it also makes a great single-layer cake (use half the ingredients) covered with Ganache (page 201).
* Allow the cake to cool thoroughly on a cooling rack before frosting.

Triple-Play Chocolate Cake

A Super Simple Way to Decorate a Cake

IT WAS MY grandmother's job to make the birthday cakes for the family. She called it a job, but she surely would have balked if anyone suggested she hand over the baton. Memere was able to make birthday cakes that looked as if they came from a bakery, even though she wouldn't think of buying cake from the store. When I was twelve she shared her secret with me, and it's a technique I use to this day.

How the cake looks may not matter except on special occasions, but it's good to be able to decorate a cake quickly, if you need to. This is a technique for those of us who haven't taken a cake decorating class and don't have the time to spend with a pastry bag and multiple frostings. This method works equally well on cakes of all shapes and sizes.

MEMERE'S METHOD FOR DECORATING A CAKE

1. Use a butter knife to smooth the frosting over the cake, being sure to cover any opaque spots. The frosting on the top of the cake should be about ¼ inch thick.
2. Using the flat edge of a butter knife, gently draw vertical lines through the frosting, from one edge of the cake to the other. Be careful not to cut into the cake. Keep the lines parallel, and about ½ inch apart. Continue drawing vertical lines until the entire cake is lined.
3. Turn the cake so that the lines you just drew are now horizontal.
4. Once again, using the flat edge of a butter knife, gently draw vertical lines through the frosting, from one edge of the cake to the other. The new lines will intersect the lines drawn in step 2. Keep the lines parallel, and about ½ inch apart. Continue drawing vertical lines until the entire cake has been crisscrossed. You will have created a grid pattern, with the edges of the lines softly folding inward as though each section of frosting has been added separately.
5. Add any additional decorations you desire. Don't forget the candles!

Ganache

Ganache is typically made with chocolate and heavy cream, resulting in a dense coating for cakes or pastries. It's pourable when slightly cooled, and hardens when completely cooled. Ganache will have a slight sheen to it when set, making it a very nice cake topping. My recipe uses a combination of shortening and non-dairy milk in place of the cream, but the result is just as good.

{ MAKES ABOUT 1 CUP OF GANACHE, ENOUGH TO FROST A SINGLE-LAYER CAKE }

2 tablespoons Earth Balance Natural Shortening (see tip)
¼ cup chocolate hemp milk
1 cup allergen-free chocolate chips

1. Melt the shortening, in a medium saucepan, over low heat.
2. Add the hemp milk and stir the ingredients together. Bring the mixture to a low boil over medium-low heat, about 3 minutes, stirring occasionally.
3. Reduce the heat to low, and add the chocolate chips. Stir until the chocolate is melted.
4. Remove the saucepan from the heat. Stir vigorously for another 2 to 3 minutes.
5. Let it cool.
6. After 30 to 45 minutes of cooling, stir the mixture gently (to ensure that no sections have hardened) and pour it over the cake. Use a spatula to spread the frosting evenly.

TIPS

* The shortening provides a thickness that oils will not. If you need to replace the Earth Balance Natural Shortening in this recipe, use a solid palm oil shortening (see page 48).
* Make sure the cake you are pouring the ganache over has cooled completely before you frost it.

Not All Chocolate Is the Same

EARLIER I TOUCHED on the fact that there is little consistency in how chocolate products are labeled, and that the quality (and taste) of chocolate can vary tremendously (see page 188). Of course, "better" is a matter of personal preference; some of us like our chocolate sweeter and smoother, and others prefer it grainier and more bitter. While you can get a sense of how sweet the chocolate is by looking at the product labels (either by the cacao percentage or the sugar content), the only way to really tell the quality of chocolate is to taste it.

It's also true that not all chocolate products perform the same way. Slight shifts in fat-to-sugar ratios, the quality of the cacao beans, and the presence (or lack of) an emulsifier (e.g., soy lecithin—see page 193) can all make a difference in your recipes. To demonstrate how chocolate can vary, I have devised an experiment for you, which tests how quickly the Eggless Chocolate Mousse (which follows) will set when made with two different chocolate chips. I have chosen the chocolate mousse for this test because chocolate is clearly the dominant taste and because this dessert can be made relatively quickly and then observed as it sets. In the first batch I use Enjoy Life Mini Chips, and in the second batch I use Schokinag Bittersweet Chocolate Chips (available in the United States from King Arthur Flour).

First, let's take a look at the ingredients as listed on the packages:

ENJOY LIFE MINI CHIPS: Evaporated cane juice, chocolate liquor, non-dairy cocoa butter (with 5 grams of fat and 7 grams of sugar)

SCHOKINAG BITTERSWEET CHOCOLATE CHIPS: Cocoa liquor, sugar, cocoa butter, soy lecithin, pure vanilla (with 6 grams of fat and 6 grams of sugar)

The ingredient lists of both products are very similar, with the Enjoy Life chips having slightly more sugar, and the other chips have a little bit more fat and soy lecithin added as an emulsifier. Now, let's experiment:

THE BEHAVIOR AND TASTE OF DIFFERENT CHOCOLATE CHIPS IN BAKING

Preparation: Prepare the Eggless Chocolate Mousse (page 204) twice, using a different chocolate chip each time. Keep all other ingredients constant. This experiment is best done with a partner, so that two batches of chocolate mousse can be prepared simultaneously. Be sure to have all of the ingredients ready to go for both batches of chocolate mousse before you begin.

After baking: Let the mousse cool and transfer it to the serving dishes. Use the same size and type of serving dishes for both batches. Mark the batches so that you will be able to tell which is which (I used a string around the base of one set of serving dishes).

Observe: Notice how each of these products behaves differently. Here's what I observed:

Prior to refrigeration: The mousse made with Enjoy Life chips appeared to be slightly thicker right after mixing. Both batches appeared to be thickening equally after cooling for 30 minutes.

During refrigeration: The Schokinag batch was gelling quite well at 1 hour, and was fully set at 2 hours. The Enjoy Life batch still had some pour up the sides of the serving bowl at 1 hour, and at 2 hours it was gelling. While there was no movement whatsoever with the chocolate mousse made from the Schokinag chips at 4 hours, the chocolate mousse made from the Enjoy Life chips never totally set, even after 8 hours.

After refrigeration: The mousse made with the Enjoy Life chips was creamy and had a smooth chocolate taste. The mousse made with the Schokinag chips was grainier, and had a hint of a bitter chocolate taste.

Besides the noticeable difference in taste, I concluded that the presence of the soy lecithin in the ingredients does help the mousse set. As a single serving dish, either chocolate chip will work equally well. If I were planning to make a chocolate mousse tart (which would require slicing), I would choose a chocolate chip with soy lecithin (unless you must avoid soy lecithin). Try the same experiment on your own, with different chocolate chips to explore the taste and properties of the chocolate.

Eggless Chocolate Mousse

Some recipes made with eggs are really all about the eggs. For example, French toast without the eggs is really just fried bread. Chocolate mousse, on the other hand, while traditionally made with eggs, is really all about the chocolate—and yes, it can be made without eggs.

While the time spent actually preparing this dessert is minimal (20 minutes, tops), it must be refrigerated prior to serving. That makes it a great choice to prepare ahead for special occasions when you'd rather spend time with family and friends than slave away in the kitchen.

Serve this plain or with Whipped Coconut Cream (page 44) and allergen-free chocolate shavings.

{ MAKES 8 SERVINGS }

4 tablespoons (½ stick) Earth Balance Natural Shortening

2 cups chocolate hemp milk

4½ teaspoons Ener-G Egg Replacer mixed with 6 tablespoons chocolate hemp milk (equal to 3 eggs)

2 cups allergen-free chocolate chips

1. Melt the shortening in a medium saucepan over low heat.
2. Raise the temperature to medium-high and add the chocolate hemp milk. Stir together completely. Whisk occasionally and bring the mixture just to a rolling boil.
3. Quickly add the egg replacer mixture, whisking to blend completely, for 30 seconds. The mixture will start to thicken.
4. Remove the saucepan from the heat.
5. Whisk in the chocolate chips, 1 cup at a time.
6. Continue whisking until the mousse is completely blended and deep chocolate in color.
7. Let the mousse cool for approximately 30 minutes.
8. Spoon the mousse into serving cups, and cover with plastic wrap. Let it set in the refrigerator for at least 4 hours prior to serving.

TIPS

* Be careful not to let the mousse set before transferring it to the serving cups and refrigerating.
* Depending on the chocolate you use, the mousse may require longer refrigeration (see "Not All Chocolate Is the Same," page 202).

Chocolate No-Nut Crisp

It can be difficult to find a chocolate bar that is made without milk (or traces of milk and nuts). This chocolate crisp is a make-your-own candy bar that can be prepared in minutes, without turning the oven on. Use your favorite non-dairy chocolate, or try this with different chocolates to see which you prefer. See page 192 for allergen-free chocolate options.

For a special treat, spread a layer of sunflower seed butter (available at the grocery store) between two pieces of chocolate crisp. Yum!

{ MAKES ABOUT 16 SERVINGS }

2 tablespoons Earth Balance Natural Shortening

1¾ cups allergen-free chocolate chips

¾ cup gluten-free crisped rice cereal (see tip)

1. Line a 9-inch square pan with wax paper.
2. Melt the shortening in a medium saucepan over medium-low heat.
3. Add the chocolate chips and use a spoon to stir continuously while melting.
4. When the mixture is completely melted, remove the pan from the heat. Let it cool for 5 minutes.
5. Fold in the rice cereal.
6. While still warm, spread the mixture in the lined pan.
7. Refrigerate for at least 2 hours. The chocolate will harden.
8. Use the wax paper to lift the chocolate block from the baking dish. Cut or break the crisp into desired-size chunks and serve.

TIPS

❋ My favorite crisped rice cereal is Erewhon Gluten Free Crispy Brown Rice cereal. It contains just three ingredients: organic brown rice, organic brown rice syrup, and sea salt.

❋ Be careful not to let the chocolate burn while it is melting. Stir continuously and keep the heat low.

Chocolate Cranberry Rice Cookies

A cookie that you don't have to bake? You betcha! This cookie reminds me of chocolate lace. My twist on that classic cookie is gluten-free and allergen-free, and adds the surprise of cranberries. Like the Chocolate No-Nut Crisp (page 205), this is made on the stovetop, and can be prepared in minutes.

{ MAKES 20 TO 24 COOKIES }

1 tablespoon Earth Balance Natural Shortening
½ cup allergen-free chocolate chips
1½ cups gluten-free crisped rice cereal
½ cup dried cranberries (see tips)

1. Line a cookie sheet with wax paper.
2. Melt the shortening in a medium saucepan over medium-low heat.
3. Add the chocolate chips and use a spoon to stir continuously while melting.
4. When the mixture is completely melted, remove the pan from the heat. Let it cool for 5 minutes.
5. Fold in the crisped rice cereal and cranberries.
6. Drop the mixture, by the tablespoon, onto the lined cookie sheet, allowing room between the cookies for them to spread.
7. Refrigerate for at least 2 hours prior to serving.

TIPS

* The dried cranberries can be sweetened or unsweetened.
* Avoid buying dried cranberries (or any other produce) from open bins or packages that have been bundled in-house. A prepackaged container is less likely to include potential contaminants (see page 13).

Basic Brownies

My all-time favorite dessert is the chocolate brownie. I love the simplicity of a brownie with a rich chocolate taste. Brownies are easy to prepare—it's a simple batter. And they're easy to serve as finger food—no plates or utensils are needed.

Most brownie recipes (including gluten-free and dairy-free versions) contain eggs—sometimes as many as three or four. The trick to making a brownie without eggs is to keep the sugar content low; too much sugar and the brownies will burn. My version uses flaxseed gel instead of eggs, which helps to give the brownies texture and hold them together. The result is the perfect medium between a fudgy and a cakey brownie. I've also chosen to use unsweetened baking chocolate—both for the low sugar content and the high fat content, which helps to give these brownies a subtle sheen.

For a great summer treat, serve brownies with dairy-free ice cream (see page 50) and Chocolate Glaze (page 177).

{ MAKES 16 BROWNIES }

¾ cup gluten-free flour blend

¼ teaspoon xanthan gum (leave out if your flour blend contains xanthan gum)

⅔ cup sugar

½ teaspoon baking powder

¼ teaspoon salt

7 tablespoons Earth Balance Natural Shortening

⅓ cup unsweetened allergen-free baking chocolate

¼ cup chocolate hemp milk

½ cup flaxseed gel (equal to 2 eggs)

1 teaspoon vanilla extract

½ cup allergen-free chocolate chips (optional)

1. Preheat the oven to 350°F. Spray a 9-inch square baking dish with cooking oil.
2. Mix the flour, xanthan gum (if needed), sugar, baking powder, and salt together in a medium bowl. Set it aside.
3. Melt the shortening and chocolate together in a small bowl. Stir these two ingredients together thoroughly.
4. Combine the hemp milk, flaxseed gel, and vanilla together in a large bowl, with a mixer on medium-low speed, about 1 minute.
5. Add the chocolate and shortening mixture and blend for 1 minute more.
6. Gradually add the flour mixture to the wet ingredients. Blend completely.
7. Stir in the chocolate chips (if desired) by hand.
8. Pour the batter into the prepared baking dish, spreading to the edges.
9. Bake at 350°F for 22 to 25 minutes.

TIPS

✳ I like to make a batch of brownies and freeze them. Slice them before freezing and you can take out individual portions as you need them. Simply let them sit out on the counter for a couple of hours or overnight in the refrigerator to defrost.

✳ Allergen-free chocolate chips may be substituted for unsweetened baking chocolate, if necessary (see "About Chocolate" page 189). If you do so, forgo the optional chocolate chips.

Basic Brownies

11

Extra Credit:

Bars, Cookies and Stovetop Delights to Round Out Your Repertoire

NOT EVERY DESSERT IS made from a batter or dough. Some of the quickest and tastiest treats are those that are practically thrown together, such as a trail mix or fresh fruit with Whipped Coconut Cream (page 44) on top. In this chapter we'll explore a handful of simple treats, including some that are baked on the stovetop rather than the oven (see "Baking on the Stovetop," page 215). The recipes in this chapter do not require a stand mixer, and many can be made in just one bowl.

This chapter is for those days when you just need

a break—the kids are sick, you've had a bad day at work, it's raining for the fifth day in a row, or you just need some comfort food. There are no rules to follow in this chapter; just use the skills you've learned, bake, and enjoy!

Rocky Oat Bars

When you think of "rocky," you might be envisioning a traditional rocky road combination of nuts, chocolate, and marshmallow in a milk-based ice cream. My version of "rocky" keeps the chocolate (dairy-free, of course), adds fruit (raisins), and substitutes hemp seeds for nuts, in an oat base. The result is a power-packed, tasty treat.

The hemp seeds add a soft crunch to these bars, which can be sliced into whatever size you need. They're great warm, and make a terrific on-the-go breakfast bar or lunchbox snack.

{ MAKES 8 TO 12 BARS }

2 cups quick-cooking gluten-free oats
½ teaspoon salt
2 tablespoons grapeseed oil
½ cup unsweetened applesauce
2 tablespoons honey
¼ cup flaxseed gel (equal to 1 egg)
¼ cup raisins (see tip)
¼ cup shelled hemp seeds (see tip)
¼ cup allergen-free chocolate chips (see tip)

1. Preheat the oven to 350°F. Spray a 9-inch square baking dish with cooking oil.
2. In a large bowl, stir the oats and salt together with a fork. Add the oil and toss to coat the oats. Let it sit for 5 minutes.
3. Whisk together the applesauce, honey, and flaxseed gel in a small mixing bowl, by hand.
4. Add the wet ingredients to the oat mixture. Mix completely with a fork.
5. Stir in the raisins, hemp seeds, and chocolate chips.
6. Pour the mixture into the pan and spread it to the edges. Press it down and fill any holes.
7. Bake at 350°F for 16 to 18 minutes, until browned.
8. Let cool and slice into bars.

TIPS

* If your raisins are very dry, soak them in warm water for 20 minutes; drain before using.
* If you prefer a bar with more of a nutty taste, substitute sunflower seeds for hemp seeds.
* Enjoy Life Mini Chips (see page 192) work really well in these bars and make them less messy to take along with you in warmer weather. If you plan to take them on the go, wrap them in parchment paper squares, then store them in a plastic sandwich bag or brown bag.
* The applesauce and flaxseed gel help to hold these together.

Banana Oatmeal Cookies

Bananas and oatmeal—of course! These cookies are a snack version of the traditional breakfast oatmeal topped with bananas.

Not all cookies need to be refrigerated before baking. Unlike a traditional cookie recipe that requires preparing dough, these cookies are super simple. Just toss the ingredients in a bowl, drop the cookies on a baking sheet, and set the timer. If you are a multitasker (like me) I think you'll find these cookies will become a favorite because they're easy to make between laundry batches (or even while you're on a conference call). Great warm, these make a terrific breakfast cookie!

{ MAKES ABOUT 24 COOKIES }

2 cups quick-cooking gluten-free oats
½ teaspoon salt
1 teaspoon baking powder
2 tablespoons grapeseed oil
3 very ripe or frozen bananas (see tips)
¼ cup flaxseed gel (equal to 1 egg)

1. Preheat the oven to 350°F. Line a baking sheet with parchment paper.
2. Toss the oats, salt, baking powder, and oil in a small bowl until the oats are coated with oil. Set it aside for 5 minutes.
3. In a large mixing bowl, mash the bananas with a fork or potato masher until they are juicy but still lumpy.
4. Add the flaxseed gel to the bananas and whisk them together with a fork.
5. Add the oat mixture to the wet ingredients, and stir together completely. The mixture should be wet but still lumpy.
6. Drop tablespoons of the cookie mix onto the prepared baking sheet. Flatten the tops.
7. Bake at 350°F for 16 to 18 minutes until browned.

* Use the ripest bananas you can find.
* When using frozen bananas, either thaw them at room temperature or place them in the microwave for 60 seconds. Use a sharp knife to slice the skin open and release the banana. (I suggest doing this right over your bowl.) The banana will be watery, and that's okay.
* These cookies are intended to be roughly formed; don't worry about the shape or size as you drop them.
* For variety, try adding ½ cup of raisins or allergen-free chocolate chips.

Mixed Berry Crumble

During the summer, fresh berries are plentiful in the Northeast; if you live near a pick-your-own farm, this is the time to stock up on berries. I freeze what I can't use in the summer for winter pies.

It really doesn't matter which berries you choose to mix in this crumble—any combination of soft berries (e.g., blueberries, raspberries, blackberries, strawberries), or even a single berry, will do. Serve this with your favorite dairy-free ice cream (see page 50).

The beauty of a crumble is that is can be served in a bowl—no need to worry about a pie crust breaking before it reaches the plate. It's just easy and suitable for kids of all ages.

{ MAKES 8 TO 12 SERVINGS }

5 cups mixed berries (see tip)

2 tablespoons fresh lime juice

¼ cup granulated sugar

¼ cup corn starch

¾ cup light brown sugar

¾ cup gluten-free quick-cooking oats

4 tablespoons (½ stick) Earth Balance Natural Shortening, cold

1. Preheat the oven to 350°F. Spray a 9-inch square baking dish with cooking oil.
2. In a large bowl, mix together the fruit and lime juice, by hand.
3. In a small bowl, mix together the sugar and corn starch. Sprinkle it over the fruit mixture and toss to coat the fruit. Set it aside.
4. In a large bowl, combine the brown sugar and oats. Break up any lumps of brown sugar.
5. Cut the shortening into tablespoon-sized pieces. Use a pastry cutter or pastry fork to cut the shortening into the oat mixture.
6. Spread the fruit mixture evenly in the baking dish.
7. Sprinkle the oat mixture on top of the fruit. Use the flat side of a spoon to lightly pack the topping.
8. Bake at 350°F for 30 to 35 minutes, until the fruit is bubbling around the edges.

TIPS

* If you are using strawberries, be sure to remove the stems and chop them (in half or thirds) so they are about the same size as the rest of your berries.
* If fresh berries are not available you may use frozen (unsweetened) berries. Thaw and drain them before using.
* This is best warm. Keep leftovers in the refrigerator and reheat for 30 seconds in a microwave.

Mixed Berry Crumble

Baking on the Stovetop

WHO SAID THAT baking has to be done in an oven? Common definitions of *baking* describe it as "cooking with dry heat." While that is most often in an oven, the principles of baking also apply on the stovetop.

In both cases, you are using dry heat, which causes moisture to evaporate and the chemical properties of the ingredients to interact. In both cases, the ingredients will solidify when heated. And of course, in both cases, you expect to create something delicious. Yup, I call that baking!

When baking on the stovetop, you must be present. Unlike putting muffins in the oven and walking away until the buzzer rings, baking on the stovetop often requires constant stirring, and always requires a watchful eye. That said, it's usually fairly quick and can be accomplished with just a few tools—the most important are a good medium stainless-steel pan and a medium whisk.

As you bake on the stovetop, pay special attention to the order in which the ingredients are added, and at what temperature. For example, if a mixture needs to be brought "just to a rolling boil," make sure you remove it from the heat or reduce the heat as soon as the bubbles are large and expanding. If the recipe says to boil until it starts to solidify, have a spoon nearby so you can test the thickness.

Pay special attention to my choice of egg substitute in the two pudding recipes that follow and in the Eggless Chocolate Mousse (page 204). Most often, egg is used in puddings and mousses to thicken the mixture. Without a traditional egg to play that role, I have chosen Ener-G Egg Replacer. Notice that when you add the egg replacer, you will see an immediate thickening—that's success. If you choose to substitute for the egg replacer, you will need to add a starch (e.g., corn starch or tapioca starch) to thicken the pudding.

Clockwise from upper left: Blackberry Jam, Raspberry Jam, and Strawberry Jam

Strawberry Jam

While it's not too hard to find jams that are free of the most common food allergens, even grocery store jams that bill themselves as "all fruit" often contain such ingredients as "natural flavor," and, regardless of the fruit on the front label, many have pear and grape juice in the first few ingredients. I have kept my recipe very simple, and have not added fruit pectin (another common ingredient in off-the-shelf jams).

I started making jam when I was able to pick my own fresh fruit at my local farm. There is nothing quite like a fresh strawberry or raspberry. Extras can be frozen for future baking projects, or made into— you guessed it—jam. I like to make my jams as needed, but if you're familiar with preserving techniques, this is the time to get those jam jars boiling.

Try these with leftover Dinner Muffins (page 162) for breakfast or in Strawberry Oat Squares (page 220).

{ MAKES ABOUT ¾ CUP OF JAM }

1 cup crushed strawberries (about 1½ cups uncrushed)

½ cup sugar

1. Crush the strawberries in a medium saucepan. They should be juicy.
2. Add ¼ cup of the sugar and bring the mixture to a rolling boil over medium-high heat, stirring occasionally.
3. Reduce the heat to medium and stir in the remaining ¼ cup of sugar.
4. Boil over medium heat for 5 to 8 minutes, until the sauce starts to thicken.
5. Use a spoon to test for doneness. If the mixture drips completely off the spoon after cooling for about a minute, boil for a few minutes longer.
6. Skim the foam from the top of the jam.
7. Let the jam cool. It will solidify further during cooling.

TIPS

* This jam contains less sugar than you would typically find in a jam recipe. If you prefer a sweeter jam, double the sugar.
* This recipe is easily scalable for large quantities of jam. Be sure to use larger pots as you scale up. The jam will increase in volume as you boil.
* Store jams in the refrigerator.

✳ VARIATIONS:

BLACKBERRY JAM: Use 1 cup of crushed blackberries instead of strawberries. Add 1½ teaspoons of fresh lemon juice with the berries.

RASPBERRY JAM: Use 1 cup of crushed raspberries instead of strawberries. Add 1½ teaspoons of fresh lemon juice with the berries.

Strawberry Oat Squares

To make these squares, you will use the same technique to cut the shortening into the flour as you did to make cookies (see page 129), but there's no need to refrigerate the dough before you bake. They are sweet and simple.

Plan enough time to let them cool before cutting. You may find that you always prefer these squares refrigerated.

{ MAKES 16 SQUARES }

1 cup gluten-free flour blend

¼ teaspoon xanthan gum (leave out if your flour blend contains xanthan gum)

1 cup gluten-free quick-cooking oats

½ cup light brown sugar

¼ teaspoon salt

1 teaspoon baking powder

8 tablespoons (1 stick) Earth Balance Natural Shortening, cold

¾ cup Strawberry Jam (page 219) (see tips)

1. Preheat the oven to 350°F. Line a 9-inch square baking dish with parchment paper. Spray a very thin layer of cooking oil over the parchment.

2. Combine the flour, xanthan gum (if needed), oats, brown sugar, salt, and baking powder in a large bowl.

3. Cut the shortening into tablespoon-sized pieces and place them on top of the flour mixture. Use a pastry cutter or pastry fork to cut the shortening into the oat and flour mixture, until it is crumbly.

4. Spread half of the oat mixture in the bottom of the prepared baking dish, spreading to the edges. Gently pat it down to create the bottom layer of the bars.

5. Spoon the jam on top of this layer, in tablespoon-sized portions, and gently spread the jam to cover the bottom layer, leaving the last ½ inch on the edges uncovered.

6. Sprinkle the remaining oat mixture on top of the jam layer to cover completely. Lightly pat down this top layer.

7. Bake at 350°F for 30 to 35 minutes, until the top is lightly browned and the strawberry filling is bubbling. It's okay if the filling peeks through the top layer.

8. Let it cool for at least an hour. Use the parchment paper to lift it from the baking dish and then use a sharp knife to cut it into desired-size bars.

TIPS

* The jam can be prepared well in advance (and refrigerated) or just before baking. Let it cool before spreading it.
* This recipe works equally well with the Raspberry or Blackberry Jam variations (page 219), or your own favorite jam.
* Err on the side of spreading more of the oat mixture on the bottom of the bars than on top.
* Refrigerate what you don't plan to eat within 48 hours.

12

Mix It Up:
Adapting Gluten–Free Baking Mixes for Allergen–Free Results

WHILE YOU MAY ENJOY spending time in the kitchen, you don't always have time to make baked goods from scratch. Sometimes you need cupcakes for a party on short notice, or a quick and easy snack for a lunch box tomorrow. Sometimes, you just need a simple answer.

Just ten years ago it seemed that a family needing to eat allergen-free had to forgo muffins, cookies, and cakes forever, or bake them all from scratch, but that's no longer the case. Today, gluten-free baking mixes are readily available on the market, and this is great news for food-allergic families. But while these mixes do not contain wheat, the recipes often require adding milk and eggs and need to be adapted for food-allergic families.

I have tried every gluten-free baking mix I can get my hands on and have selected some that I like best to share with you here. In this chapter, I'll show you how to make substitutions for those added ingredients to transform a gluten-free baking mix into an allergen-free treat. I have made these recipes many times, testing different substitutions to find the best replacements. By the time you've tried the adaptations in this chapter, you'll be ready to go out and create your own!

Selecting a Gluten–Free Baking Mix

WHEN I SEE a new gluten-free baking mix on the shelf at the health food store, I first check the ingredients to make sure that the mix itself does not contain any food allergens. The product labels for these baking mixes must follow the FDA food-allergy labeling rules (see page 6), and that's the place to start. Because they are gluten-free, we already know they shouldn't contain wheat, but they may contain milk and soy proteins, as well as other allergens, so read the labels carefully. (See page 12 for more on the proposed gluten-free labeling laws.) Some brands you'll want to explore include:

✳ **AUTHENTIC FOODS**
authenticfoods.com
Authentic Foods is a California-based company dedicated to creating gluten-free and wheat-free products. While not as readily available on the East Coast, the baking mixes from this company consistently perform well.

✳ **BETTY CROCKER** (gluten-free line)
bettycrocker.com/products/gluten-free-baking-mixes
Betty Crocker introduced its gluten-free baking mixes in 2010, and they are now available in most large chain grocery stores.

✳ **BOB'S RED MILL** (gluten-free line)
bobsredmill.com/gluten-free
Bob's Red Mill produces its gluten-free baking mixes in a dedicated wheat-free and milk-free facility. Look for packages with the gluten-free banner. Some products contain warning labels for soy and tree nuts.

✳ **GLUTEN-FREE PANTRY**
glutino.com/our-products/gluten-free-pantry
The Gluten-Free Pantry baking mixes by Glutino are produced in a dedicated gluten-free facility and undergo in-house testing for gluten. Some products carry warning labels for soy and/or milk.

CRASH COURSE

✳ JULES GLUTEN FREE
julesglutenfree.com
This company uses its patent-pending Jules Gluten Free Flour (which contains Expandex modified tapioca starch) as the basis for its baking mixes. They are available online.

✳ KING ARTHUR FLOUR (gluten-free line)
kingarthurflour.com/glutenfree
Introduced in 2010, this Vermont-based company's gluten-free baking mixes are produced in a dedicated facility that is free of gluten and the top eight food allergens. They can be found in most mainstream grocery stores.

✳ NAMASTE FOODS
namastefoods.com
Namaste Foods produces a line of gluten-free and allergen-free baking mixes that are made in a dedicated facility. The mixes contain no corn or potato, or any of the top eight allergens.

✳ ORGRAN
orgran.com/gluten-free
This Australian company creates a line of baking mixes that can be found in some North American health food stores and online. Their baking mixes contain none of the top eight allergens, but most do contain corn.

✳ PAMELA'S PRODUCTS
pamelasproducts.com
These gluten-free baking mixes include some of my family's favorites. While their facility is gluten-free, some mixes do contain milk, and others carry advisory labels.

New brands and products are popping up every day, so be sure to keep an eye out for them. While all of these listed manufacturers produce a gluten-free product line, not all of the products in these lines are allergen-free, and their food-allergen advisory statements vary. Again, make sure you always check the ingredients to determine that a product will work for your particular needs. If you live outside the United States, the concepts in this chapter should also apply to brands that you may be able to find locally.

Once you've determined that a mix is safe for you and your family, there are a couple of other things to consider. While nearly all of these

CRASH COURSE

baking mixes can be made with substitutions, some are more difficult than others to adapt. Here are a few more things to watch out for:

﹡ Brownie mixes with a very high sugar content have a tendency to burn when made with egg replacements. If you're looking for brownie mixes, I recommend choosing a gluten-free mix with less than 18 grams of sugar per serving, or where only one egg is called for.

﹡ Pancakes have a tendency to stick to the pan when made without eggs. If you choose the wrong baking mix, you could end up with a crumbly pancake mess, or waffles that won't release from your waffle iron. Try the Orgran Stonemilled Buckwheat Pancake Mix or Authentic Foods Pancake & Baking Mix to make Pancakes with Chocolate Maple Syrup (page 243) or Blueberry Pancakes (page 230).

﹡ Something else to watch out for are cookie mixes that require a lot of butter; some gluten-free cookies have a tendency to spread in an unruly fashion when non-dairy shortening is used. I recommend looking for cookie mixes that call for one stick of butter (8 tablespoons, or ½ cup) or less (and use non-dairy shortening to replace the butter; see page 50).

Choosing Replacements for Eggs with Gluten-Free Baking Mixes

AS YOU LEARNED in chapter 4, there are many options for replacing eggs, but keep in mind that no egg replacer will solidify quite the way an egg does when heated. Your options for egg replacements can help provide texture, taste, and leavening.

When leavening is the biggest concern, it's best to choose a chemical egg replacer (e.g., Ener-G Egg Replacer). This would be the case for yeast breads and pizza crusts. When texture and taste are bigger concerns (if you're making cakes, muffins, brownies, or cookies), flaxseed gel (page 58) or unsweetened applesauce (page 60) are great choices. These options both result in a denser and chewier finished product. Note the choices I have made to replace eggs in the recipes that follow.

Double Chocolate Brownies from Pamela's Products Chocolate Brownie Mix

I have made these brownies hundreds of times—more often than any other gluten-free baking mix. They are one of my go-to desserts for potluck dinners, after-school snacks, and care packages sent away to college. They are so tasty that even my kids' friends have no idea that they are made allergen-free, until they see my youngest son eating them.

I chose to replace the single egg in this adaptation with the equivalent of two eggs using applesauce because it brings a thickness to the batter, resulting in a chewy brownie. For a more cake-like brownie, use Ener-G Egg Replacer instead of applesauce. While brownies are one of the most difficult desserts to make without eggs, this is one mix that works perfectly, still resulting in a very fudgy brownie.

Be careful! You won't be able to eat just one.

{ MAKES 16 BROWNIES }

BAKING MIX USED: **Pamela's Products Chocolate Brownie Mix**

Instead of adding:	Add:
½ cup oil	½ cup grapeseed oil
1 egg	½ cup unsweetened applesauce (equal to 2 eggs)
¼ cup water	¼ cup water
	½ cup allergen-free chocolate chips (optional) (see page 192)

1. Follow the package preparation instructions, with the above substitutions.

2. Add the chocolate chips last, by hand.

TIPS

* Note that the package for this mix contains an advisory warning that the product may contain traces of milk. The folks at Pamela's Products have told me that this is due to the chocolate chunks, which are processed in a facility that also processes milk chocolate. If the "may contain milk" label is a concern for you (see page 6 to learn more about food-allergen advisory labels) this mix is available in bulk at the Pamela's Products website, without the chocolate chunks (and free of the warning label).

Mixed Berry Scones

Mixed Berry Scones from Namaste Foods No Sugar Added! Muffin Mix

While many of the muffin mixes you will find are high in sugar content, this mix from Namaste Foods has less than 1 gram of sugar per serving, making it perfect for scones. I love that I can control the sugar content by adding my own sweetener, but when these are made with fresh berries, I don't think added sugar is needed. In this recipe I chose applesauce to replace the eggs.

{ MAKES 8 TO 10 SCONES }

BAKING MIX USED: **Namaste Foods No Sugar Added! Muffin Mix (see tip)**

Instead of adding:	*Add:*
2 eggs	½ cup unsweetened applesauce (equal to 2 eggs)
¼ cup oil	¼ cup sunflower oil (see tip)
1 cup water	¾ cup water
	1 cup fresh or frozen mixed berries (see tips)

1. Follow the package preparation instructions, with the above substitutions.

2. Stir in the berries last, by hand.

3. Form the scones (see page 115).

TIPS

* Namaste Foods offers two different muffin mixes; be sure to choose the one that is labeled "No Sugar Added!"
* I prefer sunflower oil with this recipe, but feel free to substitute your favorite oil.
* Try this with different types of berries or raisins.
* If using frozen fruit, defrost and drain the fruit before adding it to your scones.

Blueberry Pancakes from Authentic Foods Pancake & Baking Mix

A great gluten-free pancake baking mix is tough to find. When made without eggs, pancakes often stick to the pan, or they're too flat and runny, but not these! Use Ener-G Egg Replacer in this recipe to create pancakes that fluff up nicely. You might not be able to tell them apart from their wheat cousins. When I make these, even the gluten-eating members of my family beg for more!

{ MAKES 8 TO 12 PANCAKES, 4 TO 6 SERVINGS }

BAKING MIX USED: Authentic Foods Pancake & Baking Mix (1 cup; see tip)

Instead of adding:	Add:
2 eggs	3 teaspoons Ener-G Egg Replacer combined with 4 tablespoons warm water (equal to 2 eggs)
1 cup milk	1 cup original hemp milk
2 tablespoons oil	2 tablespoons grapeseed oil
2 tablespoons maple sugar or brown sugar	2 tablespoons light brown sugar
	¼ cup water (optional; see tip)
	½ cup fresh blueberries

1. Follow the package preparation instructions, with the above substitutions.

2. Stir in the blueberries last, by hand.

TIPS

* You won't use the entire baking mix for this recipe; one package contains about 4 cups of baking mix. Double, triple, or quadruple the added ingredients to make a larger batch.
* I prefer these pancakes with an additional ¼ cup of water. If you like very thick pancakes you may not need to add the water.
* Serve with pure maple syrup.

Low-Sugar Chocolate Muffins from Namaste Foods No Sugar Added! Muffin Mix

Here is a second recipe made from the same muffin mix used to make Mixed Berry Scones (page 229), with very different results.

While some people like to save chocolate for dessert, I believe that chocolate can be for breakfast, too. This recipe is easy and low in calories. The flaxseed gel used to replace the eggs gives the muffins a rich flavor without making them too heavy.

{ MAKES 12 MUFFINS }

BAKING MIX USED: Namaste Foods No Sugar Added! Muffin Mix

Instead of adding:	Add:
	¼ cup unsweetened natural cocoa powder
2 eggs	½ cup flaxseed gel (equal to 2 eggs)
¼ cup oil	¼ cup grapeseed oil
1 cup water	1½ cups chocolate hemp milk

1. Blend the cocoa powder with the baking mix first, before adding it to the wet ingredients.

2. Follow the package preparation instructions, with the above substitutions.

TIPS

* Note that I have suggested replacing the water with chocolate hemp milk, adding another dimension of chocolate flavor. The additional ½ cup of hemp milk offsets the added dry ingredient (cocoa).
* To make this a sweeter muffin, add up to ½ cup of sugar or honey, and reduce the chocolate hemp milk by ¼ cup.

Banana Chocolate Chip Muffins from King Arthur Flour Gluten Free Muffin Mix

This muffin mix is from the gluten-free product line introduced by King Arthur Flour in 2010. This is definitely a sweeter muffin (sugar is the first ingredient), but one that can be made allergen-free with the right egg substitutions. Here I have used a combination of flaxseed gel and bananas to replace the eggs. These muffins also make a great dessert.

{ MAKES 12 MUFFINS }

BAKING MIX USED: King Arthur Flour Gluten Free Muffin Mix

Instead of adding:	Add:
6 tablespoons melted butter or oil	5 tablespoons Earth Balance Natural Shortening, melted
3 large eggs	¼ cup flaxseed gel (equal to 1 egg) 1 medium banana, mashed (equal to 2 eggs) (see tips)
¾ cup milk	¾ cup original hemp milk
	¾ cup allergen-free chocolate chips

1. Follow the package preparation instructions, with the above substitutions.

2. Stir in the chocolate chips last, by hand.

TIPS

* Using banana as an egg replacer gives these muffins a definite banana taste. For an even stronger banana taste, use two mashed bananas and leave out the flaxseed gel.
* To make a non-banana version of these muffins, leave out the banana and use ¾ cup of flaxseed gel.

Carrot Cake from Namaste Foods Spice Cake Mix

Ready to spice it up a bit? Carrot cake made from this Namaste Foods mix is one way to do it. The mix includes cinnamon, nutmeg, and cloves, and a single package makes two layers. This is a great way to add some vitamin A and fiber to your diet.

In this recipe I have chosen flaxseed gel to replace the eggs, which gives the cake added flavor and a nice texture.

{ MAKES 1 DOUBLE-LAYER CAKE, 12 TO 16 SERVINGS }

BAKING MIX USED: **Namaste Foods Spice Cake Mix**

Instead of adding:	*Add:*
3 eggs	¾ cup flaxseed gel (equal to 3 eggs)
⅔ cup oil	¼ cup grapeseed oil
¾ cup water	¾ cup water
	4 medium carrots, finely shredded

1. Follow the package preparation instructions, with the above substitutions.

2. Add the shredded carrots in last, using your mixer.

TIPS

* To make this as a simple spice cake, leave out the carrots and increase the oil to ⅔ cup.
* If you want just a single-layer cake, save half of the mix and use only half of the added ingredients.
* Frost with Creamy Vanilla Frosting (page 109), or use your favorite allergen-free frosting.

Choosing Replacements for Milk, Butter and Yogurt with Gluten-Free Baking Mixes

ON-DAIRY MILK CAN be substituted in equal amounts for cow's milk when baking, and it can also be used to replace water in your baking mixes to enhance the flavor.

Whether you choose rice milk, hemp milk, coconut milk beverage, or another favorite is largely a matter of discretion. I love hemp milk for the nutritional benefits it provides, and I like the flavor it adds. I also find coconut milk easy to bake with, but some people find the taste too strong for their liking. In contrast, while some allergen-free bakers use a lot of rice milk, I find it leaves a grainy taste. The choice is up to you; feel free to swap in your favorite milk in the recipes that follow. When I'm making a chocolate recipe I generally opt for a chocolate milk—I like the extra dimension and richness that it adds. For most other recipes, an original or vanilla milk will be your best bet.

Butter or margarine can be replaced with shortening or oil. I like to keep my refrigerator and pantry stocked with Earth Balance Natural Shortening and Spectrum Organic All Vegetable Shortening to replace butter. If you choose an oil to replace butter, note that you will have more spread in your finished product; this choice works best with simple batters (muffins, cakes, and quick breads). Stick with shortening to replace butter in cookies and crusts (see page 50).

My first choice to replace yogurt or sour cream is usually part unsweetened applesauce or flaxseed gel combined with non-dairy milk; this combination will bring a thickness that milk alone can't provide.

Note the choices I have made for milk products in the recipes that follow, but don't be afraid to try other options and see which you like best. For more detail on non-dairy milk and replacements for butter, margarine, and other dairy products, see pages 35–51.

Spicy Corn Bread from Pamela's Products Cornbread & Muffin Mix

I find corn bread to be the perfect complement to soup, chili, and even pasta. It's great in place of a classic dinner roll, and (being a quick bread) easier to make. I chose coconut oil as a replacement for butter in this recipe because of its light texture.

{ MAKES 12 TO 16 SERVINGS }

BAKING MIX USED: Pamela's Products Cornbread & Muffin Mix

Instead of adding:	Add:
½ cup sugar	⅓ cup agave nectar (see tip)
8 tablespoons butter, melted	7 tablespoons coconut oil, melted (see tip)
2 large eggs	½ cup unsweetened applesauce (equal to 2 eggs)
1 cup water	1 cup water
	⅓ cup jalapeño peppers, seeded and diced finely (optional)

1. Follow the package preparation instructions, with the above substitutions.

2. Stir in the peppers last, by hand.

TIPS

* Because I used agave nectar I was able to reduce the amount of sweetener.
* See page 48 for shortening alternatives if you need to avoid coconut.
* For an even spicier corn bread, double the jalapeño.

Spicy Corn Bread

Hamburger/Sandwich Rolls from Jules Gluten Free Bread Mix

If you were to stock your pantry with just one yeast bread mix to bake allergen-free, this is the one I would suggest you buy. This versatile mix is based on Jules Gluten Free All Purpose Flour, and includes the yeast packet. Although some gluten-free breads are too flat, are too dry, or become too soggy after the first day, this formula solves those issues. The directions I share here are to make buns (for hamburgers or sandwiches).

I chose a combination of applesauce and hemp milk to replace the yogurt in this recipe; any dairy-free milk mixed with applesauce would work equally well.

{ MAKES 8 TO 10 ROLLS }

BAKING MIX USED: Jules Gluten Free Bread Mix

Instead of adding:	*Add:*
2 tablespoons honey or agave nectar	2 tablespoons honey
1¼ cups yogurt	½ cup original hemp milk ½ cup unsweetened applesauce
1 teaspoon apple cider vinegar	1 teaspoon apple cider vinegar
¼ cup olive oil	¼ cup olive oil
2 large eggs	3 teaspoons Ener-G Egg Replacer mixed with 4 tablespoons warm water (equal to 2 eggs)
	1 to 3 tablespoons water (as needed)

1. Line a baking sheet with parchment paper.
2. Mix the contents of the included yeast packet with the dry ingredients in a medium bowl. Set it aside.
3. Blend the honey, hemp milk, applesauce, apple cider vinegar, olive oil, and egg replacer mixture together in a large bowl, using a mixer on medium speed, about 2 minutes.
4. Gradually add the dry mixture. Blend completely on medium speed.
5. Add up to 3 tablespoons of water, ½ tablespoon at a time, until the dough is moist and pulling away from the sides of the bowl.
6. Separate the dough into eight to ten equally sized portions. Use your hands to form them into balls. Flatten the rolls to about ½ inch thick and place them on the baking sheet.
7. Proof for 35 to 45 minutes (see "Proofing Methods," page 158).
8. With 5 minutes left to proof, preheat the oven to 350°F.
9. Bake at 350°F for approximately 24 minutes, until the internal temperature measures 200° to 205°F.

(continued)

* Wet your fingers before forming the buns to keep the dough from sticking.
* Although Jules Gluten Free recommends proofing for 30 minutes, I find that an additional 5 to 15 minutes of proofing may be needed.
* To make this as a bread loaf, I recommend using a 9 by 4-inch gluten-free loaf pan (see page 75). Bake for approximately 1 hour.

Chocolate Chip Cookies from Bob's Red Mill Gluten Free Chocolate Chip Cookie Mix

This cookie mix is different than any I have worked with. It uses a combination of garbanzo bean, fava bean, and sorghum flours and results in a chocolate chip cookie that looks just like its cousins made with wheat, butter, and eggs. Instead of butter in this recipe, I use Earth Balance Natural Shortening.

If you don't want to start from scratch to make Chocolate Chip Cookies (page 132), these are the next best thing. Be prepared to get your hands dirty.

{ MAKES 24 COOKIES }

BAKING MIX USED: Bob's Red Mill Gluten Free Chocolate Chip Cookie Mix

Instead of adding:	*Add:*
½ cup butter or margarine	8 tablespoons (1 stick) Earth Balance Natural Shortening, softened (equal to 1 egg)
1 egg	1½ teaspoons Ener-G Egg Replacer mixed with 2 tablespoons warm water
2 tablespoons water	3 tablespoons cold water

1. Soften the shortening using a mixer on medium speed (about 3 minutes).
2. Add the egg replacer mixture and water. Blend for 30 seconds.
3. Add the cookie mix. Blend on low speed about 2 minutes. The dough will be crumbly.
4. Use your hands to further blend the dough until it sticks together.
5. Roll the dough into a cylinder, wrap it in plastic, and refrigerate for at least an hour.
6. When you are ready to make cookies, preheat the oven to 350°F. Line a baking sheet with parchment paper.
7. Slice the dough into ¼-inch slices. Roll each slice into a ball. Place the cookie balls on the prepared baking sheet, with room in between.
8. Bake at 350°F for 15 to 17 minutes, until the cookies have spread and small splits can be seen on the top of the cookies.

TIPS

* Refrigerate or freeze leftover dough and use at a later date.
* These cookies are best when served warm, but they will be perfect the next day, too.
* To make these into cookie bars, use a 9-inch square pan and bake for 20 to 24 minutes.

Party Cupcakes from Bob's Red Mill Gluten Free Vanilla Cake Mix

When you need to whip up a batch of cupcakes for a classroom party tomorrow, this is an easy answer. These are sweet enough to leave unfrosted, making them great for little hands, and the colors inside are a nice surprise.

I replaced the water with vanilla hemp milk in this recipe to give the cupcakes a thicker texture and a stronger vanilla taste.

{ MAKES 12 CUPCAKES }

BAKING MIX USED: Bob's Red Mill Gluten Free Vanilla Cake Mix

Instead of adding:	Add:
3 eggs	¾ cup flaxseed gel (equal to 3 eggs)
½ cup oil	½ cup sunflower oil
½ cup water	½ cup vanilla hemp milk
	½ cup allergen-free candy sprinkles

1. Follow the package preparation instructions, with the above substitutions.

2. Stir in the candy sprinkles last, by hand.

TIPS

✳ This recipe can also be made as a single-layer cake or a loaf cake.

Favorite Chocolate Cake from Gluten-Free Pantry Decadent Chocolate Cake Mix

Some have said this is the best gluten-free chocolate cake mix available on the market, and I would be hard pressed to argue with them. When topped with Ganache (page 201), this easy dessert solution rivals a traditional "death by chocolate" cake. Prior to creating my own chocolate cake recipe (page 198), this was my go-to favorite for birthdays and parties.

Note that I have used Earth Balance Natural Shortening, chocolate hemp milk, and applesauce (with added baking powder) in this adaptation to replace the butter, buttermilk, and eggs, respectively. It's the combination of these ingredients that makes this work.

{ MAKES 1 SINGLE-LAYER CAKE, 8 TO 10 SERVINGS }

BAKING MIX USED: **Gluten-Free Pantry Decadent Chocolate Cake Mix**

Instead of adding:	*Add:*
5 tablespoons butter	5 tablespoons Earth Balance Natural Shortening, melted
2 large eggs	½ cup unsweetened applesauce (equal to 2 eggs) 1 teaspoon baking powder
1 cup low-fat buttermilk or low-fat yogurt	1 cup chocolate hemp milk
½ teaspoon vanilla extract	½ teaspoon vanilla extract
	½ cup allergen-free chocolate chips

1. Follow the package preparation instructions, with the above substitutions.

2. Stir in the chocolate chips last, by hand.

TIPS

* One package makes a single-layer cake. Use two packages for a double-layer cake.
* Enjoy Life Mini Chips practically melt into the cake, leaving tiny pockets with bursts of chocolate (see page 192).

CRASH COURSE

Make It Special

L ATELY, MY TRIPS to the grocery store and health food store feel more like a treasure hunt than a chore. Every week there's something new in the baking aisle to try. When I find a new gluten-free baking mix I ask myself, "What can I make with this?" Can that cookie mix be used to make a pie crust? Can this spice cake mix be used to make carrot cake? What about that brownie mix—can I make mini-muffins with it?

After all, sometimes a basic cookie or muffin can be, well—boring. You have already seen some ideas to spruce up baking mixes by adding chocolate chips or fruit, or using a bread mix to make hamburger rolls. Are you ready for more? Each of the recipes that follow can be made as a basic mix (with allergen-free substitutions) or kicked up a notch for a special treat.

Always remember, before you purchase a baking mix or choose ingredients to add, to check the detailed ingredients labels (see page 6 for more on reading labels).

Pancakes with Chocolate Maple Syrup from Orgran Stonemilled Buckwheat Pancake Mix

I love buckwheat and was thrilled when I discovered this Orgran buckwheat pancake mix. Buckwheat has a bold—almost nutty—taste that works extremely well in a pancake or waffle. And as I noted earlier, despite its name, buckwheat contains no wheat (see page 22). Hemp milk pairs very nicely with buckwheat and gives these pancakes a rich taste. These pancakes won't stick to your pan like some made with rice-based mixes do, making this an option to try in a waffle iron, too!

{ MAKES 12 TO 16 PANCAKES, 6 TO 8 SERVINGS }

BAKING MIX USED: Orgran Stonemilled Buckwheat Pancake Mix

Instead of adding:	*Add:*
1 cup water	1 cup water
3 ounces milk	⅓ cup original hemp milk
3 eggs	4½ teaspoons Ener-G Egg Replacer mixed with 6 tablespoons water (equal to 3 eggs)

1. Whisk together all of the ingredients, by hand, with the above substitutions
2. Add up to an additional ½ cup of water for thinner pancakes.
3. Heat a large shallow pan on medium-high heat. Add 1 tablespoon of oil.
4. Reduce the heat to medium.
5. Drop spoonfuls of batter (depending on the desired size) into the pan. Flip after 1 minute (when lightly browned).
6. Serve with Chocolate Maple Syrup (page 244).

TIPS

* Note that this mix does contain maize and is not suitable for those with corn allergies.
* The directions from this Australian company use metric measurements, which I have converted.
* I recommend using a nonstick pan with just a little bit of oil.

Chocolate Maple Syrup

{ MAKES 1¼ CUPS SYRUP }

1 tablespoon Earth Balance Natural Shortening
1 cup pure maple syrup
½ cup allergen-free chocolate chips

1. Melt the shortening with the maple syrup, in a small saucepan, over low heat, until the shortening is melted.

2. Add the chocolate chips and continue heating on low heat, stirring constantly, until the chocolate is melted.

3. Remove from the heat and continue mixing until the chocolate is completely blended.

4. Serve warm over pancakes.

Pancakes with Chocolate Maple Syrup

Marble Squares from Pamela's Products Chocolate Chunk Cookie Mix

When I was in high school, my grandmother made a treat she called marble squares. They were a cross between a brownie and a chocolate chip cookie, inspired by a recipe she found on the back of a package of Nestlé Toll House Semi-Sweet Morsels. Memere continued to make these for me and my siblings even after we moved away from home, sending us care packages at college. This recipe is my allergen-free replacement for those nostalgic bars.

{ MAKES 16 SQUARES }

BAKING MIX USED: Pamela's Products Chocolate Chunk Cookie Mix

Instead of adding:	*Add:*
8 tablespoons butter or 7 tablespoons margarine	5 tablespoons grapeseed oil
1 egg	½ cup unsweetened applesauce (equal to 2 eggs)
	⅓ cup water
	½ cup allergen-free chocolate chips

1. Preheat the oven to 350°F. Spray a 9-inch square baking dish with cooking oil.
2. Mix together the baking mix, oil, applesauce, and water, by hand, in a large mixing bowl.
3. Spread the dough evenly in the baking dish. Sprinkle the chocolate chips on top.
4. Bake for 8 minutes at 350°F. Remove the baking dish from the oven.
5. Use the back of a butter knife to swirl the melted chocolate chips into the batter.
6. Return the baking dish to the oven and bake for an additional 14 to 16 minutes.
7. The total baking time is 22 to 24 minutes. Let cool and cut into squares.

TIPS

* This mix contains an advisory warning for milk, due to the chocolate chunks. A version of this mix is available in bulk from the Pamela's Products website, without the added chocolate chunks.
* The key to achieving the marbled effect is swirling the chocolate chips into the batter, after they have partially melted.
* Be sure to draw the knife through in both an east–west and north–south direction.
* To make chocolate chunk cookies from this mix, use 7 tablespoons of oil and eliminate the water and added chocolate chips.

Marble Squares

Chocolate Mousse Tarts from King Arthur Flour Gluten Free Cookie Mix

If I'm going to have dessert, I prefer something chocolate and decadent—such as chocolate lava cake, death by chocolate cake, or a rich chocolate mousse. This is another allergen-free solution for all of the true chocoholics out there. I used a cookie mix from King Arthur Flour to make the pie tart, and combined it with Eggless Chocolate Mousse (page 204) to make a truly luscious dessert.

Note that you will need to prepare the mousse for this recipe just prior to making the tarts. Do not refrigerate the mousse until after it is added to the tarts in step 8.

{ MAKES 12 SMALL TARTS }

BAKING MIX USED: King Arthur Flour Gluten Free Cookie Mix

Instead of adding:	Add:
½ cup soft butter	8 tablespoons (1 stick) Earth Balance Natural Shortening, softened
1 large egg	2 tablespoons unsweetened applesauce (equal to ½ egg)
2 tablespoons water	1½ tablespoons water
	½ cup allergen-free chocolate chips

1. Preheat the oven to 350°F. Spray a muffin tin with cooking oil.
2. Slowly melt the chocolate chips and shortening together in a microwave. Mix together well.
3. In a large mixing bowl, combine the baking mix, chocolate mixture, water and applesauce. Stir all the ingredients together by hand. Add up to an additional tablespoon of water, if needed, to hold the dough together.
4. Divide the dough in half, then make twelve equal-sized balls with half of the dough. Save the remaining dough for a future project (see tip).
5. Mold the dough into the cups of the muffin tin as you would a cookie pie crust, flattening the bottom, and bringing the dough up the sides of the cups.
6. Bake at 350°F for 13 to 15 minutes.
7. While the tarts are still warm, gently use the back of a spoon to flatten the crusts (which may have risen a bit during baking).
8. Fill the tarts with chocolate mousse. Refrigerate to set (at least 4 hours).

TIPS

* Divide the recipe in half after mixing, and refrigerate or freeze the remaining dough for a future baking project.
* A muffin pan is an easy way to make single-sized servings. Alternatively, use any size tart dishes to vary the size of these tarts.
* You can use the same ingredients and method to create a cookie pie crust, or simply make cookies with the dough.
* One package of this cookie mix is enough to make two 9-inch pie crusts or 24 single-serving tarts.

Chocolate Mousse Tarts with Whipped Coconut Cream (page 44)

Raspberry Brownie Bites from Bob's Red Mill Gluten Free Brownie Mix

Another favorite gluten-free brownie mix that can successfully be made allergen-free is this one from Bob's Red Mill. These raspberry brownie treats are the perfect size for parties, or when you just want a hint of chocolate and sugar as a mid-afternoon snack.

One package of Bob's Red Mill Gluten Free Brownie Mix is enough to make 24 brownie bites (in a mini-muffin pan) with enough brownie mix left over to fill a 5 by 7-inch baking dish.

Note: This recipe uses Raspberry Jam (page 219), which should be made ahead of time. Alternatively, your favorite jam can be substituted.

{ MAKES 24 BROWNIE BITES, 12 SERVINGS }

BAKING MIX USED: Bob's Red Mill Gluten Free Brownie Mix

Instead of adding:	*Add:*
1½ sticks (12 tablespoons) melted butter or margarine	8 tablespoons (1 stick) Earth Balance Natural Shortening, melted
1 egg	3 teaspoons Ener-G Egg Replacer mixed with 4 tablespoons warm water (equal to 2 eggs)
2 teaspoons vanilla extract	2 teaspoons vanilla extract
¾ cup water	1 cup water
	½ cup raspberry jam

1. Preheat the oven to 350°F. Spray a mini-muffin tin with cooking oil.
2. Blend together the brownie mix, melted shortening, egg replacer mixture, vanilla, and water, using a mixer on medium speed.
3. Fill the mini-muffin tins three quarters full with brownie mix. (There will be brownie mix left over; see tip.)
4. Bake at 350°F for 10 minutes. Remove the pan from the oven.
5. Use a butter knife to make a small concave dip in the center of each brownie bite.
6. Spoon ¼ teaspoon of raspberry jam into the middle of each bite.
7. Return the brownies to the oven and bake for an additional 6 to 8 minutes. The total baking time is 16 to 18 minutes.

TIPS

* I reduced the fat in this recipe, but compensated for it by adding an extra Ener-G egg and ¼ cup more of water.
* Use the leftover brownie mix to fill a 5 by 7-inch pan. Bake for 22 minutes at 350°F. Alternatively, an additional half pan of brownie bites can be made.
* To make this as classic brownies (without the jam), use a 9 by 13-inch pan, and bake for 22 to 25 minutes.

Chocolate Blackberry Cake from King Arthur Flour Gluten Free Chocolate Cake Mix

It has a full-bodied, rich taste, with a hint of berry. I could be talking about wine; instead, I'm describing this Chocolate Blackberry Cake. If chocolate cake is good, then chocolate cake with berries inside is even better. The blackberries can't be seen with the naked eye when you cut the cake.

Many gluten-free cake mixes make a single-layer cake, but this mix is enough for a double-layer or sheet cake, making it perfect for parties!

{ MAKES 1 DOUBLE-LAYER CAKE, 12 TO 16 SERVINGS }

BAKING MIX USED: King Arthur Flour Gluten Free Chocolate Cake Mix

Instead of adding:	Add:
⅔ cup vegetable oil	⅔ cup sunflower oil
2 teaspoons vanilla extract	2 teaspoons vanilla extract
4 large eggs	1 cup flaxseed gel (equal to 4 eggs)
1⅓ cups water	1⅓ cups water
	¾ cup fresh or frozen blackberries (thawed and drained) (see tip)

1. Preheat the oven to 350°F. Spray two 8- or 9-inch round cake pans or one 9 by 13-inch pan with cooking oil.
2. Combine the oil, vanilla, flaxseed gel, and water together in a large bowl, using a mixer on medium speed, until blended.
3. Add the blackberries and continue mixing on medium-low speed. The blackberries will break apart.
4. Add the cake mix and blend well on medium speed.
5. Follow the timing instructions on the package.

TIPS

* The blackberries should still be in small bits before baking.
* Frost with Creamy Vanilla Frosting (page 109) or your favorite frosting.

A final word: create your own

As you've seen with these adaptations, there are a lot of options for replacing food allergens when using off-the-shelf baking mixes. Don't forget to read the labels, even if you've made the products dozens of times before—ingredients and preparation methods do change. Always err on the side of caution when it comes to food allergies.

If your baked goods don't turn out quite as you hoped the first time you try them, don't be afraid to try again. With the exceptions I noted earlier in this chapter, most gluten-free mixes can be made without butter, milk, and eggs. As you experiment, be careful not to change too much at once. Often just a small tweak is needed to get the results you want. Refer to appendix A for solutions to common problems.

Now that you've tried a few of these adaptations and have practiced with the different ways you can substitute ingredients, I am confident that you will be able to adapt your own recipes. I'd love to hear from you when you do.

Remember, it's an adventure!

APPENDIX

A

Troubleshooting Recipes

I'VE HAD MY share of baking mishaps. Sometimes I accidentally leave out an ingredient or skip a step. I recommend always assembling the ingredients required for the recipe before you begin and checking off each step as you go.

As you experiment and make changes, do so incrementally. Don't add more flour, change the shortening, and add more baking powder all at once. If it works you're in luck, but if not, you won't know what steps to take next. If you're working on a new recipe, try scaling it down and making just half or one quarter of the recipe (be sure to keep proportions in sync).

You should always read through the recipe instructions before you start, and have all the tools and ingredients you need ready to go. But even if you follow the recipe to the letter, things can go wrong. Keep in mind that baking is a science—and in all science we learn by making mistakes, in addition to proving what works.

I believe there is no such thing as a stupid question. While so many cookbook authors take for granted that everyone knows the basics, I strive to explain even the simple stuff. In this appendix I share some common allergen-free baking problems, and tips for how to solve them.

PROBLEM: My cakes/muffins/quick breads don't rise.
SOLUTION: First, check your baking powder or baking soda to make sure it is still good (see page 97). If you are using only baking

soda, make sure you have an acid in your recipe. If so, then add 1 to 2 teaspoons of baking powder. If you are using baking powder and you have tested it to make sure it is still good, try increasing the amount by 1 to 2 teaspoons.

PROBLEM: My cake/muffin/quick bread batter is too lumpy.
SOLUTION: Make sure you bring all of the ingredients to room temperature before you begin mixing. Blend the dry ingredients extremely well (either by hand or with your mixer) before adding any liquids. Break up any lumps. If this doesn't resolve the problem, you may be using a heavy flour blend that is absorbing too much liquid. See the next problem.

PROBLEM: My cakes/muffins/quick breads are too dry.
SOLUTION: You may be using a flour blend that is too heavy. Many gluten-free flours are considerably heavier than wheat flours, and absorb more liquid. See pages 28 and 33 for suggestions on flour blends and adjusting the amount of flour used to compensate for the weight.

PROBLEM: My cakes/muffins/quick breads fall flat before I take them out of the oven.
SOLUTION: Make sure your oven reaches the suggested baking temperature before you start to bake (this is called preheating). Make sure you don't open the oven door (to peek, or to test for doneness) until the baked goods are near the end of the suggested baking time. If you still have problems, check the temperature of the oven for accuracy. To check, set the oven to 350°F. Place an oven-safe thermometer in the center of the center rack. After 15 minutes, the thermometer should read 350°F. If it's not accurate, the next time you bake you should adjust the setting on your oven to compensate (either up or down accordingly). For example, if your oven was set to 350°F and the thermometer reads 325°F after your test, then set the oven temperature at 375°F when the recipe suggests 350°F. Conversely, you would set the oven temperature lower if your test resulted in a temperature higher than 350°F.

PROBLEM: My scone/doughnut batter sticks to my hands while I'm trying to work with it.
SOLUTION: When working with thick batters, it's better to use water to keep your dough from sticking, rather than extra flour. Run your fingers under warm water and shake off any drops. Use slightly wet hands to form your pastry. Sprinkle a few drops of warm water on your prep surface, and on your bench knife, if needed.

PROBLEM: My cookie or pie dough is too crumbly.

SOLUTION: Many dough recipes will have "1 to 2 tablespoons cold water as needed" listed as an ingredient. Cookie or pie dough should be just moist enough so the dough holds together, but not wet. Add additional cold water ½ tablespoon at a time, so you can get to just the right consistency. If having added all of the additional water suggested, your dough is still too crumbly, use a little bit less flour the next time.

PROBLEM: My dough is too sticky.

SOLUTION: You may have added too much water as you formed the dough. Work in a little bit of additional flour (go easy, add just 1 tablespoon at a time), until you achieve the right consistency. Next time, use less water or liquid, and add the water more slowly (½ tablespoon at a time).

PROBLEM: My pie dough sticks to my rolling pin.

SOLUTION: I prefer not to use flour to keep pie dough from sticking. Instead, spread a layer of wax paper or parchment paper over your dough before you begin rolling. When finished, gently peel the paper back to reveal your crust.

PROBLEM: My cookies spread too much and burn around the edges.

SOLUTION: First, make sure you are using a shortening that remains solid at room temperature (see page 48). Make sure you use the shortening cold (right out of the fridge) and that the liquids you add are also cold. Refrigerate the dough for at least an hour before forming the cookies. If you still have problems, refrigerate the dough overnight, or freeze the dough for an hour before using. Work quickly once you start forming the cookies; they should still be cool when they go into the oven.

PROBLEM: My pie crust falls apart (or my cookie dough doesn't hold together).

SOLUTION: This is one of the simplest problems to solve when using gluten-free flour. There's no need to re-roll the crust. Just use a few drops of cold water and your fingers to stick your crust or cookies back together. If the problem occurs often with the same recipe add up to 1 tablespoon more of cold water as you are forming the dough.

PROBLEM: My frosting is runny.

SOLUTION: Make sure you are using a shortening that remains solid at room temperature. Test it before use by letting it sit at room temperature for at least 2 hours. If it starts to get wet around the edges, choose a different shortening. See page 48 for shortening recommendations.

PROBLEM: My yeast dough sticks when I try to roll it out.
SOLUTION: Most yeast recipes will call for additional flour for dusting. This flour is used to coat the surface you roll out your dough on, to coat the rolling pin (if applicable), and to coat the dough so that it doesn't stick to your hands as you manipulate it. You should only need about 2 tablespoons of additional flour for most recipes to accomplish all of these things.

PROBLEM: My yeast bread crust doesn't brown.
SOLUTION: Wheat breads are traditionally browned by using an egg or milk wash. If you are using a "white" gluten-free flour blend you may find that the crust doesn't brown. If you want a brown crust, try increasing the whole grains in your flour blend. Alternatively, brush the top with a thin coating of oil or dairy-free milk prior to baking.

PROBLEM: My yeast bread crust gets soggy after a couple of days.
SOLUTION: Many gluten-free yeast breads will do that. Freeze whatever portion of the bread you are not planning to use within two or three days. If it's a loaf of bread, slice it before you freeze it and take out portions as needed.

PROBLEM: My yeast bread doesn't rise (won't proof).
SOLUTION: First, let your bread rise for 15 minutes longer. Walk away; use this time to catch up on the bills or slice the veggies for dinner. A surprising amount of the rise happens later in the cycle. Make sure you have a warm (but not too hot) spot to proof in (see "Proofing Methods," page 158). If the proof still fails, test your yeast to make sure it's still good (see page 173). Next, check to make sure your ingredients include a true sugar (one that includes fructose and glucose—see page 140 for more information on sugar). If the recipe contains salt, reduce the amount by one-half.

PROBLEM: My pudding/mousse doesn't thicken.
SOLUTION: The eggs are typically what will help hold a mousse or pudding together. Make sure you are using a chemical egg replacer (rather than a fruit puree or flaxseed gel). See page 56 to understand how the various egg substitutions behave. Make sure the mixture is at a rolling boil before adding the egg replacer. If your pudding still doesn't thicken, add 1½ teaspoons of starch (corn starch or tapioca starch) and boil for 3 to 5 minutes longer.

APPENDIX

B

Substitutions

ALL OF THE recipes in this book are made without wheat flour, cow's milk, eggs, and butter—the most common ingredients that traditional baking recipes call for. Your family may need to avoid all of these foods, like mine does, or you may be able to include some of these ingredients in your baking. If so, lucky you! The table in this appendix can be used two ways: first, to see how to substitute back traditional ingredients if you aren't allergic to them and second, to find other options for allergen-free substitutions in the correct proportions.

COMMON FOOD ALLERGENS	WITHOUT COMMON FOOD ALLERGENS
WHEAT FLOUR Most wheat flours weigh between 120 and 122 grams per cup. If you choose to use wheat flour in the recipes in this book, add one additional tablespoon per cup of flour used (or use a kitchen scale to measure 128 to 130 grams of wheat flour for each cup of gluten-free flour the recipe calls for). Leave out the xanthan gum.	**GLUTEN-FREE FLOUR BLEND** This includes any gluten-free flour or flour blend that weighs approximately 128 to 130 grams per cup. See page 33 to learn how to adjust the amount of flour you use based on weight.

COMMON FOOD ALLERGENS	WITHOUT COMMON FOOD ALLERGENS
COW'S MILK/ SOY MILK/ NUT MILKS 1 cup cow's milk can be substituted for 1 cup of non-dairy milk. 1 cup soy milk can also be substituted for any other non-dairy milk. 1 cup almond, hazelnut, or other milk derived from nuts can be substituted for any other non-dairy milk. 1 cup buttermilk (or soured milk) can be substituted for non-dairy soured milk.	**NON-DAIRY MILK** 1 cup hemp milk (all varieties) 1 cup coconut milk beverage* (all varieties) 1 cup coconut milk in the can* (diluted with equal parts water) 1 cup rice milk (all varieties) 1 cup non-dairy soured milk (see page 43) 1 cup fruit juice or water
EGGS 1 egg can be substituted for any of the options to the right. The recipes in this book note the equivalent number of eggs that it would be appropriate to substitute (if you aren't allergic to them).	**EGG SUBSTITUTES** 1½ teaspoons Ener-G Egg Replacer mixed with 2 tablespoons warm water (or non-dairy milk) ¼ cup flaxseed gel (made by mixing 1 tablespoon ground flaxseeds with 3 tablespoons warm water) ¼ cup unsweetened applesauce or fruit puree 1 tablespoon vinegar See page 65 for more detail on which substitutes are best suited for which recipes.
BUTTER AND MARGARINE 8 tablespoons (1 stick) butter or margarine can be substituted for any of the options to the right. When substituting for oil, use the butter melted.	**NON-DAIRY SHORTENING AND OILS** 8 tablespoons (1 stick) Earth Balance Natural Shortening†‡ 8 tablespoons Spectrum Organic All Vegetable Shortening (palm oil)† 8 tablespoons coconut oil* 8 tablespoons Earth Balance Soy-Free Natural Buttery Spread 8 tablespoons oil (includes grapeseed, sunflower, hemp, canola, olive)

* If you are allergic to tree nuts, check with your doctor to determine whether coconut is a concern for you.

† Use one of these options for pie and cookie doughs.

‡ Contains soybean oil. Check with your doctor to determine whether this is a concern for you.

A Blueprint for Adapting a Traditional Recipe

IN THIS BOOK I have given you recipes that are made without gluten or the top eight food allergens. But you might have a favorite recipe that's been in your family for years. Perhaps everyone is expecting Aunt Sarah's Famous Cherry Cake at Thanksgiving dinner and you want to make an allergen-free version so that everyone at the table can have the same dessert. Or you just want to adapt your favorite traditional recipe to accommodate your family's food restrictions. This appendix is intended to give you a blueprint for how to approach adapting a traditional recipe to remove gluten and the top food allergens.

Keep in mind that adapting recipes is more than just replacing ingredients; it's also about how those ingredients interact with each other. This blueprint gives you a place to start, but you may still need to tweak the formula for the recipes you have. If you need to make additional changes, change one component at a time, until you have a formula that works.

It's not necessary to follow all of these steps; choose the steps required based on your family's food restrictions.

Replace wheat and gluten with non-gluten grains and supporting ingredients.

Approach:

- Replace any gluten grains (including wheat, barley, rye,

or spelt) with a gluten-free flour blend (see page 28 for options). Adjust the weight of the gluten-free flour you choose to be consistent with the weight of wheat flour at approximately 120 grams per cup. In most cases you will be using less flour than the original recipe.

- If the flour blend you choose does not contain xanthan gum, add ¼ teaspoon of xanthan gum for each cup (or partial cup) of flour used.
- If the recipe uses baking powder, double the amount. If the recipe uses baking soda, use the baking soda and add 1 to 2 teaspoons of baking powder.

Replace the milk.

Approach: Replace dairy milk or soy milk with equal amounts of non-dairy milk (including hemp milk, coconut milk beverage, and rice milk). See pages 35–51 for more information on milk choices.

Address the oils.

Approach: Substitute equal amounts of allergen-friendly oils (including sunflower, grapeseed, hemp, and canola oil) for any nut oils. See page 44 for more on oils.

Address the shortening or butter.

Approach: Substitute equal amounts of dairy-free shortening (including palm oil shortening, coconut oil shortening, and Earth Balance Natural Shortening) for butter and/or margarine. See page 47 for a detailed discussion on shortening. Check the labels on these products to ensure that they don't contain any foods you are allergic to.

Eliminate the eggs.

Approach: Determine what role the eggs play in the recipe—leavening, texture, and/or binding—and consider the type of baked goods you are making:

- If leavening is the main concern, or your recipe uses yeast, or you are making a pudding or mousse, replace the eggs with a packaged egg replacer (e.g., Ener-G Egg Replacer) according to the package directions (see page 62).
- If texture is the main concern (or you are working with a batter), replace each egg with ¼ cup of fruit puree (see page 59), or ¼ cup of flaxseed gel (see page 57).

- If binding is also a concern (or you are working with thick batters or doughs), replace one or more eggs with flaxseed gel (see page 57).
- If your recipe requires 3 or more eggs, consider using a combination of these options.
- If your recipe doesn't require leavening or additional texture (or you are making pie crust or cookie dough), consider leaving out the egg.

See pages 53–65 for more detail on baking without eggs.

Address other food allergens.

Approach:

- Eliminate nuts. If your recipe calls for nuts, decide whether your recipe will give you a good result if you replace the nuts with raisins (this may be appropriate in some cookies and pies), allergen-free chocolate chips (appropriate in brownies and bars), or gluten-free oats (this may be appropriate instead of nut toppings). If not, leave the nuts out. If the recipe is essentially a nut recipe (such as a pecan pie) then set it aside and choose to make something else.
- Make sure you haven't introduced any soy flours or soy proteins with the ingredients you have added.

And, of course, always address any other less common food allergens that may be a concern in your recipe. Always check the labels on every product you use each time you use it (see page 6 for more information).

English Muffins (page 171)

Metric Conversions and Weights

GLUTEN-FREE FLOUR BLENDS (see page 28 for recommended flour blends and page 32 for how to measure)	
¼ cup	32 to 32.5 grams
½ cup	64 to 65 grams
1 cup	128 to 130 grams
2 cups	256 to 260 grams

ADDITIONAL FLOURS, STARCHES, AND GRAINS	
1 cup oat flour	110 grams
1 cup millet flour	120 grams
½ cup buckwheat flour	90 grams
½ cup garbanzo bean flour	60 grams
¼ cup sweet rice flour	30 grams

¼ cup corn starch	32 grams
¼ cup tapioca starch	40 grams
¼ cup potato starch	40 grams
¼ cup cornmeal	33 grams
¾ cup gluten-free quick-cooking oats	67.5 grams
¾ cup gluten-free crisped rice cereal	22.5 grams
½ cup brown rice (dry)	90 grams

EGG SUBSTITUTES (one-egg equivalents)

¼ cup applesauce or fruit puree	52.5 grams
¼ cup flaxseed gel	60 grams

SHORTENING

8 tbsp (1 stick) Earth Balance Natural Shortening	112 grams (14 grams per tbsp)
8 tbsp Earth Balance Soy-free Natural Buttery Spread	112 grams (14 grams per tbsp)
8 tbsp palm oil	96 grams (12 grams per tbsp)
8 tbsp coconut oil	112 grams (14 grams per tbsp)

SUGAR AND SWEETENERS

½ cup granulated sugar	100 grams
½ cup raw sugar	96 grams
½ cup Sucanat	96 grams

½ cup light brown sugar	96 grams
1 cup confectioners' sugar	120 grams
½ cup honey	168 grams
½ cup agave nectar	168 grams

CHOCOLATE

½ cup natural unsweetened cocoa powder	40 grams
½ cup allergen-free semisweet or bittersweet chocolate chips or chunks	120 grams
½ cup unsweetened baking chocolate	70 grams

FRUITS AND VEGETABLES

1 cup blueberries	130 grams
1 cup sliced strawberries	125 grams
1 cup soft berries (mixed or individual)	105 grams
1 cup cranberries, chopped	140 grams
1 cup apples (cored and diced)	100 grams
1 cup mashed banana (frozen or very ripe)	220 grams
1 cup raisins	160 grams
1 cup dried cranberries	120 grams
1 cup zucchini (shredded)	110 grams
1 cup mashed sweet potato	175 grams

LIQUID INGREDIENTS		
(including all non-dairy milks, fruit juice, water, and oils)		
¼ cup	2 fl oz	60 ml
½ cup	4 fl oz	120 ml
¾ cup	6 fl oz	180 ml
1 cup	8 fl oz	240 ml

TEMPERATURES		
Proofing	95°F to 100°F	35°C to 38°C
Warmed liquids (yeast baked goods)	100°F	38°C
Testing for doneness (yeast baked goods)	200°F to 205°F	93°C to 96°C
Baking and Preheating	350°F	175°C
Baking and Preheating	375°F	190°C

APPENDIX
E

Resources

Organizations

THE FOOD ALLERGY AND ANAPHYLAXIS NETWORK (FAAN)

FAAN is focused on raising public awareness, providing
advocacy and education, and advancing food-allergy and
anaphylaxis research.

foodallergy.org

FOOD ALLERGY INITIATIVE (FAI)

FAI is focused on food-allergy research and advocacy.

faiusa.org

KIDS WITH FOOD ALLERGIES FOUNDATION (KFA)

KFA is focused on education, support, and community forums
for families with food allergies.

kidswithfoodallergies.org

AMERICAN PARTNERSHIP FOR EOSINOPHILIC DISORDERS (APFED)

APFED is focused on education, research, and advocacy on
eosinophilic gastrointestinal disorders.

apfed.org

CAMPAIGN URGING RESEARCH FOR EOSINOPHILIC DISEASE (CURED)

CURED is focused on raising funds for research and awareness.

curedfoundation.org

CELIAC DISEASE FOUNDATION (CDF)

CDF is focused on awareness and support for those with celiac disease.

celiac.org

1 IN 133—IT'S A BIG DEAL

A gluten-free advocacy organization

1in133.org

Tools and Online Retailers

ALLERDINE

A web and mobile food allergy–friendly restaurant guide

allerdine.com

ALLERGY EATS

An online guide to allergy-friendly restaurants. Mobile apps are available for iPhone and Android.

allergyeats.com

AMAZON.COM

Many allergen-free and gluten-free foods can be found in the online grocery store. Use Subscribe & Save to keep costs down.

amazon.com

AUTHENTIC FOODS GLUTEN FREE SUPERMARKET

Flours, baking mixes, and more

glutenfree-supermarket.com

BOB'S RED MILL

Flours, baking mixes, and more

bobsredmill.com/gluten-free

DIVVIES BAKERY

A source for dairy-free chocolate and baked goods

divvies.com

ENJOY LIFE ONLINE STORE

A source for chocolate and packaged products

enjoylifefoods.elsstore.com

JULES GLUTEN FREE

Gluten-free flour and more

julesglutenfree.com

KING ARTHUR FLOUR

Gluten-free baking mixes, flours, and more

kingarthurflour.com/glutenfree

ONESPOT ALLERGY

Provides food-allergy training kits, EpiPen holders, and more

onespotallergy.com

THE GLUTEN FREE MALL

Carries many allergen-free products

celiac.com/glutenfreemall

Basic Brownies (page 207)

Acknowledgments

THERE ARE MANY PEOPLE who supported and encouraged me on this journey. First, I must thank my husband, Harry, who not only taught me everything he knows about photography, but took my publicity photo, and encouraged me (and asked for status) every day. To all of my friends and family who tried my recipes, gave me feedback, and tried them again until they were perfect—I thank you. Special thanks to those who regularly eat gluten, wheat, dairy, eggs, and soy, but were compelled to eat what I baked instead (especially those who did so on a daily basis). There were many who inspired me, including Kevin with his never-ending optimism, Andree with her examples of joyful living, Anna with her ease in the kitchen, and Patrick who happily embraces the foods he can eat. Thank you to my mother for sharing her love of chocolate with me.

Thank you to Shelly Loveland and Devon Wickens, who provided feedback on drafts, cheered me on, and helped to bring life to the words on the page. Thanks to my agent, Shawna Morey, who instantly recognized that this book was needed. To Matthew Lore for taking a chance on me as a new author, and providing exactly the right guidance at the right time. And to Matthew, Molly, Karen, Jack, and the superb extended team at The Experiment for making this book come alive. Thank you to Susi Oberhelman for designing a cover that I fell in love with the moment I saw it, to Iris Bass for fine-tuning my words, and to Pauline Neuwirth for a fabulous book design.

A special thank you goes to Dr. Stephen Wangen for writing an inspiring foreword, and to all of the doctors and medical professionals who take a practical approach to diagnosing and treating food-related medical issues.

Thank you to all of the mentors, teachers, and authors who inspired me and encouraged me, including Alisa Fleming, Monica Bhide, Kristin Taliaferro, Dianne Jacob, Jules Dowler Shepard, Lori Sandler, and Chef Richard Coppedge. Thank you to the many followers of Learning to Eat Allergy-Free, for reading, caring, and sharing.

Most important, I must thank my grandmother, Stella Laferriere. While she hasn't been with us in physical presence for some time, she is still here in spirit. I am quite certain she would be "tickled pink" to be able to hold this book in her hands.

Notes

1   Amy M. Branum, MSPH, and Susan L. Lukacs, DO, MSPH, "Food Allergy Among U.S. Children: Trends in Prevalence and Hospitalizations," Centers for Disease Control and Prevention, *NCHS Data Brief Number 10* (October 2008).

2   US Food and Drug Administration, Food Allergen Labeling and Consumer Protection Act of 2004 (Public Law 108-282, Title II) (Internet). Updated 2009 Aug 21; cited September 8, 2011. Available from fda.gov/Food/LabelingNutrition/FoodAllergensLabeling.

3   Lara S. Ford et al., "Food Allergen Advisory Labeling and Product Contamination with Egg, Milk, and Peanut," *The Journal of Allergy and Clinical Immunology* 126, no. 2 (August 2010): 384–85.

4   The Food Allergy and Anaphylaxis Network (Internet). Updated August 18, 2011; cited September 8, 2011. Available from foodallergy.org/page/tree-nut-allergy.

5   US Food and Drug Administration, Guidance on the Labeling of Certain Uses of Lecithin Derived from Soy Under Section 403(w) of the Federal Food, Drug, and Cosmetic Act, April 2006 (Internet). Updated June 6, 2011; cited September 8, 2011. Available from fda.gov/Food/GuidanceComplianceRegulatoryInformation/GuidanceDocuments/FoodLabelingNutrition/ucm059065.htm.

6   US Food and Drug Administration, Federal Register Proposed Rule - 72 FR 2795 January 23, 2007: Food Labeling; Gluten-Free Labeling of Foods (Internet). Updated May 20, 2009, Cited September 8, 2011. Available from fda.gov/Food/LabelingNutrition/FoodAllergensLabeling/GuidanceComplianceRegulatoryInformation/ucm077926.htm.

7   US Department of Agriculture, Center for Nutrition Policy and Promotion, Dietary Guidelines for Americans, 2010 (Internet). Updated June 9, 2011; cited September 15, 2011. Available from cnpp.usda.gov/dietaryguidelines.htm.

8   Michael Pollan, *Food Rules: An Eater's Manual* (New York, NY: Penguin Books, 2009), 15.

9   Parents of Children with Food Allergies Survey, Galaxy Nutritional Foods, available from galaxyfoods.com/landing/galaxy-faan-survey-results/; cited December 7, 2011.

10   Wheat Foods Council, Wheat Facts (Internet). Cited September 15, 2011. Available from wheatfoods.org/AboutWheat-wheat-facts/Index.htm.

11   Stephen Wangen, Dr., *Healthier Without Wheat*, Seattle, WA: Innate Health Publishing, 2009, 14.

12   Richard J. Coppedge Jr., CMB, *Gluten-Free Baking with The Culinary Institute of America* (Avon, MA: Adams Media, 2008), 23–24.

13   Scott H. Sicherer, MD, "Clinical Implications of Cross-reactive Food Allergens," *The Journal of Allergy and Clinical Immunology* 108, no. 6 (December 2001): 881–90.

14   The Library of Congress, H.R. 1831: Industrial Hemp Farming Act of 2011 (Internet). Cited September 8, 2011. Available from thomas.loc.gov/cgi-bin/bdquery/z?d112:h1831.

15   The Food Allergy and Anaphylaxis Network (Internet). Updated August 18, 2011; cited September 8, 2011. Available from foodallergy.org/page/peanut-allergy.

16   Carmen Martin-Hernandez, Sylvie Benet, and Ladislav Obert, "Determination of Proteins in Refined and Nonrefined Oils," *Journal of Agriculture and Food Chemistry* 56, no. 12 (May 2008): 4348–51.

17   US Food and Drug Administration, Guidance on the Labeling of Certain Uses of Lecithin Derived from Soy Under Section 403(w) of the Federal Food, Drug, and Cosmetic Act, April 2006 (Internet). Updated June 6, 2011; cited September 8, 2011. Available from fda.gov/Food/GuidanceComplianceRegulatoryInformation/GuidanceDocuments/FoodLabelingNutrition/ucm059065.htm.

Index

Page numbers in italics refer to photographs.

ABOUT THE AUTHOR

COLETTE MARTIN is a food-allergy mom and an expert on how to bake allergen-free. When her son was diagnosed with multiple food allergies, she had to reinvent how her family ate. Having first learned to bake in her grandmother's kitchen with wheat, butter, milk, and eggs, Colette understands firsthand what it means to transform a kitchen to accommodate multiple food allergies.

You can find her website, Learning to Eat Allergy-Free, at learningtoeatallergyfree.com, follow her on Twitter @colette-fmartin, like her on facebook.com/AllergenFreeBaker, or e-mail her at multifoodallergies@gmail.com.